The Cost of
WINNING

The Cost of
WINNING

GLOBAL DEVELOPMENT POLICIES
AND BROKEN SOCIAL CONTRACTS

MICHAEL H.
COSGROVE

TRANSACTION PUBLISHERS
New Brunswick (U.S.A.) and London (U.K.)

Library of Congress Catalog Number: 95-44246
ISBN: 1-56000-229-8
Printed in the United States of America

Library of Congress Cataloging-in-Publication Data

Cosgrove, Michael (Michael H.)
    The cost of winning : global economic development and broken social contracts / Michael Cosgrove.
        p. cm.
    Includes bibliographical references and index.
    ISBN 1-56000-229-8 (alk. paper)
    1. United States—Economic policy. 2. United States—Economic conditions—1945- 3. Economic forecasting—United States. 4. United States—Foreign economic relations. 5. United States—Social policy. I. Title.
HC106.5.C685   1995
337.73—dc20   95-44246
                                                              CIP

Contents

Part III
The Future—Change?

Figures

Tables

Acknowledgments

This book is dedicated to U.S. taxpayers and ordinary Americans who have given much, so that many people around the globe have an opportunity to enjoy freedom. The United States accomplished this by implementing policies to ensure the political and economic defeat of the Soviet Union. The cost of winning on the U.S. economy has been large, and ordinary Americans paid dearly.

Whatever the shortcomings of this book, they would have been larger without help from friends such as Tom Stewart-Gordon, who counseled me early in the book's development, as well as Dan Marsh and Joe Kottukapalli, who went through the manuscript asking questions and giving suggestions. Dan also provided valuable guidance in development of chapter 18.

My wife Kathy and children, Kelly and Sean, provided support and the time to write this book.

Introduction

The Cost of Winning is a book about the United States as an economic superpower in the post-World War II era. In particular, it addresses how (1) U.S. taxpayer power was utilized to shape global development and contain the Soviet Union through economic policies; (2) Soviet containment turned into broken promises and entitlements for U.S. citizens; and (3) policies can be implemented to reverse the U.S. decline. Many countries before the United States have held the economic-superpower mantle and lost it, and as described by Kennedy in *Rise and Fall of the Great Powers,* no previous world power has been able to reverse its relative decline.[1] Will America be the first? History suggests it won't, as a country needs to engage in a realistic assessment of where it is before changes can be undertaken to reverse the decline. The United States remains in denial. When acceptance sets in, it may be too late. That happened with Britain.

The U.S. strategy of shaping global economic development through a series of economic policies and concepts (called *building blocs* in this volume) to contain the Soviet Union is referred to as *the Creation* in this book, the term from a book by Dean Acheson entitled *Present at the Creation.* Mr. Acheson, secretary of state from 1949 to 1953, refers to the epigram of Alphonso X, King of Spain, for use of the idea of the creation: "If he had been present at the creation he would have given some useful hints for the better ordering of the universe. In a sense the postwar years were a period of creation, for the ordering of which I shared with others some responsibility."[2] Part I of this book, chapters 1–10, outlines the strategy of shaping post-World War II global economic development—The Creation.

The book opens with a brief review of the plight of two former economic superpowers that sets the stage for the U.S.'s role. The strategy of Soviet containment which took place after World War II didn't instantaneously develop but was, in part, an outgrowth of policies and events that took place before World War II. In particular, the Wilson administration made a substantial indirect contribution toward shaping post-World War II strategy. In the latter 1940s many people made a direct contribution to The Creation, including General George Marshall and President Truman. A lesser known figure but a key participant in shaping the strategy was George Kennan.

The Soviet containment objective needed to be implemented through a strategy of several building blocs over many decades. The first was the Marshall Plan which evolved over a fifteen week period and resulted from a coalescing of many events pulled together by General Marshall, then secretary of state. Jones, author of *The Fifteen Weeks*, characterizes "the Fifteen Weeks (as) one of those rare times in history when shackles fall away from the mind, the spirit, and the will, allowing them to soar free and high for a while and to discover new standards of what is responsible, of what is promising, and of what is possible."[3]

Marshall Plan assistance was effective as it was complemented by other building blocs such as movement toward free trade and a stable international monetary system. Free trade from a Soviet containment point of view meant providing U.S. allies an open door to the large and growing U.S. economy while not requiring equal access to theirs. This foreign trade-national security theme rested on the premise that stronger allied foreign economies were central to U.S. security, as economies in process of growth will resist communism much more readily than stagnating economies. The U.S. open-door trade policy was very important to growth of economies such as Japan. In 1954 John D. Rockefeller, III said, "It seems clear that the increase of Japan's exports is the key to the situation" and added with some prescience that "there is no need to be pessimistic about the future of Japan."[4]

Initial thoughts after World War II were that economic programs might be sufficient to contain the Soviets. A more realistic assessment emerged as a number of events kicked off the arms race. Large U.S. defense expenditures allowed countries aligned with the United States to spend less of their economic output on defense and to allocate a larger proportion of their economic output to business investment. The U.S. defense umbrella was another building bloc contributing to rapid growth of countries in Western Europe and the Far East.

U.S. tax policy was a central component of Soviet containment. It encouraged a high rate of consumption, low rate of savings, and high capital cost in the United States. While U.S. tax policy was *unfriendly* to capital formation, allies such as Japan and West Germany adopted a capital-*friendly* tax code to generate strong export economies, whose products could flow into the large open-door U.S. economy. The U.S. policy of deferred capital investment and high-cost capital had the effect of sharing the U.S.'s wealth with its friends through encouraging job and economic growth in their countries.

Plentiful and cheap oil, made available by U.S. oil companies operating in the Middle East and watched over by Washington, was crucial to Soviet containment policy. Private industry and government worked together to help encourage a rise in the standard of living not only in the United States but also in Western Europe and the Far East through cheap oil. The oil company role in the Middle East was to produce as much oil as possible and dispose of it. Cheap oil was very effective in encouraging global economic growth until the early 1970s. These five economic building blocs, combined, helped secure the U.S. *golden age.*

The United States was able to share wealth with allies to contain the Soviets, and at the same time U.S. citizens enjoyed a rapidly rising standard of living. There was even enough to share with the less fortunate in this country. U.S. economic-superpower status crumbled with President Nixon's August 1971 decision to abandon the quasi gold standard and Saudi Arabia's decision on 20 October 1973 to cut all shipments of oil to the United States. Loss of cheap oil crippled what had been a rapidly rising U.S. standard of living. American voters had grown accustomed to a rising standard of living and expected it to continue. When it didn't, government expenditures increased and entitlements attempted to fill the gap between expectations and what the private sector of the economy could deliver.

Lean years set in. The United States was no longer a global economic superpower in the 1980s. Other countries decided they could not depend on the United States for much help in growth of their economies. The U.S. tax code turned more friendly to U.S. capital and labor in the early 1980s, but pressures for more and bigger entitlements continued draining U.S. taxpayers. And the Soviet threat remained. A precise dating for the start of the lean years is perhaps not important, but in 1985 Western Europe announced to the world their program—Completing the Internal Market—to attempt to manage themselves. Economic events of the 1970s and early 1980s in the United States convinced the Europeans that U.S. support was waning. Western Europe's response was the creation of a single European market at a time the cold war was winding down.

The cold war ended in a tremendous victory for the U.S. building-bloc strategy. The cost to the Soviet Union, the loser, was, of course, huge. The cost of the U.S. strategy—borne by the American taxpayer—was large, both financially and socially, as it created broken promises at home. The United States had kept its international commitment but beginning in the early 1970s failed to fulfill domestic promises created during the 1950s and 1960s. The central promise was that ordinary citizens could expect a good education and a decent job, enjoy a rising standard of living, and live in a safe neighborhood.

Part II (chapters 11–20) addresses *broken promises*. This section begins by providing an overview of both various government expenditure and taxation programs and the growing gap between taxes paid and benefits received. Growth of entitlement expenditures illustrates the tendency of many citizens to turn their hands to government for assistance to resolve problems, which has been the operating theme since the time of the New Deal. Many Americans seek security in government programs as roadblocks in the form of high tax rates and mandates block the highway of opportunity in the private economy. Purchasing power for approximately 77 million private-sector jobs has been eroding since the time of the 1973 OPEC oil embargo. The U.S. economy is attempting to work itself out of this predicament through building a knowledge-based economy. This new segment of the economy rewards people working in it with an improving standard of living, while many trapped in the old part of the economy face grim futures as jobs and benefits are phased out. Some see an apparent dichotomy when high-paying jobs in one part of the economy disappear, but the corporate sector remains healthy. The reason for this is that the burden of government policies that share wealth with our allies as well as internally falls directly and/or is shifted onto the backs of taxpayers. An economy where taxpayers experience broken promises can function. But an economy cannot function for long if the business sector bears the burden of broken promises in the form of taxes and mandates that cannot be shifted backward to employees or forward to customers.

Taxpayers carry another heavy burden as real educational expenditures per pupil continue to march upward, while the quality of primary and secondary education declines. Reasons for this and possible remedies are presented in chapter 16. Crime in the United States is another broken promise as real per capita expenditures on public safety increase rapidly at the same time that violent crime increases. Major reasons for the crime wave are that perceived benefits of the criminal life-style are greater than costs, creating incentives for people to choose that life-style, and for any given benefit/cost ratio the breakdown of family and community values means that a level of deterrence won't be as effective as in past decades. Chapter 18 provides solutions to the crime problem. It is a twofold approach. One is to privatize law enforcement through use of bounty hunters to capture alleged criminals. The second aspect is move to a fixed-penalty system for violent crimes in order to make costs of committing crime clearer to everyone. The last two chapters in this section discuss more symptoms of broken promises and roadblocks to achieving the promise of a good education, a decent job, and a rising standard of living.

Part III discusses *The Future*, which will be determined by policies that the United States implements. The cold war ended with Soviet economic and political defeat and the United States in relative economic decline. In perspective the United States and the Soviet Union had filled large military, economic, and political vacuums created by removal of the great German and Japanese hegemonies in World War II. Again, there is this enormous global political, economic, and military vacuum to be filled in the last years of the twentieth century and early years of the twenty-first century. Who is going to fill it? The United States continues its external wealth-sharing policies. The U.S. military is the only superpower left, but U.S. taxpayers are tapped out. Many domestic wealth-sharing policies continue. Basic institutions are eroding. Following the same basic policies of past decades suggests that the United States will continue its relative decline. The United States could reverse this decline with policies outlined in chapter 22 that focus on wealth creation.

Part I

The Past—The Creation

1

It Has Happened Before

Reasons why particular nations rise to world dominance and then enter into an irreversible relative economic decline are always controversial, in particular in the country undergoing the decline. There is a denial stage which may last many decades as people spin reasons why it really isn't occurring. But, as described by Kennedy, great powers have always come and gone.[1] Two cases briefly summarized in this chapter are Rome and England.

Rome

At its peak the Roman Empire extended from the Atlantic Ocean to the Euphrates River in Iraq, from North Africa to the Rhine-Danube line, and included most of Britain. This area encompassed perhaps 50 or 60 million people and it operated as a unified state at its peak. The empire collapsed. Why? It wasn't outside pressure but an internal process of disintegration. There wasn't one reason but many reasons. Jones suggests a combination of factors such as excessive taxation and inflation in addition to bureaucracy and justice system inequalities, all factors contributing to the demise.[2]

The empire was built on a unite-and-share-the-plunder policy that made Rome the keeper of a military that needed feeding with plunder. This resulted in a positive balance of trade along with an ever-growing empire fed by plunder. In modern times many nations grow by an export-led policy that involves conquering other countries or industries in those countries by economic means. Japan, after World War II, utilized in part this approach, because the United States implemented policies encouraging that behavior. Japan produces high-quality products for export to other countries and brings back money. Rome exported its military and brought back plunder to expand its empire.

But nothing works forever. Plunder within any reasonable reach grew scarce, other countries learned how to better resist, and the military lost its drive, which resulted in Rome's export-led strategy becoming ineffective. Rome's domestic economy needed to replace that export-led growth; it didn't, leading to balance-of-payment problems, reflecting, in part, trade of gold for silk. In modern times, nations such as the United States are moving toward a level-playing-field trade policy. In that environment Japan's export-led policy won't be nearly as effective as it was with the United States. Japan may need to replace its export-led development with internal growth if a level playing field develops between Japan and other countries.

Revenue for Rome's treasury came primarily from plunder, port dues, and taxes on land as well as personal taxes. State revenues, which in earlier times had been adequate from plunder, were insufficient from plunder after the year 406 B.C. when the Roman state began to pay its soldiers. Rome levied a heavy tax on citizens according to their means. Wealth was generally associated with land ownership at that time, and since Rome was primarily a nation of soldiers and farmers, taxes fell heavily on landowners. Initially women were tax-exempt so taxes could be avoided by placing land in the hands of women. This tax-code loophole resulted in the disappearance of large chunks of land from the tax base and tax revenue declined.[3] Finally, in 169 B.C. the Roman state, in an effort to maintain the tax base, passed a law that prohibited a man to will more than half of his land to women. Romans had discovered that increasing tax rates on land resulted in a shrinking tax base and declining tax revenues.

Initially tax levies took the form of a land tax, but around 43 B.C. a tax on income was levied. Other sources of revenue included tax revenue from slaves (some families had several thousand slaves); salt; crops such as corn; pillars, doors, windows; harbors; livestock-per-head tax; grazing fees; license taxes on trades; inheritance tax; and taxes on imports and to some extent on exports. Taxes on imports were not meant to be protectionist but were an attempt to find revenue for the Roman treasury. As the ability to obtain plunder slowed, incremental revenues from domestic taxes were needed to support the military, welfare state, and bureaucracy.

Tax rates reached extreme levels by the fourth century A.D. Tax rates on income climbed from around 10 percent in the first century A.D. to perhaps 40 percent or 50 percent or more in the fourth century A.D., which discouraged economic production. Tax rates on crop production were punitive. Tax rates on grapevines, for example, were based on the number of vines per unit of land area. Beyond a certain number of vines the incremental tax exceeded the income gained, so owners would destroy part of their crop to avoid taxes and production declined. Roman politicians failed to learn from their previous experience as high tax rates led to erosion of the tax base.

Romans passed legislation that required cultivation of all land. This policy of forced cultivation and high tax rates reduced income of landowners, forcing landowners to resort to tax avoidance and evasion. Larger landowners could more easily work the political system to avoid taxes as key people in the political structure were also landowners and were sympathetic to issuance of exemptions. Smaller landowners were forced out of business and migrated to urban areas. The tax assessment and collection process allowed ample room for evasion. Assessments could result in ruin, so the process was ripe for collusion and fraud. Local fiscal agents were corrupt. Tax revenues of the state decreased, and later the assessment and collection process was turned over to more "trusted" officials.

But high tax rates continued, so that evasion and avoidance of taxes were built into the economic system, depressing economic production, pushing small landowners out of business, making the poor poorer, and resulting in declining revenues. Finally an attempt was made to reduce the rate of taxation with the objective of encouraging more production and economic activity. Julian, a Roman emperor in the latter half of the fourth century, reduced tax rates and cut military expenditures in an attempt to increase production. He had fewer men in the military but encouraged use of more machines. He decreased the size of the tax bureaucracy, reducing, for instance, the number of paid tax informers to seventeen. Julian died a premature death on the way back from battle. Attempts to reduce tax rates appeared from time to time in legislation of Julian's successors, but the bureaucracy came back. For instance, the number of paid tax informers rose to the thousands again within twenty years. The tax base continued to shrink, tax revenues declined, and the ability of the state to maintain public services such as roads declined.

The empire operated on a cash basis, and transactions were carried out in coins minted from silver, gold, and copper. Domestic mines, owned by the state, provided new sources. Coin prices appear to have remained approximately fixed per unit of silver and gold respectively for over two centuries up through the time of Augustus's death in A.D.14. Debasement occurred during the first and second century at about the time the rate of taxation increased sharply. Silver and gold content in coins started decreasing as the empire devalued coins in an attempt perhaps to deceive the public in order to have existing silver and gold supplies go further. Coins were issued by the state with lower nominal values without an indication on the coins. The metal content of Roman coins was reduced about 25 percent during the first century A.D. and substantially more during the second century.[4] Rapid inflation occurred during the third century A.D.

People soon learned that coins were worth less, and prices went up by the amount of the devaluation. Inflation was underway. Prices rose slowly, but old coins were melted down and stocks of silver and gold started to be hoarded. During the third century the state rapidly devalued gold and silver leading to a corresponding rapid rise in prices. This had the effect of reducing real wages of state employees, including soldiers. Some government expenditures were made in kind, but government expenditures continued to rise rapidly. Government expenditures were the mechanism that the empire used to inject new money into circulation as newly minted coins were spent by the empire for a variety of purposes including payment to soldiers. Finally, instead of devaluating coins through utilizing less metal, the empire resorted to arbitrarily assigning high nominal values to coins, and prices jumped rapidly. High tax rates and high inflation encouraged nonproductive activity, and the level of economic production declined.

Periods of high inflation and high tax rates led to concentrations of wealth, in particular to those in public service as Roman public service was extremely profitable. Regulatory schemes and the corresponding corrupt legal system helped lead to the demise of the middle class, and there is a story of one Crassus that illustrates the workings of political connections. Rome's public fire system was inadequate, so Crassus formed a slave fire brigade. When a fire occurred, Crassus and his slave brigade would rush to the house on fire and make an offer to purchase the burning house as well as those adjacent. If the offer was accepted, he proceeded to put out the fire. If it wasn't, he moved on.[5] Crassus provided a service and reaped large profits. Crassus was an entrepreneur. The state, however, regulated the number of people in this business in order to keep profits high. No doubt there were kickbacks.

Could Julian, had he lived, with his lower tax rates, reversed the fall of Rome? It is possible, but corruption was so embedded in the state that failure was perhaps inevitable. The surprising aspect might be that the Empire survived as long as it did. The power of a bureaucracy, even a corrupt one, to perpetuate itself in conjunction with a powerful military cannot be underestimated. The effectiveness of the military fell rapidly and barbarians were hired for the military as the bureaucracy became more corrupt. In the fifth century the sacking of Rome by outsiders occurred.

England

England remains a wealthy society, but that is not the issue. The issue is the relative decline in economic position for the past 100 years. Other nations, such as the United States, grew faster so that England suffered a relative decline. England's decline has been gradual and not sudden. Rome had its barbarians at the gate as did England in the form of Hitler. Some might say that barbarians also come in other forms, such as the tax man, bureaucracy, corruption, and inflation, among others, but old style barbarians are still around in modern times (e.g., Saddam Hussein). England, by conventional measures, has been in a relative decline for a long time. The British economy was roughly comparable to the U.S. economy in 1870 but had shrunk to 37 percent of the U.S. economy by 1914.[6] In 1994 England's economy was only 15 percent as large as the U.S. economy. Parallels of the British experience have been made with different empires such as Rome and Spain.

The relative decline of an empire is due to a unique set of circumstances, but the decline for each empire is perhaps inevitable. Empires have their golden age and the British golden age was in the nineteenth century, from the end of the Napoleonic Wars to the latter part of that century. A unique set of events seems to take place during the golden years that ensures decline will follow, but it is probably unreasonable to expect that an empire, once in its golden years, can do anything but enter a relative decline as competing countries grow and expand. The British began to pursue an outward-looking policy from around 1650 on and emerged in the 1800s as the overwhelming victor. England met with huge success by focusing on her navy and maintaining relatively small land forces while building a solid economic foundation—England was the first major economy to industrialize.

Countries, once in their relative decline, remain in denial for many decades. It no doubt was incomprehensible to many British citizens that their country could be victorious in major wars, but then lose the commercial challenge from rivals they had defeated in war. As recently as 1900 the world was under British hegemony. England had the largest empire in the history of the world, amounting to one-fifth of the world's land surface and a quarter of globe's population. British military power was viewed as invincible and London was the financial center.

It is no different for the United States. Some people no doubt find it inconceivable that the United States, which was the dominant economic power after World War II, could suffer large commercial losses relative to countries such as Japan. Furthermore, the United States followed policies in the post-World War II period encouraging West Germany, Japan, and others to gain economic advantage at the expense of itself. The United States responded to the Soviet threat after World War II by developing a set of building blocs encouraging market economies surrounding the Soviets to grow and expand in order to contain the Soviets. This process, explained in following chapters, made possible rapid development of market economies around the globe. The United States shouldered the burden during its golden years, but eventually policies and events turned golden years into lean years and broken promises. England experienced a somewhat similar set of events.

A common explanation of England's decline is one of an antimarket economy, which is ironic since the industrial revolution and free-market system originated in Great Britain.[7] But the argument is made that British culture regards free market economics as unfair because the working class comes out losers. British culture, the argument goes, is antibusiness, in particular via its educational system, which results, over time, in the belief that a market economy is inherently unfair and requires governmental intervention, regulation, and mandates to make the system less unfair. Great Britain was the first country to industrialize, but this antibusiness climate was held by both the British Left and Right. Resulting high tax rates, burdensome regulations, and mandates become roadblocks for business to grow and people to get ahead, so production slows. Government mandates and taxes, in many instances, hurt the groups they were designed to help and end up solidifying the class structure. People at the bottom have more and more difficulty climbing the income ladder because of taxes and mandates.

The United States is also becoming a much more rigid economy where roadblocks confronting the ordinary American are much higher and make it more difficult to advance and obtain an improving standard of living, points demonstrated in the following chapters. Americans turned more and more toward government in the anticipation that government could meet their expectations through entitlements and mandates when the lean years started. What was great about the U.S. franchise is that it allowed ordinary Americans the opportunity to obtain a good education, work hard, and enjoy a rising standard of living. That roadway is littered with roadblocks and potholes, making it more and more difficult for ordinary people to travel. It is becoming more difficult as the U.S. educational system moves toward a curriculum of equality of cultural outcomes. A market economy can't provide that. Instead, governmental mandates are required to achieve cultural outcomes.

Another common explanation for the British decline is that the British consumed too much and worked too little,[8] and, in addition, British investment went overseas to profitable locations such as the United States to fund expansion. The idea was that people and institutions in Great Britain obtained their profits through capital investments in other countries. These other countries then became stronger and stronger rivals of the British economy. Countries such as Germany and the United States, aided by exports of machine tools and capital from Great Britain, industrialized rapidly and became commercial threats to England. The British, perhaps, should have been investing in the British economy to develop new industries at home. Furthermore, the British, in the previous century, were busy promoting and implementing the idea of free trade or an open-door trade policy from the British perspective, while not necessarily requiring other countries such as the United States to open their markets. That allowed the United States, Germany, and France to enjoy net gains from trade that England didn't share.

The United States is going through a somewhat similar process, as many opportunities are outside this country and investments go where opportunities are. High taxes, mandates, and a relatively high cost of doing business in the United States mean that a portion of U.S. investment dollars go outside the United States in search of more profitable opportunities. But the U.S. economy has remained more fluid than the British. U.S. business responded to changes taking place around the world and became more competitive, whereas less-flexible British corporations languished for a longer time. The United States, as later chapters illustrate, started implementing a movement toward free trade after World War II, but it was primarily from a U.S. perspective, as other countries were not necessarily required to open their economies. This allowed other countries such as Japan to enjoy net gains from trade that the United States didn't.

Rubinstein suggests the British decline reflected the point that England was never an industrial economy but was always financial and service-based.[9] What people observed was a manufacturing abnormality due to the industrial revolution that gradually declined as other economies around the world adopted British technology and grew; thus, the industrial decline in England involved a shifting of resources from the industrial segment to financial and service-based segments. It was this factor, rather than the cultural one or sending investment dollars overseas, that contributed to the perception that Great Britain had manufacturing-based difficulties. Rubinstein's argument is that manufacturing was never a British skill.

Another explanation for England's decline, which is developed in succeeding chapters for the United States, is that once a country takes a world-leadership position, that position cannot be sustained indefinitely. Other countries, as suggested above, become commercial competitors and want to participate in the wealth of the world leader. England shared her wealth with others, but to a much lesser extent than the United States did as the world leader, through movement toward free trade and by maintenance of a massive navy and a network of bases around the globe. England failed to share wealth with her colonies as they were part of the British plunder system. But the commitment by the British to keep ocean highways open and maintain order required tax revenues, and England moved toward a progressive income tax system around the turn of the century. This had the added effect of sharing wealth with other countries such as the United States. The progressive income tax was modest by today's standards, but it had a wealth-sharing effect nonetheless. The core premise of this explanation, which is covered in this book, is that the very fact of becoming a world leader sets in motion a process by which the country moves into a relative economic decline. A world economic leader, when taking a positive approach, shares wealth with other countries. A country can take a world-leadership role and not share wealth, but then such a country or group of countries is viewed as an unfriendly one. A world leader and keeper of the peace, by definition, must stand ready to help other countries, which requires sharing of wealth. That was the role England held into the early part of this century.

World War II ended British dominance and pushed England to the brink of collapse. World War II illustrated the extent of British relative economic decline to the world as it ended the British Empire and cleared the stage for U.S. and Soviet ascendancy. The United States undertook the role of rebuilding the world economy, and the baton for policing the world was transferred from England to the United States shortly after World War II. England attempted to act as a junior partner to the United States at that time and continues to do so by politically and militarily supporting the United States when possible. England continues to make a sizeable military commitment of more than 3.5 percent of economic activity compared to over 4.5 percent for the United States in 1994.

England, in spite of handing the world-leadership role to America, continued to lose relative economic position after World War II. Labour won a decisive and unexpected victory in 1945. Victory in Europe came in May 1945, and in July British voters said goodby to Sir Winston Churchill. On 25 July 1945 Churchill told King George VI that he "confidently expected a Conservative majority." On 26 July 1945 at 7 p.m. Churchill saw the king and handed in his resignation as prime minister. Churchill was "saddened and surprised by the electoral results." The results, at that time of the evening, showed the Conservatives with 189 seats and the Labour party with 392. The king was also saddened at the unexpected dismissal of his great war prime minister. The British electorate seemed to him (the king) "very ungrateful." The winner, Clement Attlee, was just as surprised by the results.[10]

Large and enthusiastic crowds had turned out to see Churchill when he toured England during the campaign in June and July. That, as it turned out, was their way of saying goodby. It was not that they were ungrateful to him for saving them, but they felt his great ability as a war leader didn't fit their domestic needs (Churchill did return to power in October 1951). England had been a world power for 100 years, and British taxpayers probably thought they had given enough. The majority, since they elected Mr. Attlee, wanted a more activist domestic government to attempt to improve the overall standard of living. The British knew their country was nearly bankrupt and finished as a world power. They had sacrificed much in the struggle for peace and, in return, expected the government to produce an improved domestic postwar economy. A contract had no doubt evolved between the people and the government during the two world wars that sacrifices of the people would be remembered. John Maynard Keynes, in conjunction with the Labour party, had set forth an agenda of both comprehensive welfare services and government involvement in delivery of goods and services. The Labour party offered a contract of "security" and "care" in exchange for higher taxes, higher spending, more government involvement, and a relatively less-fluid economy. British voters signed on.

President Bush never caught on that the cold war was over, and voters wanted a president who would focus on domestic concerns. Candidate Bill Clinton offered the idea that we must care about each other, we must include all segments and groups within our society, and we must protect our environment. That is the contract that Clinton offered—security and care—in exchange for higher taxes, higher spending, more government involvement, and a relatively less-fluid economy. American voters, 43 percent of them, signed on. President Bush gave Americans the same in his one term in office—higher taxes and spending, more government involvement, and a more rigid economy—but he was perceived as not offering security or caring. And his strength—foreign policy—was not deemed critical by voters in the post-cold war era.

U.S. taxpayers had given much during the cold war. They funded a worldwide defense program, an economic policy that helped contain the Soviets and eventually end the cold war (as explained in succeeding chapters) and a large and growing entitlement-based economy. During the golden age a contract evolved between the American people and their government that the economy would provide decent jobs, education, safety, and rising standard of living. These were provided at the same time the United States fought a cold war. The cold war ended. Voters had difficulty understanding why President Bush did not have a set of policies in place to deliver a decent job, safety, and a good education for their children. American voters were perplexed. The United States won the cold war, but my neighbor is unemployed and his neighbor is working part-time, the streets aren't safe, and the public school system

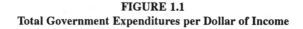

FIGURE 1.1
Total Government Expenditures per Dollar of Income

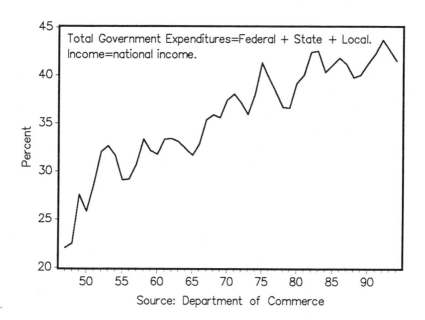

Source: Department of Commerce

is falling apart. Americans in the 1990s, like the British in the 1940s, know something is wrong. Sacrifices such as taxes for national defense were made for decades. Americans shared their wealth with other nations. The United States provided a large portion of the security blanket for the rest of the free world. The United States won, but the domestic economy can't deliver. Many Americans feel they are entitled to a good job, education for their children, safe streets, health care, and retirement. So did the British.

The United States appears to be on the road that England followed in the 1940s by turning more and more toward government. England traveled this road for decades in an attempt to halt the relative British decline. Mrs. Thatcher dismantled part of the welfare economy. More and more involvement of government in the U.S. economy has also been underway for decades. The end of the cold war opened up domestic problems for everyone to see. It perhaps is a situation that all great powers eventually find themselves trapped in. There are examples in the United States where government has been pushed back. The November 1994 election results could be interpreted in such a fashion. But in the aggregate, the public sector is winning and pushing the private sector back. Figure 1.1 erases any doubt about what Americans wanted over the past fifty years. It says in election after election Americans vote for representatives that give voters what they want—more and more government spending and involvement in the economy. Americans made a series of decision to increase the role of government in the economy. But key societal and community values such as family, the educational process, and safety can't seem to adapt to the many changes thrust upon them by government. This breakdown of core community values, and their replacement by more and more government involvement and a bigger and bigger safety net is not working.

2

The Foundation Years

The post-World War II period saw major U.S. policy initiatives as the United States ascended along with the Soviets to fill the large power vacuum created by defeat of the Germans and Japanese in World War II. The economic building blocs that the United States used to create and shape global development to contain the Soviet Union didn't instantaneously develop after World War II. The foundations for policy development of free trade, investment, foreign aid, development of multilateral institutions, and arms control had been laid over previous decades with various parties and presidents. The focus of this book is on post-World War II policies, but chapter 2 provides a very brief overview of (1) the Wilson presidency and its building-bloc foundations; (2) the Great Depression in the 1930s, FDR's response in particular, and how that experience influenced post-World War II policies and domestic economic parameters; and (3) the global shifts wrought by World War II.

Wilson Presidency

During Woodrow Wilson's campaign for President in 1912 he met in August with Louis Brandeis, a leading progressive lawyer of the day who helped shaped Wilson's early economic policy—the New Freedom—and whom Wilson later appointed to the Supreme Court. Brandeis wanted Wilson to encourage competition within the United States by reducing or eliminating measures that gave monopoly power to U.S. business and to encourage competition with foreign companies through reduced tariffs. Brandeis felt that competition was the basis of U.S. greatness.

During the nineteenth century the United States imposed high tariffs on European imports to protect U.S. manufactures and Britain didn't retaliate. U.S. industry grew and prospered under that arrangement. The

U.S. economy grew rapidly relative to other economies, in particular, that of England, as the British had taken the world-leadership position. American taxpayers, over the years, viewed tariffs as a subsidy to business. U.S. industry became increasingly stronger, but part of that strength was paid for by U.S. consumers in the form of higher product prices. The Payne-Aldrich Tariff of 1909 raised tariffs to their highest point in U.S. history. Tariffs were a primary source of federal tax revenue, but they also kept out lower priced goods from abroad, which worked to raise U.S. cost of living—a process similar to that in Japan today.

Woodrow Wilson was inaugurated on 4 March 1913. While a student at Princeton, he had begun formulating future political plans, which included his ambition of being a U.S. Senator from Virginia, and after graduating from Princeton in 1879, he obtained his law degree from University of Virginia Law School. Wilson's health was rather frail through college as well as in later life, particularly so during a part of his presidency. He practiced law in Georgia, but then decided to pursue a Ph.D. degree in history at Johns Hopkins. Upon graduation he began his career as a teacher at Princeton. He was elected president of Princeton in 1902 but resigned in 1911 to run for and become governor of New Jersey. While at Princeton Wilson had written a friend that the governorship of New Jersey was a step along the way in what would be an upcoming bid for presidency of the United States in 1912.

Wilson almost ran for U.S. senator from New Jersey in 1907 but decided against it in order to avoid a fight with some Democrats who would oppose his nomination. Instead Wilson was able to orchestrate the politically powerful of New Jersey to support his run for governor in 1910. He was inaugurated governor in January 1911, earned the reputation of a progressive and independent during his first year, and became a leading contender for the 1912 Democratic presidential nomination.

Wilson went through the primary process, but by the June convention he was behind, and it wasn't until the forty-sixth ballot that Wilson was declared the Democratic nominee for president of the United States. Franklin Delano Roosevelt, a state senator from New York, campaigned for Wilson and participated in swinging the New York delegation to Wilson on the forty-sixth ballot. FDR became assistant secretary of navy in the Wilson Administration.

After inauguration on 4 March Wilson called Congress into special session on 7 April for the express purpose of tariff reform. Tariff reduction and banking reform were the major components of the New Freedom. Congress passed the Underwood Tariff Act of 1913 which reduced tariffs. An offset to that federal government revenue loss was implementation of a progressive income tax that was included as part of the tariff reduction package. It was argued that the tariff tax was a tax on consumption, and that revenue to support the federal government should be based on income. Earlier attempts at instituting a progressive income tax had been declared unconstitutional by the Supreme Court. The Sixteenth Amendment, providing for a tax on income, was passed by Congress and ratified by states in February 1913.

Along with tariff reduction Wilson established the Federal Reserve system in 1913. The recession of 1907 raised questions about effectiveness of the national banking system established in 1863. Congressman Carter Glass, chairman of the House Banking Committee, was the primary initiator of the Federal Reserve regional banking structure, while Brandeis and others put together the Board of Governors that kept the banking system under federal control. The tariff-reduction issue was argued primarily as a domestic tax issue; not a trade issue with other countries. Also the decision concerning the Federal Reserve was argued strictly on domestic grounds. Spillage on other nations was ignored.

In November 1916 Wilson narrowly won a second term with the campaign slogan "He kept us out of war." Wilson obtained concessions from the Germans after a German U-boat sank the *Lusitania* in 1915, but in January 1917 the Germans announced they would resume unrestricted submarine warfare. In April the United States declared war. World War I suddenly altered the U.S. position in the global economy from one of isolation to one of involvement. Munitions were produced in the United States for European Allies as well as for itself. The U.S. private financial system provided financing for British and French private borrowing. The U.S. government also financed public Allied borrowing.

President Wilson traveled to Paris to meet with leaders of other countries in an attempt to shape the postwar world three weeks after the 11 November 1918 armistice. This was a break with precedent as no sitting U.S. president had ever traveled to Europe. Earlier that year President Wilson, in a speech to Congress, had outlined his Fourteen Points as a basis for peace. Eight of the fourteen pertained to territorial adjustment after the war; others called for such things as freedom of the seas, removal of economic barriers, and equality of trade and reduction of armaments. The fourteenth point related to a league of nations which Wilson felt was the most important point.

President Wilson helped in drafting the Treaty of Versailles and League of Nations Covenant. During months of negotiations he compromised on many points with foreign leaders to keep alive his idea of the League of Nations, as it had become of central importance to him. Domestically, Republican senators were busy organizing opposition to the League of Nations as Wilson had outlined it. On 8 July 1919 President Wilson attempted to sell the Treaty of Versailles to the Senate. The votes were not there, and Wilson tried to sell it directly to the people but became ill during that process. The United States refused to ratify the Treaty of Versailles or to join the League of Nations.

The 1920 presidential election confirmed the rising mood of U.S. isolationism. Candidate Warren G. Harding campaigned on old-fashioned nationalism. He won in a landslide, announced that the League was now deceased and turned the United States inward. The United States was a world economic power following World War I, but it primarily followed inward-looking policies over the next two decades. The United States insisted European Allies pay all of their debts. In addition, the Fordney-McCumber tariff of 1922 was passed to provide tariff protection to nurture a new crop of U.S. wartime infant industries. Tariffs were raised around the world in response. A pullback from Wilsonian principles occurred, but during the Wilson administration tariff reduction and a progressive income had been implemented, while the idea of a League of Nations in which the United States would take a major leadership role was planted. These policies and ideas formed the cornerstone of the post-World War II Soviet containment strategy.

The Great Depression

Another major force for U.S. international and domestic involvement was the depression in the 1930s. The U.S. economy peaked in September 1929, and a month later the stock market crashed in response to the economy going into recession. The economic boom during the 1920s occurred as tax rates were reduced, in steps, from a top rate of 73 percent in 1921 to 24 percent in 1929. Lower tax rates provided incentives for workers to work, for new businesses to start up, and for existing businesses to produce.

In 1928 Benjamin Strong, president of the Federal Reserve Bank of New York, faced a decision—whether to lower interest rates in New York to assist the British with an inflow of capital to their country or to raise rates in an attempt to slow the domestic rise in stock prices and economic expansion. Mr. Strong chose lower interest rates and the stock market boomed, but later that year the Federal Reserve raised interest rates and significantly slowed money growth, which may have been one factor in the economy turning down in September 1929, as has been argued by Milton Friedman and Anna Schwartz.[1]

But the more important factor in turning the recession into a depression were efforts of the Republican party to raise tariffs on foreign agricultural products in the name of protecting domestic producers. Farmers felt left out of the boom during the 1920s, and protecting U.S. farmers from imports became imbedded in the 1928 Republican platform. Herbert Hoover promised farmers help while campaigning for president. Stock-market participants sent a signal to Hoover and the Republicans in autumn of 1929 not to implement tariffs. On 21 October the tariff bill written by Senator Smoot in the Senate Finance committee was being discussed on the Senate floor. Over the next few days the Senate discussed tariff hikes on specific proposals.

On 24 October, Black Thursday, the stock market made a rational adjustment to the possible implementation of tariffs and their detrimental influence on the economy and corporate profits. The next day saw a market rally supported by Wall Street bankers, and many felt the worst was over. But Tuesday, 29 October, was a day of devastation. The market crashed as the increasing likelihood of tariffs finally hit investors. President Hoover responded to the crash by quickly proposing a very minor tax cut to increase purchasing power. This step, while too small, was a positive step, and by the spring of 1930 the stock market had nearly recovered the losses of 1929.

But a Republican-dominated Congress ignored the stock-market warning in the fall and passed, with President Hoover's support, the Smoot-Hawley Tariff Act. President Hoover signed that measure in June 1930 with the idea of helping farm income. In addition, he expected the tariff to bring in additional revenues necessary to balance the budget as tax revenues were down owing to the shrinkage of the tax base in the recession. Instead of helping farm income, the Smoot-Hawley tariffs started a worldwide depression. By the time it passed Congress Smoot-

FIGURE 2.1
Percent Unemployment and Real Economic Activity

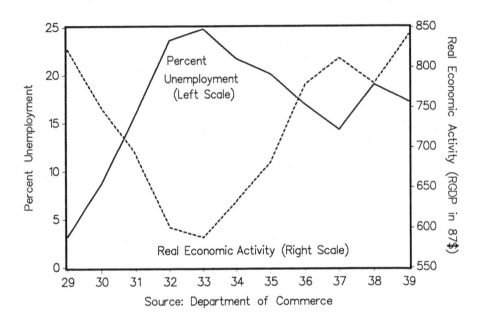

Source: Department of Commerce

Hawley had become a tariff on both agricultural and nonagricultural products. Congressional members from agricultural states needed to support tariffs on nonagricultural products in other states to garner the necessary political support from other members to pass the tariff.

The stock market fell 80 percent over the next two years. The depression was in full swing in response to the 55 percent average import tax on dutiable imports. Hoover regarded his decision to raise tariffs as a domestic measure in spite of formal protests from thirty-four nations. A tariff is a tax on international transactions. Italy, for instance, imposed tariffs of over $1000 on some U.S. autos exported to that country. President Hoover failed to see the Smoot-Hawley Tariff as a major action setting off a retaliatory tariff war. Other nations retaliated and both the quantities and prices of traded commodities went into a downward spiral. The U.S. economy crashed (figure 2.1). Unemployment climbed to

25 percent in 1933, while the level of economic activity, adjusted for inflation, fell by nearly one-third from 1929 to 1933. No one could have expected it would be ten years before economic activity again reached its 1929 level. Perhaps no one understood what happened, least of all President Hoover, and no one was prepared for the economic pain and suffering that would follow.

The Smoot-Hawley Tariff decimated the world economy since U.S. manufacturing accounted for 39 percent of world manufacturing output in 1928, according to Kennedy.[2] President Hoover failed to understand what he had done and instead came to believe that his minor tax rate cut of around 1 percent had something to do with domestic economic problems. He succeeded, with the help of Congress, in raising the top tax rate from 24 percent to 63 percent, signing this tax bill in June 1932 and making it retroactive to 1 January 1932. Real economic activity didn't reach its 1929 level until 1939—a ten-year period of economic terror brought about by implementation of the Smoot-Hawley Tariff and higher tax rates.

In response to the depression he created, Hoover started the Reconstruction Finance Corporation having a credit pool of $500 million to lend to agricultural agencies, banks, and railroads. But, as it required firm collateral before making a loan, it only helped the strong. Will Rogers described this as "The money was all appropriated for the top in the hopes it would *trickle down* [italics added] to the needy." President Hoover's two main legislative acts, Smoot-Hawley and higher tax rates, were gifts to Franklin Roosevelt.

Franklin Delano Roosevelt campaigned against Hoover promising action on reducing unemployment, lowering tariffs, and cutting government spending. Roosevelt attacked Hoover's deficit spending and at the same time promised to use government funds to aid those in need. Hoover advocated lower tariffs but also promised continued protection of U.S.industry. It was clear to most by this time that tariffs were not a domestic issue but an international one.

FDR led the United States in a new direction after he was inaugurated. He was fifth cousin of Theodore Roosevelt, the twenty-sixth president, and had been born on 30 January 1882 into a family of wealth. At his college-prep school, the Groton School in Massachusetts, he and other students received moral instruction in the responsibility of the wealthy to aid those less fortunate. At Harvard he majored in political history and government, graduating in 1904. He married Eleanor Roosevelt, his distant cousin, in 1905, attended Columbia University Law School, and worked as a lawyer after he passed the bar exam. In 1910 he won the New York state senate seat from his district, honed his political skills, and won reelection in 1912. At the 1912 Democratic presidential convention in Baltimore, he pushed for the nomination of Woodrow Wilson and assisted in moving New York delegates to Wilson. FDR was later offered and accepted the position of assistant secretary of navy in the Wilson administration, remaining in that post until 1920. Along the way he took time out in 1914 to run unsuccessfully for nomination for U.S. senator from New York and represented the navy as an observer at the Versailles Peace Conference.

FDR participated at the Democratic convention in 1920, where he seconded the presidential nomination of Al Smith. The convention selected James M. Cox as their Presidential banner carrier and he chose FDR as his running mate. Roosevelt campaigned for the League of Nations, but in the end Cox lost the race to Warren Harding. Roosevelt joined a law firm, and in August 1921 he was stricken with poliomyelitis. He fought his way back to resume his legal career and on 26 June 1924 made the Democratic nomination speech for Al Smith who was then governor of New York. His nomination speech received a one-hour-and-thirteen-minute ovation, reflecting acknowledgment for the courage FDR had shown in his comeback from disease, but Smith still lost the nomination.

FDR was asked by Al Smith to run for governor of New York, but he declined to do so. FDR was nominated anyway in 1928, ran a vigorous campaign, and won by a small margin. In his reelection bid in 1930, Roosevelt said he had answers to the depression, won in a landslide, and was busy during his second term as governor in running for the presidency.

Roosevelt won the Democratic nomination on the fourth ballot. To do that, he denounced the League of Nations in its 1932 form to gain William Randolph Hearst's vital support and in addition agreed to offer the vice-presidency to John Nance Garner of Texas. Texas, California, and others pushed FDR over the 770 votes needed for nomination. Roosevelt accepted the nomination and pledged a New Deal for the American people. He campaigned on lower tariffs, unemployment relief, repeal of Prohibition, a cut in government spending, and the idea that the country needed bold experimentation—it needed above all to try something.

After his inauguration on 4 March 1933, he initiated the Bank Holiday almost immediately, which closed banks for four days. President Roosevelt summoned the seventy-third Congress into special session on 9 March. Congress adjourned 100 days later on 16 June after creating what is called the "New Deal"—the precedent for social and economic legislation that we have today. The New Deal was a sizeable effort undertaken in an attempt to induce growth in the economy. Unemployment was 25 percent in 1933, prices were falling rapidly, people had lost confidence in the banking system, and bread lines were getting longer. But the New Deal was not a carefully thought-out plan. Rather, it was a makeshift series of experiments put together to stimulate economic activity. As FDR said, "It is common sense to take a method and try it. If it fails, admit it frankly and try another."

Some Americans regarded the New Deal as dangerous. It was argued that FDR was attempting to push the country toward Marxism, while others argued that it was a push toward U.S. fascism. The fodder for this latter concern came from the successes of Mussolini and Hitler, but those concerns were rather silly since the New Deal was simply a series of experiments in which FDR was trying to find something that worked. It is also well to remember that the most controversial issue at both the Democratic and Republican conventions in 1932 was the question of Prohibition repeal. In hindsight, the specific programs of the New Deal were probably not very important in ending the Great Depression. What was important is that the various programs told the American people that their government was attempting to direct the economy and was concerned about the plight of the American people. President Hoover failed in that effort. Tariffs were reduced, confidence started to return, and the economy bottomed in 1933 before most of FDR New Deal programs had a chance to take hold.

Following FDR's inauguration, a great deal of legislation was enacted in what came to be known as the "Hundred Days," of which but a partial list is described below. In March alone, the Emergency Banking Relief Act was passed and signed within eight hours, reopening banks and placing an embargo on exports of gold and silver (9 March); the Economy Act reduced salaries of all appointed federal personnel by 15 percent (20 March); the Beer-Wine Revenue Act legalized those beverages adding to the nation's tax base (22 March); and the Civilian Conservation Corps employed young men in work projects such as planting trees and building dams and parks (31 March).

In April the United States went off a true gold standard as gold was effectively nationalized and the dollar devalued (19 April). By the end of January 1934 the New Deal's definitive gold policy appeared in the form of the Gold Reserve Act of 1934. The official price of gold was set at $35.00 from $20.67 and the gold standard was effectively dead as U.S. citizens on longer had the right to convert currency into gold. Holders of gold, the U.S. Treasury, and foreigners, won with the dollar devaluation. Foreign governments, however, still had the right of conversion. The net result was a limited gold standard, which existed until President Nixon ended it in 1971.

In May the Federal Emergency Relief Act provided direct relief to cities and states (12 May); the Agricultural Adjustment Administration provided subsidies to farmers to limit crop production (12 May); the Emergency Farm Mortgage Act stopped foreclosures and authorized federal refunding of mortgages (12 May); the Tennessee Valley Authority Act called for the rehabilitation of the Tennessee Valley basin—40,000 square miles (18 May); and the Truth-in-Securities Act was passed in an attempt to provide more reliable information to investors (27 May).

In the virtual half of June that comprised the remainder of the Hundred Days, the Home Owners Loan Corporation authorized refinancing of mortgages at more reasonable rates for nonfarm homeowners (13 June); the Glass-Steagall Banking Act created the Federal Deposit Insurance Corporation, separated investment from commercial banking, restricted use of bank credit for speculation, and gave regulatory authority to the Federal Reserve (16 June); the Farm Credit Administration centralized provision of farm credit, provided for refinancing of mortgages, and established local adjustment committees (16 June); and the National Recovery Administration developed codes of fair competition, guaranteed labor's right to organize and bargain collectively, and created the Public Works Administration (16 June).

After the first 100 days Roosevelt kept the New Deal moving forward. In August 1933 the National Labor Relations Board was established to back collective bargaining by labor; in November 1933 the United States also normalized relationships with the Soviet Union, having withheld recognition since the 1917 Revolution on grounds that World War I debts to the United States needed to be paid; on 5 December Prohibition, which had been the major topic of discussion at the 1932 conventions, was repealed; in December 1933 Roosevelt also initiated the good neighbor policy to the south by agreeing to a pledge of non-intervention; in June 1934 the Securities Exchange Commission was established to curb stockmarket malpractice; also in June 1934 the Federal Communication Commission was established to regulate interstate communications; and, also in June 1934, a bill was signed into law that lowered tariffs up to 50 percent on a bilateral basis. In August 1935 the Social Security Act was passed . Other programs established in 1935 included the Works Progress Administration to provide loans for nonfederal projects, the Motor Carrier Act to place interstate truck lines under the I.C.C., and the Wealth Tax Act which hiked surtaxes on individual incomes of $50,000 and on estates over $40,000. In September 1936 the Tripartite Monetary Agreement was agreed to, and though mostly symbolic, it did indicate the United States taking a role in stabilizing the world economy. In particular, it allowed the French to stabilize the franc for a very short period.

The economy grew rapidly in real terms from early 1933 to the middle of 1937, an average annual rate of 12 percent over the four years. But the economy remained below its peak level of 1929, and in the meantime the population had grown. The decision to start lowering tariffs in 1934 as well as the confidence generated by the New Deal programs helped the economy grow. The Reciprocal Trade Agreements Act of 1934 was a signal that the United States was again interested in both economic and political foreign policy. But the overwhelming interest of Roosevelt was the domestic economy. FDR's programs, taken together, provide the framework for the model of increasing governmental involvement in the economy—what is now called the "welfare state." Government actions and the Smoot-Hawley Tariffs led to the depression; government actions helped pull the economy out of depression. Massive government involvement in the economy relative to earlier years told people that government programs and involvement were effective in helping to improve the private economy.

The New Deal established a promise or expectation or entitlement with groups of citizens such as farmers, the elderly, and unions that when things go terribly wrong, a benevolent government would be there to help. Constituencies and entitlements evolved out of the New Deal model, which set the stage for rising expectations in later years. What was left out of this understanding was that it was the same government that had created the Great Depression to begin with. But the New Deal became the model for a larger governmental role by both political parties in the following decades. Presidents and members of Congress harken back to the New Deal when referring to good deeds done by government. The New Deal demonstrated that the federal government could come to grips with serious economic problems, alleviate them, and/or move toward helping to resolve them.

The model evolved, continually fed by politicians, that says: Don't worry, the government will take the initiative and responsibility to solve your group's problems. The result is a nation that has drifted from the individual taking responsibility for his well-being to society taking responsibility for constituencies. The success of this model started breaking apart in the 1970s and imploded on itself in the 1980s and 1990s for everyone to see and feel.

World War II

Warnings started as early as 1933. Germany, Japan, and Italy formed their Axis in 1936, and in 1937 Roosevelt began sounding warnings, as FDR may have been more concerned than Western European leaders about potential actions of the three powers. In 1938 the United States cut off exports of scrap iron and steel to Japan, though oil to Japan wasn't cut off until the summer of 1941. Roosevelt, in 1939, asked Congress for additional money to strengthen naval and air defenses. Hitler's invasion of Poland on 1 September 1939 resulted in Britain and France declaring war on Germany.

But Congress and the American people remained opposed to involvement in a European war. A poll taken in 1940 showed that nearly 80 percent of the population opposed involvement, even if Britain and France were defeated. Pearl Harbor changed that. World War II ended with the United States an economic and military power while Western Europe was devastated. The relative strength of the United States was a key element in building the framework for U.S. leadership. FDR made major contributions through personal efforts at major wartime conferences along with his push for the United Nations and impassioned pleas for the United States to lead the battle for reason in world affairs.

3

Prelude to the Creation

Among the many who participated at the start of the Creation were President Harry Truman; General George Marshall; George Kennan, State Department policy planning head; Leo Pasvolsky, principal speech writer for Cordell Hull, who was then secretary of state; Will Clayton, an assistant secretary of Commerce who later became under secretary of state for economic affairs; John Maynard Keynes of the British Treasury; and Dean Acheson, to name but a few.

Many who came before—President Wilson, FDR, and others—helped lay the foundation that started the Creation. For instance, tariff reduction, one of President Wilson's key domestic economic programs, was a key building bloc in post-World War II foreign policy. Countries taking the world-leader role in previous times, such as England, served as role models for the United States. FDR led the United States toward the world-leadership role by building on President Wilson's ideas.

The Great Depression provided the environment for understanding the critical economic link between the United States and the rest of the world. FDR's New Deal served as the model for domestic wealth-sharing that subsequent political leaders followed. Many people over the years kept the Creation going—in particular, the U.S. taxpayer. In 1990s the United States can see the victory of international wealth sharing but is saddled with broken promises of domestic wealth sharing, a situation explained in later chapters.

Leo Pasvolsky was chief lieutenant for Cordell Hull and helped decide what the secretary of state would say. One of Pasvolsky's key personal goals in his job was to promote the idea of free trade. Of Pasvolsky, Dean Acheson said, "He wrote Mr. Hull's speech; for, whatever the occasion or title, the speech was apt to turn into a dissertation on the benefits of unhampered international trade and the true road to it through agreements reducing tariffs."[1] Acheson, an assistant secretary of state at that time, would be summoned to Mr. Hull's office to review Pasvolsky-proposed speeches—line by line but never the theme—as Hull and Pasvolsky both shared the same central political purpose, the idea of free trade.

Secretary Hull's appearance was that of a statesman and he had considerable clout with both the House and Senate. But his influence in the administration was not great because FDR was willing to utilize trade levers to fulfill domestic needs that conflicted at times with Secretary Hull's free-trade agenda. For example, FDR depreciated the dollar in 1933–34 which resulted in U.S. exports becoming more competitive and making it more difficult for foreigners to sell their products in the U.S. market. The Agricultural Adjustment Act gave the president power to exclude foreign products, but Hull opposed this, gradually losing favor with the president. Hull was a main contributor to the London Economic Conference in 1933, which was a smaller and more narrow version of the International Monetary Conference at Bretton Woods eleven years later.

But in 1940 before the U.S. entered the war, Hull and Pasvolsky were given an assignment of preparing postwar plans for the United States in the world economy. A plan and organization for delving into postwar problems were outlined by Pasvolsky and Hull in 1941 and a number of task forces resulted from their work that developed into detailed postwar plans. One outgrowth of that work was the foundation for the United Nations charter. Another was a somewhat broader-thinking document on the ways the United States could influence global postwar development and the destiny of the world.

Postwar preparations, independent of State Department efforts, were ongoing in other parts of government as well. These included those of Harry Dexter White at Treasury who led U.S. planning for monetary reconstruction, and Emilio Collado at the Agricultural Department who spearheaded efforts on food. In May 1943 Collado with assistance of Dean Acheson organized a United Nations conference at Hot Springs,Virginia, on food requirements in the postwar period. Collado and Pasvolsky also participated in the Bretton Woods meeting to continue their dialogue on exchange rates and free trade among countries. Acheson later worked on duties of an international bank at Bretton Woods. Independent preparations for eventual surrender and occupation of Germany were, of course, underway. Britain engaged in similar efforts—the future restocking and supplying of Europe once it was freed from German occupation.

Efforts on monetary reconstruction had been ongoing since 1941 with John Maynard Keynes of the British Treasury and Harry Dexter White exchanging ideas and drafts. In early summer 1941 Keynes made a visit to Washington as a representative of Churchill on lend-lease matters, and talked to a number of people in explaining issues and complexities of an international monetary system, the tremendous capacity of the United States to export goods in the post-war period, and the world's need for U.S. goods as well as problems of payment. The dialogue on international monetary arrangements between Britain and the United States continued up to the Bretton Woods meeting.

One outcome of that process was a draft statement for an international monetary fund that had clearance from U.S. congressional committees and U.K. Parliament in the spring of 1943. Sections on commercial policy, commodity agreements, and employment were added. A proposal for an international bank for reconstruction and development was also published by the Treasury with input from congressional committees. These drafts led to further work and in May 1944 the State Department issued invitations to forty-odd governments to meet on 1 July at Bretton Woods, New Hampshire. The purpose of this meeting was twofold: (1) to finalize the character of an international monetary fund and (2) to explore the possibility of establishing a bank for reconstruction and development or world bank.

There was no international system in existence prior to World War II that was acceptable to the economic and political powers. But before World War I there was a gold-standard system that worked well for about forty to fifty years up to the time of World War I. Countries such as Britain, France, Germany, Spain, and Russia were trading partners in which their relevant currency contained specific amounts of gold. London was the world financial center and Britain dominated international investment. Britain supposedly made the lion's share of its foreign investment during this time period in developing countries such as Canada and America—geographic areas called by the British "regions of recent settlement." Britain's commitment to free trade and a fixed gold value of sterling meant that sterling could act as an international money. The sterling was as good as gold.

After the international system was disrupted by World War I, most currencies fluctuated and attempts to establish an order among trading nations never resulted in any serious agreements. Conditions worsened with implementation of tariffs and the Great Depression. Some currencies lost their convertibility. In Europe, Germany was building itself for war, while the United States was involved in putting together a national consensus of action for rebuilding the domestic economy. But it was up to the newly emerged power, the United States, to provide the leadership for an international financial system in the 1940s.

Bretton Woods was selected because of its fine climate in the White Mountains of New Hampshire and the availability of a summer hotel of adequate size and condition. The hotel had been closed for three years, however, and problems of staffing and operation were present as it was still wartime. Meetings went on all day and often far into the night for nearly four weeks. Keynes and White provided the intellectual leadership, and according to Keynes, the pressure was "quite unbelievable."[2] Keynes, after attending night sessions against orders of his physician, suffered a heart attack during the period.

The conference led to formation of the International Monetary Fund (IMF), Bretton Woods exchange-rate system and the International Bank for Reconstruction and Development. The objective of the IMF, as described in Article I of Articles of Agreement, is to facilitate achieving full employment and growth. This was to be done through creating a stable international monetary system for investment and trade and by promoting international monetary cooperation. Development of the IMF at Bretton Woods was watched over by Pasvolsky and Collado, and policies were established that are still in place today. Member countries subscribe to the IMF by lending their currencies and borrowing foreign currency. The IMF lends funds to help countries in balance of payments difficulties. Major changes in IMF policy need a majority 85 percent vote; thus, the larger, richer nations, which have the larger share of votes, dominate voting.

Gold was established along with the dollar in a dual system in the Bretton Woods framework for managing exchange rates. Instead of using gold as the only international money, which Keynes did not want to do again, each currency had a set parity that was established in terms of both gold and the U.S. dollar. The dollar was the reserve currency, so it was pegged in terms of gold, initially at thirty-five dollars per ounce.

The United States agreed to buy and sell gold from monetary authorities of other countries at that price. But U.S. citizens didn't enjoy convertibility as convertibility didn't apply to the private sector. Other currencies were defined relative to both the dollar and gold. This meant a set of exchange rates among currencies was fixed by international agreement. The exchange-rate system was part of the IMF.

Members agreed to maintain their currency value within 1 percent of their chosen value. The British pound was set at 12.5 pounds per ounce of gold. This implied an official exchange rate between the dollar and pound of $2.80 per £. The Bretton Woods system was successful in keeping exchange rates fixed for much of the period from 1945 until 1971. Member countries could change the value of their currency after discussions with the IMF if they had fundamental problems with their balance of payments. The German mark was adjusted upward on several occasions, while the British pound was devalued in 1967 from $2.80 to $2.40 per £.

The International Bank for Reconstruction and Development (or World Bank) had responsibility for reconstruction and development of countries that were in early stages of industrialization or had not begun to industrialize. The bank was to make loans directly to member nations and/or to guarantee loans made by private bankers. The United States provided about one-third of the seed money for the bank and therefore had the greatest voting power. The bank is capitalized by lending nations who subscribe in proportion to their economic importance. An International Trade Organization (ITO), also established at Bretton Woods, had responsibility for lowering trade restrictions. The ITO had a short life and was replaced in 1948 by the General Agreement on Tariffs and Trade (GATT), which was signed by 23 countries.

The Bretton Woods institutional framework acted as a foundation for coordination and in particular, acted as a jumping-off point for the U.S. effort at directing global economic development to contain the Soviets. The experience of the years between the two world wars illustrated the fact that when countries pursue their own national interests without regard to other countries' interests, all countries suffer. To prevent this from recurring, Bretton Woods participants developed ground rules for a stable international monetary system (the dollar became as good as gold for a number of years), a dependable exchange rate-system, and movement toward free trade—institutions and agreements in the inter-est of all nations.

Meanwhile Roosevelt met Joseph Stalin, the Soviet leader, for the first time at the Teheran Conference in November 1943. FDR and Churchill wanted a commitment from Stalin that the USSR would open a second front against Japan as soon as Germany's defeat was assured, which was to be when Germany was invaded through France. FDR and Churchill received such an understanding from Stalin at the Teheran meeting. Stalin's impression was likely that an exchange had been made.[3] Stalin could have portions of eastern Europe for opening a front with the Japanese. Kennan suspected this arrangement from an article that appeared in *Pravda* in 1944.[4] He later found out that some borders had been substantially agreed to by Churchill, Roosevelt, and Stalin at the Teheran Conference. As it turned out, Roosevelt may have already written off eastern Europe by early 1943 before he went to Teheran Conference.[5]

There were a number of people already sounding warnings about the Soviets. One of these was George Kennan who, in 1942, felt that there were no grounds for the United States and the USSR to ever have meaningful economic trade. Kennan also argued that the Soviets held a conviction that they someday would rule the world.[6] Of Irish ancestry on his father's side, George Kennan had been born into a Milwaukee family of no particular traits, fame or fortune, his father having worked in various modest occupations such as farming and the ministry. Kennan entered Princeton in 1921, contracted scarlet fever as a freshman, developed only a few friendships, and did not partici-pate in activities outside the classroom during his stay at Princeton. Upon gradation in the spring of 1925, he entered the Foreign Service, which had only been established in 1924. Kennan indicated he chose this career because he "did not know what else to do," except he knew he enjoyed international politics.[7] He had stints in Geneva and Ham-burg and had been prepared to resign from the Foreign Service in 1928, when his application for special training in Russian was accepted. The biggest portion of that training was several years of graduate study at a European University in addition to practical training. Five and a half years elapsed from the time he was chosen to be trained as a Russian specialist until Kennan began his service in Moscow as an aide to William C. Bullitt, who was U.S. ambassador to the USSR and FDR's leading advisor on Soviet relations. A holdover from the Wilsonian days, ambassador Bullitt resigned his Moscow post in 1936 and was given the Paris job.

Kennan was appointed a regular diplomatic secretary in the mission in March 1934 and worked as part of the Soviet division until the summer of 1937. Kennan states that "no experience in life did more to sharpen my mind and refine my judgements on the whole problem of Russian communism" than working in Moscow during that period.[8] The Soviet division was abolished very suddenly in 1937 on Washington orders. The U.S. library on the USSR that had been built by Kennan and others was shipped back to the United States or destroyed. Kennan said he never learned the reason for the purge other than Kennan and others working there were felt to have "taken Russia too seriously."[9]

Kennan's next foreign assignment was Prague in 1938–1939; after that was Berlin, which is where he was, in December 1941, when the United States declared war on Japan. From December to May, Kennan and others were held under Gestapo supervision until their release was negotiated. His next assignments were Portugal and London, before being reassigned to Washington in 1944. The Ambassador to Moscow, Averell Harriman, was seeking a minister-counselor, and Kennan was given the assignment. The U.S. embassy in Moscow was split in two parts. One was the civilian which Kennan headed beginning in July 1944 and the other was the military mission.

Kennan wrote about his concerns with the Soviets in Poland and other areas of eastern and central Europe during 1944 and 1945. The USSR, Kennan argued, was after power and control and viewed U.S. efforts in creating the United Nations as a sign of weakness (the United Nations Charter was signed in June 1946). In this period Kennan's advice had no effect on FDR as Roosevelt had already made his decision on Eastern Europe.

FDR again met with Stalin and Churchill at Yalta in February 1945 in order to get Stalin to firm up a date for the USSR's entry into the Japanese war. There were a number of concessions made to Stalin for that Soviet agreement to engage Japan including (1) interim governments in eastern European countries such as Hungary, Czechoslovakia, Austria, Bulgaria, and Rumania could be represented by communists as well as noncommunists; (2) eastern Poland was to be placed under Stalin's protection; and (3) the southern part of Sakhalin Island, which was occupied by the Japanese, was to be given to Stalin after the Japanese were driven out. An understanding reached between Stalin and FDR was that the Kremlin could cautiously expand their influence over neighboring countries in eastern Europe through democratic procedures. Stalin wanted this understanding from the United States in order to establish a buffer along his boundaries. With that understanding, eastern Europe belonged to the Soviets.

FDR died in April 1945, which made acceptance of the United Nations by the American people an almost certainty. The war in Europe ended in May, while the Japanese surrendered in August. Kennan's concern about the U.N. was the "expectation that it could serve in any significant way to mitigate the consequences of the forthcoming communizing of Eastern and parts of Central Europe—that it could serve, in effect, to contain and to correct the imbalances bound to flow from the foreseeable outcome of military operations."[10] Kennan indicates that Woodrow Wilson had expected something similar of the League of Nations in 1919, only to be disappointed.[11]

An effective U.N. depended on cooperation among the great powers. Stalin was interested in European hegemony, not cooperation. Stalin's only interest in an international organization was to further his goals in eastern and central Europe. His influence in that geographic area was agreed to by FDR in 1944 and 1945. Stalin's next geographic target, according to some, was Western Europe.

Kennan, during the summer of 1944, became convinced that U.S. perceptions of Soviet intentions were dangerously wrong and that Stalin and other Soviet leaders were intent on ruling the world. In September of that year, Kennan completed a thirty-five-page essay entitled "Russia—Seven Years Later." The paper was Kennan's assessment of the evolution of Soviet foreign policy and provided the basis for Kennan's subsequent work on the USSR. In that paper he explained Russian culture and beliefs, described personalities, and explained how men in the Kremlin never abandoned their faith in a program of territorial and political expansion or their commitment to becoming a dominant power in Europe. Kennan gave the paper to Harriman, who apparently sent it on to Washington, but the climate in Washington was not receptive for concerns Kennan had for potential Soviet intentions.

Peace in Europe produced a larger and growing area of Soviet power, and Kennan again expressed his concerns about Soviet intentions in so-called "satellite" areas in a paper written in May 1945 called "Russia's

International Position at the Close of the War." One point in the paper was that the USSR might not be able to retain control in eastern Europe without U.S. assistance, and Soviet leaders were expecting that assistance. But Kennan also indicated he didn't think the Kremlin planned a further military advance into Europe. Kennan continued to make observations about likely hostile intentions of the Soviets over the remainder of 1945 and need for the United States to develop a policy to counter those intentions.

The Truman administration, in early 1946, didn't have a firm idea of what their Soviet policy should be. Kennan states that in February the U.S. Treasury sent a message to the U.S. embassy in Moscow requesting an analysis of Soviet behavior. Treasury said the Soviets were unwilling to adhere to World Bank and IMF guidelines, and Treasury officials wanted to know the reasons behind this unwillingness. People in the U.S. Treasury, according to Kennan, had a naive expectation that the United States and Soviets would work together. Stalin also made a speech in February 1946 to the effect that eventually a Soviet-capitalist showdown must occur.

Kennan's response to the Treasury was made in the form of an 8000 word telegram that came to be called the "Long Telegram." Many points in this report had been covered by Kennan in previous years, but the timing for discussion of issues was previously not right. The Treasury request and Stalin's speech changed that. The report was divided into five separate parts: (1) features of the Soviet postwar outlook; 2) background for that outlook; (3) its projection on an official policy level; (4) its projection on an unofficial policy; and (5) implications for U.S. foreign policy. Kennan suggested that the United States answer the Soviet challenge by planning as if for war, although it wouldn't necessarily be a violent war.

Copies of Kennan's response were given to many, including President Truman and James Forrestal, secretary of the navy. Kennan thinks Forrestal had hundreds, if not thousands of higher officers in the armed services, read the Long Telegram. Forrestal recalled Kennan from Moscow and assigned him as first deputy for foreign affairs at the National War College. That college was intended as the senior establishment for training in issues of politics and military for armed services. Kennan's assignment was to devise and direct the political portions of the combined military-political course of instruction, which meant not only writing and lecturing at the college but going on public speaking tours as well.

Kennan, when speaking, felt that the audiences having the best ability to understand his philosophy on the Soviet Union and the United States were groups of business people. He believed they could understand that "you could oppose a competitor without finding it necessary, or even desirable, to destroy him, and therefore capable of understanding the Soviet-American antagonism might be serious without having to be resolved by war."[12] Academics, according to Kennan, had the most problems with what he talked about.

Kennan was at the War College from September 1946 to May 1947 and developed ideas that were central to his views on the warfare portion of U.S. foreign policy. The experience of the United States in two world wars, the war with Spain, and the American Civil War had left in the minds of many the idea that total destruction of the enemy—his capital and will—was necessary. Kennan said the atomic age changed that—in particular the atomic bomb meant a doctrine of limited warfare, the United States should never use atomic weapons except in retaliation, and the United States would need "small mobile forces" capable of combat on very short notice.[13]

U.S. policy toward the Soviets started to harden in 1946 when Soviet expansion efforts in areas such as Bulgaria, East Germany, Poland, Romania, and Iran altered U.S. perceptions of Soviet intentions. The U.S. administration took actions demonstrating strong opposition to Soviet demands on Turkey in August 1946. When Soviet troops massed along the Turkish border threatening the Black Sea coast, a U.S. naval task force was sent on training maneuvers along the Turkish coast. President Truman sent another signal in 1946 when he fired then secretary of commerce, Henry Wallace, who had openly criticized the U.S. "get-tough-with-Russia policy" in a speech at Madison Square Garden and also suggested that Soviets imperialism was no worse than Western imperialism.[14] Averell Harriman replaced Wallace as Commerce secretary.

James F. Byrnes, the secretary of state, was replaced by General George Marshall when Marshall returned from the Far East in January 1947. During late 1946 the Truman administration viewpoint shifted to perceiving Soviet actions as being a possible forerunner to the Soviets extending their influence and control over Western Europe. An official move to contain the Soviets came in late February 1947 when Great Britain's ambassador advised Secretary of State Marshall that Britain was no longer capable of providing aid to Greece or Turkey. Dean Acheson, undersecretary of state, asked Kennan to serve on a task force being established to study the question of assistance to Greece and Turkey.

The Greek government had been under heavy attack by leftist and communist guerrillas since the spring of 1946. In March 1947 President Truman requested that Congress grant $400 million in aid to Greece and Turkey. (That $400 million was equivalent in purchasing power to $2.6 billion in 1994.) Truman asked for aid to Greece and Turkey within a broader context of containing the Soviets before a joint session of the House and Senate. That aid was granted within the context of what came to be called the Truman Doctrine—aiding free people (anywhere) who resist outside pressure as well as inside pressure by armed minorities. The working premise of the Truman Doctrine was containment, and it signalled the beginning of the United States as global watchdog. George Kennan supported aid but didn't support the sweeping nature of the Truman Doctrine, as he felt a time would come when that open commitment would not fit U.S.interests.[15] Dean Acheson also told members of Congress that President Truman did not intend the Truman Doctrine to be interpreted as it read.[16]

Kennan sent Forrestal a paper on the nature of Soviet power relative to U.S. policy in January 1947 and later asked Forrestal if it could be published. After going through appropriate channels it was published in the July 1947 issue of *Foreign Affairs* with the name of the author listed as "X". The now-famous piece led to the general use of the term "Soviet Containment."

Kennan later stated, after critical writing appeared, that the paper had three serious defects.[17] First, it had failed to address Soviet power and influence in Eastern Europe. Kennan later indicated he fully supported the "importance of achieving, someday, the retirement of Soviet military power from Eastern Europe," though Soviet influence in Eastern Europe had been covered in detail in his earlier writing. Secondly, Kennan felt he failed to clarify what he meant by Soviet Containment. What Kennan said he meant was containment of a political threat by political means, not military, and that a hot war could be avoided. Kennan changed his mind at a later date, according to Mark, as he supposedly told secretary of state George C. Marshall on 15 March 1948 "that a Russian invasion of Western Europe might be imminent."[18] Kennan indicated his third defect in the paper was again something to do with containment. He didn't believe "containment" meant containing the Soviets everywhere in the globe but rather making sure that certain key areas didn't come under Soviet control. Kennan discussed four such areas: the United States, Britain, Japan, and the Rhine valley and its associated areas. The essence of the X-Article, Kennan said, was to "Stand up to them [the Soviets],...manfully but not aggressively, and give the hand of time a chance to work."[19]

4

The Creation—Building Bloc I, the Marshall Plan

The United States was in a unique position to take a world-leadership role as the nation was the dominant economy in the world in terms of industrial strength and technology at the close of World War II. In 1950 after economic recovery had taken hold in the USSR and Europe, the United States remained the dominant economy (figure 4.1). The U.S. economy dominated other economies in the post-World War II period in terms of absolute size. Economies of the Big Four in Europe—U.K., Germany, France, and Italy—combined, were approximately half the size of the U.S. economy. In comparison, in 1994 the Big Four combined economies were nearly 80 percent as large as the U.S. economy. The U.S. economy relative to Japan's economy was larger by a factor of nearly 12 in 1950. In 1994 the U.S. economy was larger than Japan's by a factor of only 1.5. Japan enjoyed remarkable growth during that period, in part because of U.S. trade, tax, and military policy. Growth of the West German economy led the European recovery. Countries suffering war damage grew relatively faster than the United States during the 1950s, as would be expected when countries rebuilt with U.S. help.

The United States held a dominant economic position after World War II because a major barrier prevented Europe and Japan from entering the global marketplace. That barrier was a destroyed capital stock as World War II decimated large chunks of their basic industries. Likewise the Soviet economy suffered severe losses. U.S. industry, in comparison, emerged unscathed from the war, as wartime pressures led to massive levels of research in new technologies and major advances in production techniques. However, an economically dominant United States didn't alleviate U.S. fears of Soviet ability because of the USSR

FIGURE 4.1
Relative Economic Importance in 1950

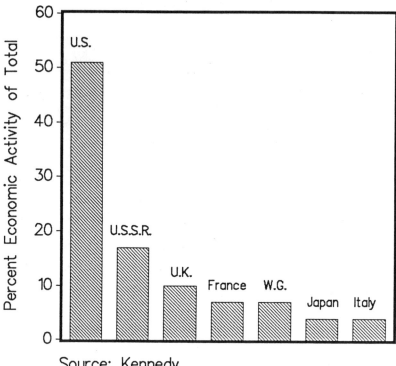

Source: Kennedy

economic success during the 1930s. The United States and Western Europe suffered severe economic depressions during the 1930s, while the Soviet economy enjoyed strong growth under Stalin's forced economic-input growth policies. The Soviet labor force increased rapidly as millions of people were moved from farms to work in the cities, and millions of women were forced into the labor pool. Factories were constructed to produce industrial output.

Soviet economic output is estimated to have grown between an average annual 4 percent and 9 percent from 1928 to 1940. This rapid growth occurred as inputs of labor and capital increased sharply. In comparison, the U.S. economic pie was no larger in 1939 than it was in 1929 while Stalin's economic policies met with success. That's why Western concerns about Soviet economic ability existed in spite of the massive destructive blow to their economic base during the war. Kennedy estimates that 20 million to 25 million Soviet citizens died premature deaths in the 1941–45 time frame.[1] Damage to the Soviet physical capital base was as crushing. It wasn't clear to U.S. analysts, at that time, that Soviet output growth reflected rapid input growth, not productivity growth, and therefore could not be sustained. Growth in the United States, in comparison during the 1950s and 1960s, reflected growth in inputs as well as growth in output per unit of input or productivity.

But as concerns about Soviet intentions increased, so did concerns about European recovery. The bitter European winter of 1946–47 brought Europe's economic recovery to a grinding halt. Europe needed rebuilding, but capital available through the IMF and the World Bank was inadequate. European countries were devastated by war with masses of refugees and bombed-out capital equipment. The IMF and the World Bank, while helpful, simply could not provide enough capital for Europe's massive needs.

Britain issued a white paper on 20 January 1947 describing the seriousness of her economic situation. The U.K. continued to go deeper in debt, and U.S. and Canadian loans of $5 billion ($33 billion in 1994 dollars) the previous year were being exhausted. The U.K. needed to increase production and exports to gain breathing room. The coal shortage in Britain was nearing disaster proportions, and coal allocations to factories were cut by half. Britain indicated she was going to have to reduce military commitments both abroad and domestically. In February the weather worsened, half of British industry closed, and Britain's hopes for increasing exports were dashed. Britain was finished as a world power, and this was widely recognized when Britain asked the United States to provide aid to Greece and Turkey in February. Reduced commitments and troop withdrawals over the previous sixteen months from India, Egypt, and Burma were obvious characteristics of an empire that was disintegrating. Britain faced economic and financial ruin—the final chapter in the collapse of the once great Empire.

Conditions on the continent were not as bad as in Britain, but the extreme weather conditions had a devastating impact, and the feeble economic recovery was coming to a halt. Shortages of labor and capital were creating major production problems, and pockets of consumers, not finding products on the shelf to purchase, were going hungry. Concerns about social unrest and communist gains in France and Italy increased U.S. concerns about Western Europe, in particular concerns about steps Soviet leaders might take to capitalize on burgeoning problems in Western Europe. Meanwhile, in Congress President Truman's proposed budget was being reduced by Republicans, which would require cuts in the operating budgets of the army and navy. Decisions made at the end of World War I were in danger of being repeated in the face of the near collapse of Britain and major economic and social problems on the Continent.

Postwar plans discussed at Bretton Woods were not capable of addressing the magnitude of problems developing in Western Europe. Plans for postwar Europe had greatly underestimated the destruction of transportation facilities, factories, and mines as well as the time and capital necessary to rebuild. The State Department announced in November 1946 that a meeting in April 1947 would take place among eighteen countries in an attempt to reduce trade barriers, a move that would be expected to assist Europe's recovery. By January 1947 it was becoming apparent to many in Washington that a much greater effort on part of the United States was needed in the near term for Western Europe.

U.S. concern about Western Europe was twofold: (1) possible meaningful social discontent and (2) and an increasing Soviet threat. General George C. Marshall took the oath of office as secretary of state in January 1947. Dean Acheson was made under secretary of state and chief of staff by Marshall. The Marshall and Acheson team was the right team for that time period. General Marshall's decisions "had every appearance of being right in their political, social and economic contexts."[2] Marshall, according to Jones in *The Fifteen Weeks*, illustrated his breadth and depth when talking to the graduating class of Princeton on 22 February 1947 which was fifteen weeks before the historic speech at Harvard on 5 June.[3] One of Marshall's favorite expressions according to Jones and Acheson was "Gentlemen, don't fight the problem, solve it!"[4]

Dean Acheson, a successful lawyer, came to the State Department in December 1940 when Secretary of State Hull asked him to be assistant secretary of state for economic affairs. Acheson had been under secretary of Treasury in 1933 but resigned after a conflict occurred with FDR. In the early weeks of Marshall's service, it was Acheson who usually briefed the president, and if Marshall did, he took Acheson along.[5]

The British ambassador met with General Marshall on 24 February and informed him that Britain was no longer capable of providing aid to

Greece and Turkey. Marshall and Acheson presented the case for aid on 27 February at a White House meeting with leading members of Congress. President Truman formally asked Congress for aid to Greece and Turkey on 12 March within the broader context of the Truman Doctrine. The Truman Doctrine—its public discussion at the same time of dire conditions in Western Europe and a more complete understanding of the intentions of the Soviet leaders—was rapidly moving toward what was to become known as the Marshall Plan, an idea not new as such ideas had been floated before. For instance, John Maynard Keynes had wanted something like it for Europe after World War I, and during the 1920s and 1930s, large-scale aid packages had been discussed along with an end to trade barriers.

U.S. leaders didn't want to repeat mistakes of post-World War I such as isolation and movement away from open trade. Many felt that U.S. isolationism after World War I was the main reason Hitler was able to embark on World War II. Economic and military disorder was due, in part, to this vacuum of world leadership after World War I. That vacuum was filled, of course, by Germany and Japan. Countries such as Britain and France sharply increased tariffs during and after World War I. Great Britain increased tariffs by one-third on items such as motor cars in an effort to reduce imports of luxury items. France increased minimum tariff rates from 5 percent to 20 percent and maximum rates from 10 percent to 40 percent in 1918. The United States passed the Fordney-McCumber Act that increased tariffs on certain products coming into the United States.

Acheson and Kennan, as well as others, had been actively pushing for assistance to Western Europe before, during, and after Bretton Woods. The difference at this time was that Acheson was working directly for Secretary Marshall. Acheson met with both the secretary of navy and secretary of war on 5 March as well as sending them identical letters suggesting that problems with Greece and Turkey were forerunners of likely larger and growing problems around the globe that had resulted in part from Britain's loss of strength and in part from increasing Soviet aggression. The question was the type of aid the United States should provide to Europe. A task force was formed involving State and Treasury along with Navy and War Departments with several sub-task forces to do the necessary studies. They addressed economic, financial, technical, and military aid that might be needed by European countries and

Japan in the near term. Longer-term programs of U.S. assistance were also developed. Private groups in the United States were also pushing for aid to Europe, and their efforts fed State Department activities. Concerns of private groups as well as government leaders were no doubt influenced by fears of a potentially deep domestic recession, as U.S. economic activity declined and went into recession after the war ended. Many in the private sector felt export markets were needed to utilize U.S.industrial capacity and the European market, if growing, would provide a major outlet for both U.S. capital and consumer goods.

While Secretary Marshall was in Western Europe and Moscow during part of March and April, Acheson was left to address the response to the Truman Doctrine along with day-to-day problems in addition to his continuing involvement in the task forces. The task forces were doing detailed work that included surveys of how much food, energy, machinery, and other items would be available for export from surplus countries such as the United States for Europe as well as for Japan. This was for the short term. Longer term involved revival of production and trade on a world basis and the U.S. role in that process. Special emphasis was given to Germany since its recovery would speed up the European recovery.

In early April President Truman asked Acheson to go to Cleveland, Mississippi, on 8 May to speak at a conference on behalf of the president. It was decided to use that occasion as a way to expand on the economic intent of the Truman Doctrine together with initial task force recommendations. That combination would provide a more comprehensive statement of U.S. foreign-reconstruction policy. This involved discussion of the bleak economic environment in Europe including Soviet activities and gains by communists in France and Italy. The U.S. response would likely involve extending major aid to Europe for large-scale reconstruction as well as accepting more imports from Western Europe and Japan. This work fed into what came to be called the Marshall Plan.

General Marshall returned from Moscow on 28 April 1947 fully aware of seriousness of economic problems in Western Europe. The Moscow meeting was the Moscow Conference of the Council of Foreign Ministers. It ran from 10 March to 27 April. Marshall met with Stalin on 15 April to discuss the economic plight of Germany and Western Europe. Stalin counseled patience. On the return trip Marshall reviewed the lessons of Moscow with his staff, concluded that the Soviets were stalling, and became convinced that the Soviets wanted to see Western Europe fall apart. Marshall decided the United States must take action to start the European recovery. The Soviets, at an earlier date, had refused to join the International Monetary Fund and International Bank for Reconstruction.

Meanwhile, the State Department was coming under criticism for not being more comprehensive in its approach to European problems. The gravity of economic conditions in Western Europe was being understood by more people as coverage of European problems increased. Secretary Marshall told Kennan on 29 April to set up a policy-planning staff in the State Department as a plan needed to be developed for the United States to take the initiative in Europe. Marshall told Kennan that "it was so clear that the world was falling down around our ears,…that Congress would soon be demanding action, suggesting all kinds of bright and unworkable ideas in an effort to force the Department's hand."[6] Marshall asked Kennan to provide him a paper with an analysis of problems in the reconstruction of Europe along with recommendations for action within two weeks. It was a formidable task in a short time frame, but many ideas and preliminary work had already been done by Acheson and others. In addition, others such as General Eisenhower had already suggested a request to Congress for funds for other countries in Europe and in the Far East to help resist communism.

George Kennan had been working on such a program, so that his previous work as well as the work of others was quickly assembled. Kennan was still at the War College but had begun to move to the State Department, assembling a staff in mid-April in anticipation of the request. Secretary Marshall had sent messages from Europe stating that he wanted such a policy-planning staff established. Kennan finished the draft of what became the Marshall Plan on 23 May. As Kennan said, "The authorship of the Marshall Plan has been variously claimed (and) Messrs. Acheson, Clayton and Bohlen were only the most senior and distinguished."[7] (Charles "Chip" Bohlen had been trained as a Soviet specialist along with Kennan and was with Marshall at the Moscow meeting.)

Will Clayton, assistant secretary of commerce, had been pushing a general recovery plan for Europe. He returned from a trip to Europe on 19 May where he had been negotiating for lower tariffs. His proposal for a European recovery plan was also reviewed by Marshall. Clayton's proposal, which he prepared on the way back from Europe, dealt with the imperative need for the United States to take immediate action to shore up the European economy. Clayton stressed economic conditions in Western Europe so dire that millions were starving along with a lack of confidence, low production, and dislocations. Clayton's point was that U.S. action in Western Europe didn't require more study; the situation was critical and Europe needed massive amounts of funding along with capital and consumer goods. Kennan's plan, in comparison, was more strategic and dealt with risks and difficulties; Clayton's plan was action oriented. In addition, Clayton's personal description of European conditions was very effective with both Secretary Marshall and Acheson. Some of Clayton's people in the economics offices of the State Department, such as Charles Kindleberger, also made an outline of their work available to Kennan in early May. Their idea was to push the Soviets to cooperate on Western Europe in exchange for aid to the Soviets and their satellites. If the USSR should decline, then the United States should work to strengthen Western Europe.

The work of Kennan, Clayton, and Acheson as well as that of others was utilized to put together the Marshall Plan framework. By early May it was widely understood in the United States that a large recovery plan for Europe was forthcoming. General Marshall decided to utilize his upcoming Harvard speech as the place to discuss U.S. plans on aid for Europe and asked Bohlen to draft the speech for him. Bohlen utilized the Kennan and Clayton frameworks to prepare the speech, and Marshall made changes to it as he saw fit with approval of the President. No discussions with European governments had taken place prior to the 5 June 1947 speech to the Harvard graduating class. Within the State Department itself, not many people knew that the upcoming Harvard speech was the occasion chosen to launch the dimensions of the European recovery plan that became known as the Marshall Plan. In the June 5 speech, Marshall only had dimensions of a plan, and plan details were developed after that speech. Gimbel suggests that it was Marshall's growing concern about Soviet intentions in Western Europe after his meetings in Moscow that led to his decision to roll out dimensions of the plan on very short notice with lack of details.[8]

The purpose of the Marshall Plan was to build a working economy in the world with the United States providing all funds necessary to nations wanting to reconstruct their economies. The USSR denounced the plan as an imperial plot to capture Europe. Marshall Plan benefits were available to all European nations, whether communist or not. This was done so the United States could not be blamed for the division of the world into blocs. Both Kennan and Acheson argued that it should be the Russians, not the United States, dividing Europe.

Secretary Marshall in his Harvard speech said:

> The truth of the matter is that Europe's requirements for the next three or four years of foreign food and other essential products—principally from America—are so much greater than her present ability to pay that she must have substantial additional help or face economic, social, and political deterioration of a very grave character.

> Our policy is directed not against any country or doctrine but against hunger, poverty, desperation, and chaos. Its purpose should be the revival of a working economy in the world so as to permit the emergence of political and social conditions in which free institutions can exist.

> Furthermore, governments, political parties, or groups which seek to perpetuate human misery in order to profit therefrom politically or otherwise will encounter the opposition of the United States [See Jones for speech at Harvard].[9]

Fear of the USSR and chaos in Western Europe had driven the United States to develop and implement the Marshall Plan, which was the first building bloc of the Creation. Without the perceived Soviet threat, it is unlikely that the Marshall Plan would have developed and perhaps mistakes similar to those that occurred after World War I would have occurred again after World War II.

The Marshall Plan premise was that people living in growing economies would resist communism much more readily than those in stagnating economies. Kennan argued that key areas such as Germany and the U.K. could not fall into Soviet hands. Keeping these areas on the U.S. side of the field in addition to building up their economic strength would place Soviet forces at a disadvantage. Economic growth, to be effective in developing stable democratic societies, needed to be accompanied by growth in democratic institutions. It evolved over time that the United States seemed willing to support almost any regime (democratic, totalitarian, dictatorship) as long as it was perceived as anticommunist.

The idea of the Marshall Plan was that the Soviets could be contained by having strong economies around the USSR and that the Marshall Plan would be sufficient for that purpose. That belief, of course, turned out to be false as the Marshall Plan was only the first large step in a series of major policy moves by the United States to contain the Soviets, who were a much more formidable competitor than the one some had initially expected them to be. The Soviet economy had grown faster than European and U.S. economies during the 1930s and continued to do so after World War II during the 1950s and into the 1960s as the Soviets forced input growth in the capital sector at expense of productivity gains and production of consumer goods and services. The Soviets gained, in a relative sense, on the United States. In comparison, industrial output in Western European countries in 1947 was in cases substantially below 1937 levels. U.S. economic activity increased by 50 percent in real terms during the war, while Europe's decreased by nearly 25 percent. Per capita GNP in Europe was about half that of the United States in 1950 (figure 4.2).

Support for the Marshall Plan needed to be developed within the United States in order to get Congress to act. Truman appointed three major commissions to study the feasibility of the Marshall Plan and to generate support for the plan. Clayton argued that Western Europe might crumble before Congress could act on the Marshall Plan. President Truman called a special session of Congress on 17 November to consider a $597 million ($4.0 billion in 1994 dollars) emergency aid program for Italy, France, and Austria. The aid package was approved by 15 December.

Meanwhile, members of Congress had been visiting Western Europe, and many returned expressing concern about the communist threat through the election process, in particular in countries such as Italy and France. On 9 December 1947 President Truman submitted to Congress the request for the first four years of the European Recovery Plan (ERP)—the Marshall Plan—and asked Congress to have the legislation through by 1 April 1948. The administration kicked off its campaign to win approval in Congress. The package was sold by promoting the Marshall Plan as a security measure. General Marshall testified in January 1948 to the Senate Foreign Relations Committee that "the way of life we have known is literally in balance."[10] Marshall also talked about possibility of a third world war. The *Saturday Evening Post* was fueling speculation about a war with the Soviet Union over Western Europe, which had the effect of generating bipartisan support for the program. President Truman, on April 1, signed the Foreign Assistance Act.

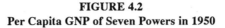

FIGURE 4.2
Per Capita GNP of Seven Powers in 1950

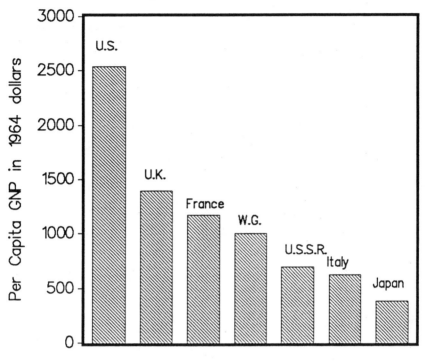

Source: Kennedy

The Marshall Plan involved grants and loans of approximately $13 billion over its life to sixteen countries. Europe received most of that in grants and loans by the end of 1951. In addition, some $10 billion in aid and loans was estimated to have been channelled to Europe before the launching of the Marshall Plan. From 1948 to 1950 Marshall Plan aid amounted to between 5 percent and 10 percent of European GNP or a quarter of Europe's imports of goods and services. Marshall Plan aid was massive, amounting to over 1 percent of U.S. GNP in the period from 1948 to 1951. Aid and loans to Western Europe following World War I were also large. In 1919 such aid was estimated to have amounted to 4.5 percent of GNP, but that aid was not effective as it wasn't followed by other building blocs such as tariff reduction to promote growth. The Marshall Plan was effective in helping reconstruct Europe because of the additional building blocs of movement toward more open trade, U.S. tax policy, and U.S. defense policy. But the Marshall plan failed to live up to its expectations of Soviet containment, and U.S. taxpayers had to pay for additional building blocs for many decades to allow, as Kennan indicated "the hand of time a chance to work."

5

The Creation—Building Bloc II, Trade Policy

The development and implementation of the Marshall Plan marked a significant directional change for U.S. foreign policy. Before World War II, the United States utilized diplomacy and the military to further U.S. foreign policy. The Marshall Plan was the first major move by the United States to utilize economic policy as a method of implementing its foreign policy. The Marshall Plan, as it turned out, was a starting point as it provided the capital equipment, foodstuffs and raw materials required to build confidence in Western Europe and to bring about production increases. By 1952 when the Marshall Plan ended, industrial production in Western Europe greatly exceeded prewar figures. Robert Pollard states that "Its (Marshall Plan) most important achievement was to restore West European self-confidence and to lay the basis for a long-term political, economic, and military association of the United States with Western Europe."[1] But the Marshall Plan was not enough by itself to bring about Soviet containment.

Countries in Western Europe, to rebuild their economies, needed markets in which to sell their products. The United States, to further their foreign-policy objective, encouraged countries and companies in the Far East and Western Europe, in rebuilding, to export to the U.S. market. Trade policy became the second major economic building bloc in Soviet containment. Trade policy, in conjunction with encouraging development of democratic institutions, turned into a major segment of U.S. overall foreign policy.

Trade policy can be subdivided into four aspects: (1) commercial policy—actions that affect imports and exports of goods and services; (2) foreign investment policy—actions taken to influence direct and portfolio investments; (3) foreign-aid policy—the Marshall Plan falls in this category, although the size of the Marshall Plan dwarfs the intent of this subdivision; and (4) balance-of-payments policy—this is influenced by actions of the previous three and includes those steps that influence a country's international monetary reserves. The United States utilized all aspects of trade policy to help achieve their foreign-policy objective.

Cordell Hull and Will Clayton had been actively pushing for movement toward free trade during the 1930s as well as the 1940s. Their idea of free trade involved reducing trading barriers among nations. The U.S. trade policy that was followed in the post-World War II period was different from their idea of free trade. Trade policy, after World War II, became a major crutch of foreign policy as U.S. trade policy tilted toward allowing other countries and companies access to U.S. markets while not necessarily requiring similar access to their markets. Post-World War II trade policy took place in an environment where countries exporting to the United States had larger net gains than the United States, but that was the objective of utilizing trade as a foreign-policy tool. U.S. trade policy was a method for the United States to share her wealth with allies. The world gained from the U.S. trade policy, and U.S. allies had major net gains. U.S. trade policy was not a zero-sum game but a net gain for the world with our trading partners capturing the lion's share.

The United States wanted to avoid post-World War I mistakes when aid to European countries was not effective as it was not complemented by trade policy. Military commitments, as well, needed to be complemented by economic policies for military expenditures to be effective. The idea of having forward attack bases in places such as Japan, France, and Britain without attempting to help those countries economically would have had limited merit. After World War I the United States returned to economic isolationism, which didn't take account of economic-policy spillage on other countries. The U.S. Fordney-McCumber Tariff of 1922, for example, increased the average tariff rate on goods subject to duties to nearly 45 percent by 1930. The Smoot-Hawley Tariff turned a recession into a depression, which spread to Europe as Europeans retaliated. In 1932 the U.S. tariff rate on dutiable imports averaged nearly 60 percent (figure 5.1).

The Reciprocal Trade Agreements Act of 1934 began U.S. tariff reduction. Cordell Hull, when talking about tariff reduction, would do so in the context that it would reduce the risks of war. Usually tariffs and trade were discussed within the context of selling more U.S. goods to

FIGURE 5.1
U.S. Tariff Rates, 1920–1987

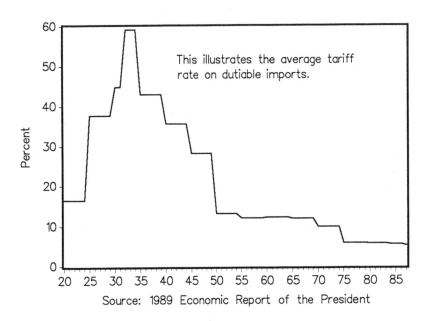

This illustrates the average tariff rate on dutiable imports.

Source: 1989 Economic Report of the President

foreigners. It was not until World War II and after, that a chorus of voices was heard echoing the theme of foreign trade and national security. This theme went along the line that access of foreign countries to U.S. markets would achieve three objectives. It would (1) reduce the risk that countries would become trapped in trade ties with the Soviets, (2) build up strength of foreign nations aligned with the United States, and (3) create a mutual economic and defense self-interest. The driving force was the familiar premise that stronger allied foreign economies are crucial to U.S. security as economies in process of growth will resist communism much more readily than stagnating economies. In addition, if a war occurs, economically stronger economies are more effective allies. In late 1945 Congress gave the administration authority to reduce U.S. tariffs up to 50 percent of rates in existence at the beginning of that year, according to the 1989 *Economic Report of the President*.[2] The United States provided the leadership over the following decades to conduct those reductions within a multilateral framework.

Along with the IMF and World Bank, the International Trade Organization (ITO) was a world organization created at Bretton Woods in 1944 with the purpose of lowering trading restrictions and establishing rules for commerce. John Maynard Keynes had argued for an understanding at Bretton Woods that the United States would maintain high domestic employment to encourage imports from Britain. Will Clayton, under secretary of state for economic affairs, continued pushing for the concept of free markets and the preamble to the European Recovery Act of April 1948 emphasized the reproduction in Europe of a Continental market such as that in the United States. Free trade within Europe developed slowly, and the framework was finally implemented in 1992 with the European free-trade zone. The ITO agreement had been reached in Havana in 1948, but the State Department did not submit it to Congress for ratification as they feared the agreement would be rejected. Many in Congress were opposed to trade liberalization, in particular when led by reduction in U.S. barriers. Instead the State Department worked out an executive agreement—not requiring congressional approval—with twenty-three other nations in Geneva later in 1948. This agreement was called the General Agreement on Tariffs and Trade (GATT) and consisted of four elements: (1) the rule of nondiscrimination in trade relations between participating countries, (2) commitments to observe negotiated tariff concessions,(3) prohibitions on use of quotas on imports and exports, and (4) special provisions to promote trade of developing countries. The focus of GATT was on achieving more trade among countries as well as encouraging capital mobility. A series of tariff reductions has been negotiated in the post-World War II era via GATT. These negotiations were carried out under names such as the Geneva Round (in 1949) and succeeding ones such as the Dillon, Kennedy, Tokyo, and Uruguay Rounds.

Progress toward free trade was slow as European countries resisted U.S. pressure for a speedy transition to free trade. European nations felt their economies were too weak to compete in open markets. Exports from U.S. industries were making inroads in countries where European exports might normally have gone. In addition, U.S. multinationals made large direct investments in Western Europe following World War II.

Mobility of capital and technology from the United States to Europe was aided by Marshall Plan investment along with development of democratic institutions. U.S. public investment in Europe calmed fears by multinationals of nationalization and propelled U.S. companies to lead in direct foreign investment in Europe. European exports to the United States lost share in the U.S. import market from one-fourth in 1936–38 to one-seventh in 1947.[3] But the Truman administration wanted European imports to increase into the United States. Progress was made in tariff reductions in the late 1940s as the United States made tariff cuts of about 20 percent on dutiable imports, while participating European countries made smaller percentage reductions. Substantial impacts of European tariff reductions were not felt by U.S. companies until European currencies were made convertible in the latter 1950s and quantitative restrictions were removed. The United States effectively engaged in unilateral tariff reductions during the latter 1940s and 1950s in an effort to help promote stronger European economies.[4]

Opposition to both tariff reduction and movement to free trade was high in the United States. Jacob Viner, a distinguished economist, said in 1947 that "there are few free traders in the present-day world, no one pays any attention to their views, and no person in authority anywhere advocates free trade."[5] Many in Congress also opposed movement toward free trade. Politically, there weren't large and powerful constituencies to push for expansion of imports into the U.S. market.

At the same time that attempts to expand trade between U.S. and Western Europe were ongoing, the United States rapidly reduced trade with Eastern European countries. Part of U.S. foreign policy was to limit exports of U.S. produced equipment and technology to the Soviet bloc. By 1948 most U.S. economic ties had been cut with Soviet Eastern European satellites. But U.S. policy didn't attempt to hinder sales of Western European equipment and technology to Eastern European countries. Exports from Western Europe into Eastern Europe were viewed as critical to continuing the Western European recovery. In addition, Western European countries were receiving essential imports such as coal and timber products from the Eastern European countries. Western Europeans were much more relaxed about exporting equipment and technology to the East than the United States was.[6]

Europeans attempted to help themselves by creating the Common Market or European Economic Community (EEC), which was signed in Rome in 1958 (also called the Treaty of Rome). France, West Germany, Italy, Belgium, Luxembourg, and the Netherlands agreed in principle to (1) reduce or eliminate tariffs and import quotas among themselves; (2) allow movement of labor, goods and capital among members; and (3) set common tariffs for nonmembers. The EEC model was a forerunner of the complete European integration framework in 1992. Countries not included in the EEC such as the U.K., Norway, Denmark, Austria, Sweden, Switzerland, and Portugal created the European Free Trade Association in 1960, which encompassed principles of the EEC but whose focus was only on movement of goods.

Earlier attempts at a European Common Market occurred both in 1948 when, as a by-product of the Marshall Plan, a sixteen-nation agreement was reached to reduce tariffs among European Nations, reflecting efforts of Will Clayton, and again in 1952 when the same six nations that started the EEC created the European Coal and Steel Community. Clayton and others wanted to prevent Western Europe from falling into pre-World War II arrangements when unity in Europe was usually the result of conquest or creation of alliances to fend off conquest. Reduction of tariffs was geared toward integration through economic self-interest.

Major U.S. aid to recovering economies of the Far East, Europe, and other areas through U.S. tariff reduction allowed companies in those countries access to the large and rich U.S. economy. That access encouraged growth of their economies. According to Vernon, the general economic security theme—economies in process of growth would resist Communism—came to dominate presentation of trade agreements to Congress and the American public.[7] In the same piece he makes the following observation:

> As one Administration after another was confronted with the task of obtaining Congressional consent to the program's renewal, the emphasis on its security aspects was gradually increased. A trade program which once was justified to the Congress largely because it might sell more American goods to foreigners began to be based on the contention that it built up defense strength, increased the mutuality of interest of the free nations and reduced the risk that any of them would be trapped by economic dependence on the Soviet bloc.[8]

Another familiar economic argument utilized to overcome protectionist sentiment existing in Congress was that foreign competition would encourage U.S. firms to become more competitive by reducing selling prices.

U.S. open-door trade policy was a crucial element in foreign policy during the 1950s. Europe benefited greatly from capital flows such as the Marshall Plan, IMF, World Bank, and private sources in rebuilding their economies. But export of goods to U.S. markets was perhaps a more important part of U.S. aid to growth in Far East and Western European economies. Vernon stated it well in 1955: "The basic pattern of United States security planning is too obvious to demand much recapitulation. Our evident strategy, as reflected in our NATO commitments and other military arrangements, is to maintain a solid coalition of nations against the Soviet bloc.... The economic counterpart of these policies of global defense is to be found in various programs of our government."[9] But Vernon, in describing the Marshall Plan and trade policies, characterized U.S. trade policies as "schizophrenia" in their defense applications compared to those of the military. As another example, he cited the fact that while imports into the United States were encouraged, there was also "buy American" legislation.[10]

W. Averell Harriman, in an article in *Foreign Affairs* in 1954, wrote:

The central objective of all-out Kremlin policy is to divide the Western Alliance.... The crucial test of our [U.S.] leadership is therefore the degree to which we are able to maintain unity in the free world.... The long-range strategy of the Soviet Union for overcoming the West is explicitly based upon the assumption, stated by Stalin and Malenkov in 1952, that the free world will not be able to maintain in the years ahead a rate of economic growth comparable to that which will be forced in the Soviet bloc. That our [U.S.] margin of industrial and overall economic superiority will decrease; and that our [U.S.] capacity to defend ourselves and dominate the world economy will correspondingly decline. There is therefore this point of agreement, that the security of the free world depends upon maintaining a wide margin of economic superiority.[11]

Harriman then goes on to list some of the more important programs and policies the United States must implement to promote world economic growth and democratic political development. A summarized and shortened list follows: (1) a strong U.S. economy to act as a locomotive for the rest-of-the-world free economies; (2) removal of trade barriers; (3) resource flows at stable prices (Harriman, at the time, probably didn't realize it but failure to do this altered, forever, world power in the 1970s); (4) promotion of capital flows to developed countries; (5) the giving of aid as needed; and (6) the provision of technical assistance to developing countries. Harriman's major point is that these are the type of long-range economic objectives and policies that the United States decided on in 1950s when the Marshall Plan was coming to an end. On trade policy Harriman, as did Vernon, mentions inconsistencies.

Part of the problem of administrations in dealing with economic parameters of foreign policy is the public perception aspect. It is relatively easy for the voter to understand the military provision aspects of equipment and manpower in foreign countries. That process, while costly to U.S. taxpayers, provides jobs in production and support roles in the United States. Taxpayers supported relatively large defense expenditures because it was in the self-interest of taxpayers to do so. It is also easy to talk about the importance of a strong U.S. economy as that means more jobs for American workers. But it is a very different matter when it comes to economic parameters of foreign policy such as trade. Taxpayers find it hard to buy into the argument that U.S. tariffs should be reduced on a unilateral basis so that other countries find it easier to export to the United States. Administration after administration talked about free trade and the point that the United States had to lead in that effort. Free trade can be talked about if it sounds like a win-win situation.

But the United States did more than talk about implementing a level playing field. It reduced tariffs on a unilateral basis. The United States was the world leader for the free world in the post-World War II era and that is what a world leader does—leads. Reduction of tariffs on a unilateral basis leads to an environment in which the playing field is tilted in favor of foreign competitors and eventually leads to relative loss of U.S. jobs. Taxpayers would find it very difficult to support such a trade program. Instead of talking about trade in such terms, administration after administration talked about trade policy in terms of free trade. Attempts to talk about a playing field tilted against American workers in the name of foreign policy would have been a loser.

The United States, for many years, was a relatively rich country compared to the rest of the world, so that economic policies tilted in favor of foreign countries seemed to have a relatively minor negative impact on domestic economic performance. By the time effects of this economic-defense policy were evident for taxpayers to see and feel, other major economic and social problems tended to override economic-defense policies; thus, economic-defense policies continue in effect today—long after the need for such policies existed. Core support for economic-defense policy continues as it is very difficult for a country to let go of its world-leadership role. Britain finally let go of their leadership role but not before it was on the edge of bankruptcy. Perhaps the United States will take the same stance.

Japan's economy also received its major external boost in the 1950s and in later decades through having access to the U.S. economy as Japan's economic growth was highly dependent on trade. George Kennan's policy planning staff, in general, focused on the grave situation in Western Europe until late summer 1947. After that they focused on the Far East, in particular Japan where General Douglas MacArthur was in charge. James Forrestal, secretary of defense at that time, had a role in directing Kennan's group to take a look at the Far East. Also Kennan previously had indicated that West Germany and Japan were two geographic areas that the United States could not allow to go to the other side.

Kennan believed the difficulty with both West Germany and Japan was that, even though the United States was in charge to a degree, Washington had limited control over internal workings of both countries.[12] Kennan's decision on West Germany was that the Marshall Plan and trade policy would, hopefully, allow the West German economy to, "progress in the desirable direction: toward the recovery, that is, of its own productivity, the development of its ability to contribute to the recovery of the remainder of Europe, and the achievement of a reasonable measure of domestic-political stability."[13]

The environment in the Far East wasn't nearly as positive. China was in the process of going communist, but at that time China was not a strong industrial power or strong military power. The United States may have provided nearly $3 billion of economic and military aid to China after World War II to mid-1949, but Kennan had already written China off in 1947. Kennan's thinking was that the loss of China did not constitute a threat to U.S. security, but the loss of Japan would be a very different matter. In particular, he felt that of the two countries Japan was much more important to the economic-political world and he decided Soviet analysis had reached the same conclusion.[14]

The Planning staff developed several papers on the world situation and dangers relating to Japan. Kennan was extremely troubled by General MacArthur's March 1947 public views that the United States should leave Japan on her own, even calling it "madness," that the United States should think about "abandoning" Japan with the Soviets in North Korea and Japan disarmed.[15] Kennan felt that what MacArthur had done to Japan was a road map for a communist takeover as reforms MacArthur implemented created social and political unrest. Japan did not even have a strong central police force so the country was defenseless. MacArthur had done little or nothing to help in Japan's economic recovery. Nearly 40 percent of Japan's urban areas were destroyed or seriously damaged during the war. Japan's industrial production at the end of 1947 was about half what it was in the 1930–34 time frame, while exports were only back to one-tenth of their level.[16]

General MacArthur, the supreme commander for the Allied Powers, his staff, and occupation regime wanted to break apart Japan's highly concentrated and centralized economy and make it entrepreneurial. But the Japanese felt their oligopolistic economy enabled them to compete effectively in international trade. The Japanese felt their way of running the economy, society, and political environment was sound—everything, that is, except the military. Both sides agreed on the dissolution of the Japanese military. U.S. business people returning from Japan had informed different cabinet officials of MacArthur's attempts to dismantle the Japanese economy. One of those officials was James Forrestal, who feared a breakup might further hinder Japan's economic recovery.

Kennan prepared a paper for General Marshall by October 1947 pointing out problems with current U.S. policy. Kennan was sent to Japan in late February 1948 to meet with MacArthur to evaluate U.S. policy in Japan. Before leaving for Japan, he completed two more papers on the world situation and difficulties for U.S. policy. In one of those, Kennan suggested that prospects for U.S. policy in the Far East didn't appear good, but that if the United States could influence the direction of Japan and the Philippines by economic and military means, they "would eventually constitute the cornerstones of a Pacific security system adequate for the protection of our interests.... If we could retain effective control...there could be no serious threat to our security from the east within our time."[17]

Initially, MacArthur was hostile to Kennan but later was agreeable to policy changes toward Japan such as movement away from his "trustbusting" economic reforms for the Japanese economy. According to Kennan, MacArthur's people had identified the top 260 Japanese companies as "excessive concentrations of economic power" and suggested they be sold and split up.[18] Kennan was extremely concerned about the "purging" taking place by MacArthur's occupation forces of people in education, business, and government who were thought to have been involved with or friendly to the Japanese military. Kennan thought the process resembled what had gone on in totalitarian practices and that it was creating significant unrest.

Pollard states that Kennan concluded that "economic recovery should be made the prime objective of U.S. policy in Japan for the coming period."[19] The State Department attempted to steer MacArthur toward policies that would allow Japan to develop as a key to U.S. Far East containment policy. Other recommendations Kennan made were that (1) control over the Japanese government be relaxed; (2) occupation costs reduced; (3) Japan be helped into a position where they could handle their independence; 4) forces remain in Japan until a treaty is signed, and the treaty be nonpunitive; but 5) significant forces remain in Okinawa for a long time, while only tactical forces remain in Japan.[20] Kennan's idea was that Japan would develop into a major U.S. ally. Kennan also felt that Japan needed, at this stage, to strengthen her internal security forces to cope with domestic instability, created in part by efforts of Japan's communists. He didn't think Japan needed foreign military bases on her soil. But it was later decided that U.S. forces would be retained indefinitely in the post-treaty period. The Korean War and the necessity to utilize U.S. military facilities in Japan for support of hostilities converted everyone into a believer about the need for U.S. military presence in Japan. Kennan indicated that his part in developing a national policy toward Japan was the second-most constructive contribution that he made in government.[21] The first was his role in the Marshall Plan.

In the 1950s the favorable environment existing for Japanese exports of manufactured products to the United States was an important factor in Japan's rapid economic growth. John D. Rockefeller, III said in 1954, "It seems clear that the increase of Japan's exports is the key to the situation."[22] He indicated that Americans must understand this. Mr. Rockefeller said that Japan was running a trade deficit with the United States, Canada, and Europe. This placed Japan in major economic difficulty as she drew on her reserve of foreign currency to pay for imports. Japan, he said, was also facing severe price competition in areas like steel, machinery, and equipment from countries such as West Germany and that Japan needed to take necessary steps to increase efficiency and productivity. That combined with an open-door trade policy in the U.S.

would suggest, he said with some prescience, that "there is no need to be pessimistic about the future of Japan."[23]

Okita, in a 1960 article on Japan's economic prospects in *Foreign Affairs*, mentions work done by the Japanese Economic Planning Agency 1960 and goes on to discuss key items in Japan's rapid growth during the 1946 to 1960 period, in particular

> The generally favorable environment for exports of manufactured industrial products, particularly to highly industrialized countries, including the United States.... In these countries such factors as...free trade policies contributed to increasing Japan's exports of industrial products....
>
> [Other points were that] Japan's economic future, therefore, will depend very much upon her success in modernizing her economic structure and in developing lines of industry which require high technological standards and are relatively capital-intensive....
>
> [Also, Japan's economic growth from 1953–1960] is about 8 percent per year—more than double that of Western countries, and even higher than that of the Soviet Union, whose rate of growth in recent years is estimated by Western experts at about 6 to 7 percent.[24]

Maintaining a faster growth rate in the USSR than in the West was key to Stalin's premise for overcoming the West.

Figure 5.2 illustrates the trade balance (merchandise exports minus imports)that the United States ran with Japan from 1946 to 1994. The Japanese, after the war, needed to rebuilt their economy. They did with the intent of exporting to the U.S. economy because of the U.S. open-door policy. The other side of this transaction is sending dollars to Japan that the Japanese recycle. Access to the U.S. market continues to be a growth segment for the Japanese economy. Japan also contributed to its economic growth by implementing tax policies that encouraged saving and discouraged consumption, which created high rates of capital formation. Japan benefited from both the Korean and Vietnam wars. The United States spent enormous resources in both wars, which helped Japan build their industrial base by Japan supplying support needs in both wars. The Japanese government through the Ministry of International Trade and Industry (MITI) encouraged exports with other countries. But it also encouraged an environment in which it was difficult for other countries to export their products and services into Japan.

One can argue about the effectiveness of MITI in helping to develop firms and industries. MITI recommended to Japan's auto manufacturers

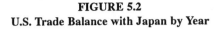

FIGURE 5.2
U.S. Trade Balance with Japan by Year

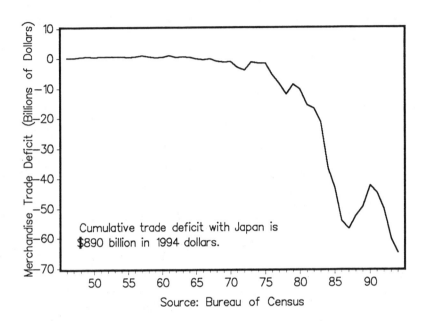

Source: Bureau of Census

in the 1960s that they should not export cars to the U.S as MITI felt Japan couldn't compete in the global auto market. It is hard to be more wrong. Peter Drucker says, "Japan's industrial policy of attempting to select and support 'winning' business sectors is by now a well-known failure. Practically all the industries MITI picked—such as super-computers and pharmaceutical—have been at best also-rans."[25] MITI, in the 1970s, suggested to Japanese producers that they increase their global market position in semiconductors and assisted them toward that end by helping to arrange financing, encouraging cooperative research efforts among Japanese firms, and limiting imports of chips. That was one success story, but it may have developed without MITI.

MITI probably achieved its biggest impact in creating a difficult en-vironment for other countries to export to Japan. The result was that

TABLE 5.1
Manufacturing Exports and Imports as a Percent of Total

	1970		1992	
	Exports	Imports	Exports	Imports
Japan	93	24	97	45
Germany	89	53	89	75
U.S.	67	61	78	77

Source: CIA

Japan was very effective in achieving economic power through project-ing that power into the U.S. economy and, at the same time, not allow-ing other countries access to their markets (table 5.1). This allowed them to gather the lion's share of trade gains.

This gets at the nub of the trade problem. Japan doesn't let in what it produces. It's an island with an island orientation to the rest of the world. Japan has to import food, raw materials, and fuel. Therefore, Japan limits imports of what it produces—manufacturing products. Both Japan's and Germany's exports consisted primarily of manufactured goods, but Germany's markets are much more open than are Japan's to manufactured imports. Japan built a competitive advantage in manufacturing through uti-lizing policies to encourage exports and limit imports. Japanese consumers, as a result, pay more than they would if Japan opened her economy.

Providing foreign countries such as Japan access to U.S. markets helped economies around the globe to promote their economic devel-opment and dependence on the U.S. economy, while at the same time reducing their dependence on the Soviet bloc. The United States' path of sharing its economic wealth was not smooth and U.S. protectionist sentiment remained strong through post-World War II years. U.S. lead-ership in the international monetary system and free trade, however, dramatically impacted world economic growth and trade. World real GDP increased 350 percent from 1950 to 1986 while world trade, in real terms, increased by more than 800 percent, according to the 1989 Economic Report of the President.[26] World output expanded at an aver-age annual percentage growth rate of over 4.2 percent compared to 2.2 percent over the period from 1870 to 1950.

Table 5.2 illustrates results of the U.S. policy of providing access to the U.S. market while not necessarily requiring similar access for U.S.

Table 5.2
Market Share and Cumulative Market Share (Percent)

| | 1950 | | | 1987 | |
Country	Market Share	Cumulative Share	Country	Market Share	Cumulative Share
U.S.	17.2	17.2	W.G.	12.5	12.5
U.K.	10.6	27.8	U.S.	10.6	23.1
France	5.2	33.0	Japan	9.8	32.9
Canada	5.1	38.1	France	6.3	39.2
W.G.	3.3	41.4	U.K.	5.6	44.8
Australia	2.8	44.2	Italy	4.9	49.7
Belgium	2.8	47.0	Canada	4.2	53.9
Netherlands	2.4	49.4	Netherlands	3.9	57.8
Brazil	2.3	51.7	Belgium	3.6	61.4
Italy	2.0	53.7	Hong Kong	2.1	63.5
Argentina	2.0	55.7	Korea	2.0	65.5
S. Africa	1.9	57.6	Switzerland	1.9	67.4
India	1.9	59.5	Sweden	1.9	69.3
Sweden	1.8	61.3	Spain	1.4	70.7
Singapore	1.7	63.0	Singapore	1.2	71.9

Source: Cosgrove.

exports to other markets, with the 15 countries listed having the largest market shares of world exports out of 157 countries the International Monetary Fund follows (excluding the communist countries during this time frame).

In 1950 the United States had the dominant market-share position in exports followed by the United Kingdom. Britain didn't have the resources to continue as world leader, and America stepped into that leadership vacuum. Results of that leadership are evident as countries made major strategic and economic moves to alter their trade position without retaliation from the United States. Both Japan and West Germany, for instance, were in the top four in 1987 but not in 1950. Japan wasn't even in the top fifteen in 1950 but by 1987 had moved to third position in terms of market share. Countries that increased their market share of trade are ones that captured the majority of trade gains.

Providing foreign countries such as Japan access to U.S. markets allowed them to dramatically alter their economic position. Five countries on the top-fifteen list in 1950—Australia, Brazil, Argentina, South Africa, and India—failed to make the top fifteen in 1987, while the new entrants were Japan, Hong Kong, Korea, Switzerland, and Spain. Countries such as Brazil, Argentina, and India made a decision not to focus their exports on the U.S. market and instead followed an inward-looking trade policy called import substitution. As a result they lost relative position. The key to foreign-country growth in the post-World War II period was to take advantage of the U.S. open-door trade policy, foreign aid, and global defense strategy.

6

The Creation—Building Bloc III, Military

Immediately after World War II there was perhaps some thought that economic aid without military involvement might be able to contain Soviet expansion efforts. The Marshall Plan and U.S. trade policy attempted to bring Western Europe up to an economic level where their economies would enable them to resist the Soviets better. According to John Lewis Gaddis this idea faded rapidly, and by the latter 1940s, "dominant opinion in Washington no longer held that the policies of 1947—economic aid without military involvement—would suffice to contain Soviet expansion."[1]

Brzezinski in 1972 said that "Two great powers, differentiated by divergent centuries-long experience and separated by sharply differing ideological perspectives, yet thrust into political proximo as a consequence of the shattering of the earlier international system, could hardly avoid being plunged into a competitive relationship."[2] W.W. Rostow in 1987 suggested, "It was historically understandable, if not quite inevitable, the Soviet Union would make a bid for hegemony after 1945 and the United States would react, even if belatedly."[3]

Britain's role as a world leader in free trade, promoting a system of stable currencies and maintaining a strong military, helped provide a relatively peaceful international political climate lasting from 1815 to 1914. The post-World War I experience in which the United States returned to isolationism was the lesson that U.S. economic and political policy actions in the post-World War II era, by themselves, would be inadequate. The United States also needed a strong military to follow Britain as the world leader.

As was expected after World War II ended, U.S. military personnel were cut very rapidly. U.S. armed forces numbered 12.3 million at the wartime peak, and in 1948 the number was under 1.5 million with ground forces under 700,000. But U.S. power remained dominant in the world with the air force having over 2,000 heavy bombers and 1,000 long-range B-29s. The navy with its 1,200 major warships was the premier navy. The United States also had an inventory of atomic bombs, and the bomb, for a few years after World War II, was U.S. property. In 1949 the U.S. monopoly on the atomic bomb was broken by the Soviets. The Soviets also demobilized but this demobilization was kept secret, and as a result Western estimates of Soviet strength were somewhat higher than what the actual numbers were in the latter 1940s. Soviet armed forces numbered approximately 11 million at their wartime peak, but by 1947 the Soviet actual count was slightly less than 3 million men under arms. Because of several factors—overestimation of Soviet strength, U.S. movement to become the world leader, changing technological requirements of a world leader, and post-World War I experience—the United States didn't cut military expenditures as a percent of government spending after World War II as much as it had after World War I (table 6.1)

Defense spending falls into a classification of a public good, that is, a good the consumption of which by any one person or group does not diminish its consumption by others. Countries aligned with the United States could therefore spend less of their economic output on defense as long as U.S. defense expenditures remained relatively high. Some countries in Europe and the Far East did that. U.S. defense spending allowed other countries to allocate a larger proportion of their economic output to business investment and consumption. U.S defense umbrella was yet another building bloc contributing to rapid growth within countries in Europe and the Far East. Marshall Plan assistance came to an end for practical purposes by mid-1951 and was officially terminated in 1952. During the early 1950s, as Marshall Plan aid dried up, the Truman administration supported allied countries through direct spending by maintaining foreign military bases.[4]

The Korean War in 1950 hiked military expenditures, but had the Korean War not developed, a number of events occurred suggesting the United States would have to take a much more active military role in the world. Stalin concluded, in his Moscow speech of February 1946, that no peaceful international order was possible and that the USSR must therefore be prepared. Stalin wanted production of iron, steel, and national defense materials tripled, while sources of energy, coal, and oil needed to be doubled. Production of consumer goods for Soviet citizens would need to wait on rearmament.

TABLE 6.1
Defense Expenditures as a Percent of Federal Government Expenditures

Number of years After last war	Post-WWI	Post-WWII
0	73.4%	72.5%
1	62.9	35.4
2	51.0	35.8
3	28.3	32.3
4	21.7	31.1
5	22.4	49.2
6	20.5	64.8

Source: Webber and Wildavsky

Kennan felt the Soviets would use every means possible in their attempt to divide and weaken the West such as not only blocking what they didn't want through diplomacy and international organizations but also expanding weak spots in the West through funding and subversion. Kennan, according to Acheson, indicated that the driving force of the Soviets was their centuries-old fear of physical and political insecurity and also that the USSR perceived its greatest danger as the Western World. As such, Acheson says, "In the name of Marxism *they sacrificed every single ethical value* [italics added] in their methods and tactics.... Soviet policy would be to *use every means to infiltrate, divide, and weaken the West* [italics added]."[5] Kennan's assessment suggested the United States needed a strong military. In Kennan's thinking on the basic purpose of warfare (explained in chapter 3), whereas warfare formerly meant total destruction of the enemy's ability and his unconditional capitulation, those goals, in the atomic age, were unnecessary and suicidal. Kennan therefore argued for three central warfare concepts: (1) a doctrine of limited warfare; (2) atomic weapons to be used by the United States only in retaliation; and (3) "small mobile forces" would be needed.

The United States had agreed to take responsibility for providing aid to Greece and Turkey from Britain in 1947 and took the leadership in developing Western strategy. U.S. strategy at this stage, according to Brzezinski, "rested on two premises[:] that Soviet expansion must be halted, by both military and political means; and this turn would create the preconditions for an eventual mellowing or even breaking up of the Soviet system."[6]

In June 1948 the Soviets closed off the autobahn through their occupation zone in Germany and blocked Allied access to Berlin. The blockade was a clever diplomatic move as it made the United States take the first military move. President Truman responded by airlifting supplies over the Soviet zone and into West Berlin. Soviets could stop the resupply effort, but it required them to fire the first shot; they didn't. The Berlin Blockade helped solidify the twelve-country constituency forming the North Atlantic Treaty Organization (NATO)—the United States, France, Britain, Italy, Canada, Belgium, Denmark, Norway, The Netherlands, Luxembourg, Portugal, and Iceland in spring 1949. NATO integrated the European defense against the Soviets in that as an attack on one would be considered an attack on all. The NATO military alliance also cemented the Marshall Plan economic split of Europe by dividing Europe into two camps since communist countries chose not to participate in the Marshall Plan. Switzerland and Sweden were neutrals. The USSR created the Warsaw Pact as an offset to NATO. When Hungary withdrew from the Warsaw Pact in 1956, Soviet troops moved in and crushed their attempt at independence. Khrushchev's order to erect the Berlin Wall in 1961 in order to stem the flow of talent to the West was another major symbol of European division.

The U.S. position toward the Soviets hardened when the USSR detonated an atomic bomb in 1949 and when North Korea attacked across the 38th parallel in June 1950. President Truman sent U.S. ships and planes to Korea hours after the invasion took place. According to Brzezinski, the West was underestimating Soviet strength in this time period. Soviet forces were being rapidly built to offset the West's atomic threat. The Soviet development of an atomic bomb came earlier than the West expected, and by 1951 the Soviets had a modest stockpile of sixty atomic weapons or roughly 10 percent of the U.S. stockpile. The United States, at that time, interpreted the Korean attack as part of a Soviet master plan of grand expansion (information from the Soviet Union after her collapse suggests this may have been the case).

The United States embarked on rearmament and military-territorial guarantees to prevent more so-called dominos from toppling. The cold war was being fought in Europe, but after North Korea the cold war extended around the world as the two powers expanded the battleground.

Economic and military support was given Taiwan while China was regarded as the enemy. In August 1951 a treaty reaffirming U.S. air and naval-base rights to the Philippines was entered into, and the United States made commitments concerning defense of the islands. Shortly after that, an agreement was entered into with Australia and New Zealand, and a peace treaty with Japan restoring sovereignty was signed about the same time. In addition, a security pact was signed that kept U.S. forces in both the Japanese home islands and in Okinawa.

Dean Acheson, who had been appointed secretary of state in January 1949, made a number of trips to various U.S. locations in 1950 to explain U.S. foreign policy. His talks repeated essentially the same message: "What we expected to achieve by the creation of strength throughout the free world—military, economic, and political—to replace the inviting weak spots offered to Soviet probing was to diminish further the possibility of war...to show the Soviet leaders by successful containment that they could not hope to expand their influence throughout the world and must modify their policies."[7] In a March 1950 speech at Berkeley, he gave the audience hope that some improvement in the U.S.-Soviet confrontation might be possible in a few years, but he added, "I must warn you not to raise your hopes, I see no evidence that the Soviet leaders will change their conduct until the progress of the free world convinces them that they cannot profit from a continuation of these tensions."[8]

The arms race was underway and the Soviet economy in the latter part of the 1940s and early 1950s grew 1.5 times faster than the U.S. economy, according to Harriman.[9] Concerns about the Soviet threat kept U.S. defense expenditures at a relatively high level. Some optimism about a thaw in the cold war occurred in the mid-1950s as both sides announced troop cuts following the Geneva summit conferences, and it appeared Soviet rule of Eastern Europe was faltering, according to Brzezinski.[10] Such hope was short-lived. In November 1956 Soviet troops moved into Budapest. The Hungarian people had been led to believe the West might help if they declared their independence from the USSR as in January 1953 John Foster Dulles had announced by radio that the people of Eastern Europe could count on U.S. help in getting rid of the Soviets. U.S. inaction in Hungary led the Soviets to doubt U.S. intentions, so the Soviets increased defense spending.

During the 1950s U.S. military plans developed into a well-defined global strategy. President Truman in his inaugural speech of January

1949 discussed four major guidelines for his foreign policy: (1) continued support of the United Nations; (2) continuation of the European economic recovery plan; (3) a strengthening of the free nations against aggression; and (4) making benefits of U.S. scientific advances and progress available to developing countries. The U.S. containment policy appeared to be working in Europe, while Truman's four guidelines were essentially an effort to have a global-containment policy. Rapid Soviet technological advances such as Soviets testing of an H-bomb in 1953, Sputnik in 1957, and testing an intercontinental ballistic missile (ICBM) in the same year propelled the United States to continue military spending at high levels. Also the United States realized that its cities were vulnerable to a first strike with resulting massive destruction.

Technological advances on a variety of methods to launch nuclear weapons from submarines and battlefields—and eventually multiple nuclear warheads—created a mutual balance of destruction. Each side continued its effort to gain technological advances on the other, which called for continued massive spending. Each side wanted to form alliances with new partners around the globe to prevent the other from doing so. This was inherent in Truman's fourth point. The United States had already committed itself to NATO and various countries in the Far East. The Rio Pact further committed the United States to defense of the Western hemisphere. The Eisenhower Doctrine offered U.S. aid to Arab states after President Eisenhower in 1957 became concerned that the Middle East was open to a communist take-over.

Soviet defense expenditures were increasing relative to U.S. expenditures in the latter 1950s and matched those of America by the early 1960s, but the U.S. economy was two to three times as large as the Soviet economy. The defense-expenditure strain on the Soviet economy was much more severe than that on the United States as both powers continued to expand their influence.

The United States spent more than the Big Four—U.K., France, Italy, and West Germany—by a factor of four during the 1950s (table 6.2 and figure 6.1)—while USSR defense-spending levels caught U.S. levels by the early 1960s. But at the time of the Cuban missile crisis in 1962, the United States was still positioned "to deliver several times as devastating an attack on the Soviet Union as the Soviet Union would on the United States," according to Brzezinski.[11]

TABLE 6.2
Defense Expenditures, 1948–1970 (Dollars)

Year	U.S.	USSR	France	U.K.	Italy	W.Ger.	Japan	China
1948	10.9	13.1	0.9	3.4	0.4			
1949	13.5	13.4	1.2	3.1	0.5			2.0
1950	14.5	15.5	1.4	2.3	0.5			2.5
1951	33.3	20.1	2.1	3.2	0.7			3.0
1952	47.8	21.9	3.0	4.3	0.8			2.7
1953	49.6	25.5	3.4	4.5	0.7		0.3	2.5
1954	42.7	28.0	3.6	4.4	0.8		0.4	2.5
1955	40.5	29.5	2.9	4.3	0.8	1.7	0.4	2.5
1956	41.7	26.7	3.6	4.5	0.9	1.7	0.4	5.5
1957	44.5	27.6	3.6	4.3	0.9	2.1	0.4	6.2
1958	45.5	30.2	3.6	4.4	1.0	1.2	0.4	5.8
1959	46.6	34.4	3.6	4.4	1.0	2.6	0.4	6.6
1960	45.3	36.9	3.8	4.6	1.1	2.9	0.4	6.7
1965	51.8	62.3	5.1	5.8	1.9	5.0	0.8	13.7
1970	77.8	72.0	5.9	5.8	2.4	6.1	1.3	23.7

Source: Kennedy

FIGURE 6.1
Defense Expenditures, 1948–1970

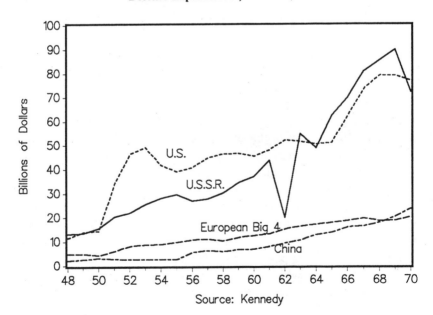

Source: Kennedy

U.S. commitments around the globe continued to mount, and Paul Kennedy noted that in 1970 "the U.S. had 1,000,000 soldiers in 30 countries, was a member of four regional defense alliances and an active participant in a fifth, had mutual defense treaties with 42 nations, was a member of 53 international organizations and was furnishing military or economic aid to nearly 100 nations."[12] This indicates the effort U.S. taxpayers made to support U.S. military around the globe in an effort to contain and defeat the USSR. The Soviets also expanded their influence and commitments through the 1950s which included providing aid to India, Egypt, Iraq, Afghanistan, African states, and in 1960, Cuba, as both superpowers were enlisting countries to join their side.

By the 1960s the United States learned from their experience that for capital to be effective in the developing countries, technical and managerial competence must precede capital loans and aid. Developing countries had their own self-interest, which was not necessarily that of the United States or the USSR, so instead of two distinct sides in the world, there was a splintering of political allegiance in the 1960s as countries followed their internal needs.

U.S. involvement in Vietnam resulted in a splintering of the United States as sizeable segments of the population did not support U.S. efforts in Southeast Asia. The Vietnam War was one indication of the decline of U.S. dominance, not because of the war itself, but because of the effect on the U.S. economy and on its other commitments. Vietnam illustrated the limitation of U.S. economic as well as military power. It brought both a reassessment of the U.S. military and economic role in the world and a movement away from the focus of an idealist (a holdover of the Wilson era) to one more of a realist.

The foreign-policy guide that evolved was based on a realist's approach of (1) a balance of power and that balance of power is a military one; (2) friends and enemies should be chosen primarily on the basis of their power, rather than on ideology; (3) assessment of foreign threats should be judged primarily on what a country has done and its military capabilities rather than intentions; and (4) a need to exclude moralism in foreign policy. Thus, for example, President Nixon could order a massive bombing of North Vietnam in 1972 in order to pull Hanoi closer to the U.S. bargaining position and also make a trip to China that same year to mend fences with Mao Tse-Tung—or President Bush in the Gulf War could work a deal with Syria, a terrorist supporter, to pull them to

FIGURE 6.2
U.S. National Defense Purchases

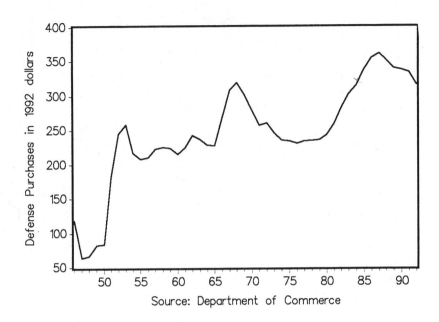

Source: Department of Commerce

the U.S. side to fight Iraq. Practicality took the place of ideology in foreign policy. A central cog in that foreign policy was a strong U.S. military. Figure 6.2 illustrates U.S. annual defense purchases from 1946 through 1992—the beginnings of the cold war through the Bush administration when the cold war ended (historians may decide the cold war ended when the Berlin Wall began to crumble in 1989). With the effect of inflation taken out, cumulative annual spending amounted to $11.5 trillion over that time period.

Dollars spent on defense don't capture opportunity cost—that is, could this money have gone for more productive uses? Could that $11 trillion or some proportion of it have been more effectively utilized? According to Pollard, "Like Truman, Eisenhower believed that American national security depended upon a healthy domestic economy and that high defense spending hurt the economy by generating less real growth than an equivalent amount of private sector expenditures would create."[13] Some have argued that the Pentagon is coordinator of U.S. industrial policy or that the Pentagon serves a somewhat similar purpose to Japan's MITI. National defense is a public good and other countries won't pay for it since they can't be excluded from sharing the benefits. The United States supplies a military umbrella to our allies, who don't have to purchase it.

In contrast, MITI was oriented to attempting to provide an environment where Japanese companies could produce and sell private goods and where if the customers want them, customers can purchase them. If someone doesn't purchase a private good, that someone is excluded from utilizing that good. MITI was engaged in attempting to induce private companies to follow their directions or incentives in order to create wealth for Japan. The Pentagon is in an entirely different business of building buffer zones and, if necessary, fighting wars as well as wealth sharing. Other countries such as Canada, Mexico, Japan, and Germany—as well as many others—obtain benefits of U.S. tax-payer-supported defense but do not pay. Another way of looking at it is the common-sense point that it is better to spend too much rather than not enough.

7

The Creation—Building Bloc IV, Tax Policy

The Marshall Plan encouraged Europeans to rebuild their economies while the U.S. open-door trade policy provided an incentive to export to the United States. U.S. military strength and the world-watchdog role provided a security umbrella for nations and businesses in conducting long-term business relationships with the United States. Another very important policy, the U.S. tax system—in particular, the federal personal income-tax code—has the effect of encouraging economic growth in capital-friendly countries, while discouraging U.S. production, work, and capital formation that collectively generate the wealth the United States shares.

The Sixteenth Amendment, providing for a tax on income, was ratified by the states in 1913. The federal income tax, enacted after the Sixteenth Amendment, levied a flat 1 percent tax rate on all income over $3000 (equivalent to $44,900 in 1994 dollars) and had a top rate of 7 percent for income over $500,000 ($7.5 million in 1994 dollars). Before 1913 other forms of taxation generated revenue for the federal government. From 1789 to 1909 the Federal Government source of revenue was primarily tariffs and excise taxes. The Continental Congress levied a tariff of 5 percent across the board and the Tariff of 1789 had 5 percent duties on most items except on a list of manufacturing imports where rates went up to 15 percent. Until 1800, 30 percent of the federal budget went for interest payments on the national debt, and 55 percent for maintaining the militia. [1] President Jefferson abolished excise taxes in 1801, downsized the army and navy, and reduced compensation as well as number of federal employees.

The embargo of December 1807 and the War of 1812 accelerated economic development of the domestic cotton and woolen textile mills and also iron foundries. As Kindleberger states,"War is the ultimate protective tariff,"[2] and following the war, tariffs increased to protect expanding domestic industries. During the War of 1812 excise taxes came back but were dropped in 1817 and weren't implemented again until the Civil War. Tariffs were the primary source of federal revenue in the intervening years and were viewed as a domestic issue—a method to protect domestic industries and raise revenue as needed. Tariffs were hiked during the Civil War, later lowered, and raised again in 1890 to help pay off Civil War debt. Excise taxes during the Civil War were placed on items such as manufactured goods, advertising, licenses, and legal documents, as well as on standard items such as liquor and tobacco. An income tax was also implemented from 1862 to 1871 on wages, salaries, interest and dividends and at its peak accounted for nearly 25 percent of revenue[3] with the tax ranging from 1 percent to 10 percent of income. An income tax was reenacted in 1894 but declared unconstitutional by the Supreme Court. From the Civil War until the early twentieth century, the private-sector economy grew faster than the federal sector. Excise taxes and tariffs are consumption taxes and can become very noticeable to people purchasing the impacted products and services. Hikes in consumption taxes are equivalent to price increases, so consumption taxes served as a major constraint on growth of federal spending during that time period as consumers and businesses fought increases. Webber notes that in 1902 Federal spending accounted for 2.4 percent of economic activity.[4]

In 1909 the corporate income tax began at 1 percent. Implementation of that tax resulted from continuing efforts to reduce tariffs as consumers of products affected by them felt high tariffs were an unnecessary subsidy to U.S. business. President Taft suggested federal revenue loss from tariff reductions could be offset by a tax on corporate profits. The proposal passed both houses of Congress almost unanimously, and the corporate income tax became law. Taft also believed the corporate income tax would give the federal government an opportunity to secure valuable information in respect to conduct of corporations, such as their financial condition.

During 1909 President Taft was a driving force behind drafting of a constitutional amendment with the express purpose of bypassing the Supreme Court's 1894 decision that the income tax was unconstitutional. Many joined the effort to pass the Income Tax Amendment. Some elected officials looked at what governments in Europe were doing and felt the

U.S. government could provide more services, but tax revenue was needed for that. Representatives of urban areas felt their constituents were hurt more by high tariffs than they would be with a low income tax rate. Businesses feared that if they didn't support the amendment, tax rates on corporate profits would rise. Many voters also felt that a majority of wealthy Americans were living in New York, New Jersey, and Massachusetts and the rich were not paying their fair share. Raising revenue according to one's ability to pay has always been a strong rationale for taxation. A number of diverse movements contributed to ratification of the Sixteenth Amendment and enactment of the 1913 personal income tax, which applied to wages, salaries, dividends, interest income, rents, and capital gains. It allowed deductions for personal interest expense and tax payments as well as for business expenses. Exemptions included federal, state, and local government bond interest as well as personal exemptions. But excise and tariff taxes remained the major source of federal revenue until expenditure-revenue needs of World War I kicked in.

World War I, as all wars, required massive increases in federal spending and taxes. In 1916 the top income-tax rate hit 15 percent, and an inheritance tax was levied at rates from 1 percent to 10 percent with an exemption of $50,000 (equivalent to $680,000 in 1994 dollars). In 1917 the top income-tax rate hit 67 percent and in 1918, 77 percent. Exemption limits such as the personal exemption were reduced to generate more revenue. An excess-profits tax was also implemented on businesses. One percent of individual returns filed from 1917 to 1919 had incomes over $20,000 (equivalent to $196,000 in 1994 dollars), but this 1 percent generated 70 percent of the income-tax revenue collected. After World War I there was general agreement among political parties that personal income-tax rates were too high and the tax code was revised in 1921, 1924, 1926, 1928, and 1929 with tax-rate reductions. Lower personal tax rates resulted in vigorous economic growth and, in turn, more tax revenue, which prompted still lower tax rates.

Andrew Mellon, who became Treasury secretary in 1920, served three presidents over a twelve-year period and felt that personal income-tax rates should be modest as well as creating minimal interference with market incentives. In 1924 he said, "High rates of taxation do not necessarily mean large revenue to the government, and...more revenue may often be obtained by lower rates."[5] By 1925 the top marginal income-tax rate was cut to 25 percent. Personal income-tax rate cuts created a rapidly growing tax base, and the federal budget surplus grew. Congress granted more exemptions, and in 1926 the oil industry was granted a 27.5 percent oil-depletion allowance. The inheritance tax was also reduced. Mellon argued for an increase in corporate income tax rates on grounds that investment income should be taxed at a higher rate than earned income. Mellon based this idea on the ability-to-pay rationale. The corporate income tax which reached 12 percent in 1918 went to 13 percent in 1925 and 13.5 percent in 1926.

The U.S. tax system was fundamentally altered to an income-based tax system from a consumption-based tax system in the early part of the twentieth century. The stage was being set for the United States to take the role of a global leader. "Up to 1914, dominant economic issues were argued in terms of domestic interests in a world taken as given.... Feedback to other nations was ignored," according to Kindleberger.[6] World War I changed that. A country progresses through a series of stages from young debtor, to mature debtor, then young creditor, and finally to mature creditor, and Kindleberger says, "The United States went from the first to the fourth in three years, from 1914 to 1917."[7] He goes on to cite examples such as the expansion of assembly-line methods devised by Henry Ford for car production that were utilized for production of munitions and equipment for the Allied powers of Europe as well as the United States. Other examples include J.P. Morgan and Company's financing British and French private borrowing in the United States and the U.S. government financing Allied borrowing in dollars.

The highly progressive personal income-tax system that the U.S. devised during World War I was a tax system that allowed U.S. wealth to be shared with other countries. But the United States refused to accept the world-leadership role, rejected the Treaty of Versailles, would not join the International Labor Organizations established at Geneva, and, in general, refused to participate in the world political and economic system. In addition, the sharply progressive tax system was flattened and the United States moved away from wealth sharing to domestic wealth generation. Tariffs were also increased during the 1920s. This was in sharp contrast to the portion of Wilson's Fourteen Points that called for "removal, so far as possible, of all economic barriers and the establishment of an equality of trade conditions among all nations consenting to the peace and associating with its maintenance." President Harding signed the Fordney-

McCumber Tariff of 1922, which raised tariffs. The purpose of this tax on imports was to help nurture U.S. infant industries. Higher tariffs and lower personal tax rates were major steps backward from being a world leader, as the United States turned inward. President Hoover moved the United States even further from a world-leadership role when he signed the Smoot-Hawley tariff in June 1930, but that tax hike had such an adverse effect on the world economy and political events that it set in motion the U.S. transition to global leadership.

A return to soak-the-rich-mentality started in 1931 when Andrew Mellon advised Congress to increase personal and corporate income-tax rates in order to restore budget balance, reversing his 1920s position on lower tax rates, more rapid increases in production, and more tax revenues. The depression created a tax base shrinkage, and both President Hoover and Congress made an attempt to balance the budget by increasing tax rates. Franklin D. Roosevelt, in 1935 and in later years as well, lashed out at wealthy taxpayers as being able to avoid paying their fair share. President Roosevelt implemented surtaxes, raised tax rates, and closed so-called loopholes—for instance, taxing undistributed corporate profits. In 1936 U.S. individual income-tax rates ranged from 4 percent to 79 percent with the 79 percent for incomes over $5 million. During peak-tax World War II years, tax rates went from the lowest bracket of 23 percent to the highest at 94 percent on adjusted gross income of $200,000 (approximately $1.68 million in 1994 dollars). After World War II top income-tax rates declined slightly but remained very high, at or near 91 percent until the 1964 change in the tax code.

Table 7.1 shows select tax rates in effect in 1949 for a married couple with two dependents, approximate rates that were in effect until the mid-1960s. Average and marginal rates were clearly sharply progressive. The average effective rate (in table 7.1) is the percentage of total income, before taxes, taken by federal income taxes. A married couple with two dependents in 1949 with an income of $10,000 paid 11.7 percent of their income in taxes. The marginal rate, in comparison, is the tax rate applicable to the last dollar of income. The marginal dollar was subject to a 19.4 percent tax for the same $10,000 couple.

Impacts on production, savings, and investment of high marginal income-tax rates in the United States are clear. An investor (married) with an income of $25,000 in 1949 needed a before-tax rate of return of 7.5 percent to obtain an after-tax yield of 5 percent (table 7.2). An investor

TABLE 7.1
Average and Marginal Federal Income Tax Rates in 1949

Income	Average Effective	Marginal
$5,000	7.0	16.6
10,000	11.7	19.4
25,000	18.6	33.4
50,000	28.0	49.3
100,000	39.3	60.7
200.000	50.7	73.9
500,000	63.5	82.1

Source: Brookings Institution

(married) with an income of $50,000 in the marginal 49.3 percent tax bracket that has an additional $1,000 to invest would need a before-tax return of 9.9 percent to obtain an after-tax yield of 5 percent. An investor (married) falling into the top tax bracket (not shown in table 7.2) would need a before-tax rate of return of 27.9 percent to obtain an after-tax yield of 5 percent.

Required before-tax yields are calculated from marginal tax rates rather than average effective tax rates. The reason for this is that a marginal tax rate is key when considering an incremental investment. In deciding how to invest an additional $10,000, an investor does not refer to the return on his existing portfolio. Rather an investor makes his decision on returns available in the market on an after tax basis for that incremental $10,000. The average net return after taxes on an investor's portfolio is only important after the asset becomes a part of it.

High U.S. marginal personal income-tax rates were central to the Soviet containment strategy. General Marshall spelled out the framework of the European-reconstruction effort to the Harvard graduating class in June 1947. A key component of that process, not mentioned, was U.S. domestic tax policy, and the 1949 tax code, which remained more or less in effect until 1964, may have done more to assist Far East and European economic growth than other building blocs.

In his 1950 Brookings Institution book entitled *Taxes and Economic Incentives,* Lewis H. Kimmel lists a number of effects of U.S. tax policy. These effectively benefit other countries. Among these were "high personal taxes [which] reduce the net return to an investor and may cause

TABLE 7.2
B.T. Returns Required to Obtain an A.T. Return of 5% at Various Incomes

$10,000	25,000	50,000	100,000	200,000
6.2%	7.5	9.9	12.7	19.2

Source: Brookings Institution

him to seek relative safe uses for funds becoming available for investment."[8] That means a major flow of potential equity capital for U.S. company expansion and production was siphoned off to safe uses or was consumed. "The steeply progressive income tax rates on middle- and high-bracket incomes constitute a serious barrier to the flow of investment funds."[9] The effect is that U.S. companies, which would have been producing a product or producing more of a product, did not expand or begin production. This allows foreign producers to expand or start producing the product and employ their workers. In short, high personal income-tax rates in the United States are a vehicle utilized to shift production offshore, a process by which the U.S. tax code helped European and Far East countries and thereby led to Soviet containment.

Kimmel also said that, in conjunction with the above effect, "the shortage of venture or equity capital is regarded as the most serious problem in the entire field of business finance. High income taxes are regarded as the principal factor militating against a more abundant supply."[10] Potential stockholders are one source of capital for start-up businesses, but potential investors facing steep marginal income-tax rates demand a higher before-tax rate of return on their incremental investment. Higher marginal personal income-tax rates effectively translate into a higher incremental cost of capital for U.S. businesses. In short, high personal income-tax rates result in a high cost of capital for U.S. businesses, thus allowing businesses outside the United States the opportunity to expand as opposed to domestic businesses.

Kimmel also pointed out that high marginal personal income-tax rates without a sizeable exclusion for income from savings translate into a lower national savings, investment, and production rate which is another effective benefit to other countries. Higher-income savers have the ability to save at a high rate, but high tax rates at high-income levels nullify savings—what would be saved goes to pay taxes. In addition, a saver with an incremental $1000 to place in a savings account who falls into a 91 percent tax bracket will retain nine cents out of each dollar of income from savings. Why save and invest? High tax rates are an incentive to spend and obtain a product or service, "a substantial part of personal income taxes is paid from funds which otherwise would be saved.... It is probable that in the period 1946–49 somewhere between one fourth and two[-]fifths of personal income taxes were paid at the expense of savings."[11] High tax rates therefore diminish the quantity of personal savings, investment, and production in the United States and increase the difficulty of companies to raise capital. "In short, the tax situation has lessened the supply of equity money."[12] The Brookings study found that nearly 77 percent of manufacturing companies surveyed felt they had difficulty raising capital to expand production due to the high personal income-tax rates. U.S. manufacturing businesses having trouble raising capital for expansion amounted to a plus for foreign-based companies that could raise capital to expand. That suggests other economies with high personal-saving rates could fund their business needs and enjoy increases in production and employment to fill needs that could have been produced in the United States.

Another of Kimmel's observations was that "it is widely believed that high taxes on personal incomes have an adverse effect upon the incentive to work.... Earlier retirement and unwillingness to assume the burden of more responsible positions may be among the consequences of high personal income taxes."[13] Remember that this was a 1950 study and data utilized in the study were for the latter 1940s. The work ethic and production were already being altered by high personal-income tax rates, and high tax rates had only been in effect for a few years. This is also a positive for other economies producing products and services that compete with U.S. producers as companies in other countries can produce more.

Spending through increasing debt use was subsidized in the United States until 1986 when a change in the tax code starting phasing it out. Taxpayers were given a deduction for interest expense when utilizing borrowed funds to make a purchase of an auto, television, or other item. That deduction was another line in the tax code to encourage spending. In particular, it encouraged spending on durables such as autos, which were one of the products shipped to the United States. In essence, the Japanese economy had a subsidy from U.S. taxpayers for American consumers to purchase Japanese products. This line in the U.S. tax code encouraged growth in Japan as well as other U.S. trading partners.

U.S. homeowners, except for those in the state of Texas, continue to have their spending subsidized through use of home-equity loans. Homeowners borrow on their home equity and use proceeds to purchase durables and other goods and services. Home-equity loans and the home mortgage deduction encourage use of debt. The cost of the home-mortgage interest deduction was roughly $186 billion in 1993. The idea of the home-mortgage deduction is to encourage home ownership. But Canada, which does not have a mortgage-interest deduction, has a comparable rate of home ownership. The effect of this deduction is to encourage potential home buyers to purchase a larger home and/or more amenities for that home than would otherwise be the case. In 1993, 27 million couples and individuals claimed a mortgage-interest deduction, and the $186 billion deduction is a subsidy to these homeowners. Homeowners use this deduction if the tax benefit is greater than they would receive with the standard deduction. In France, by comparison, mortgage interest is deductible as a separate line item and does not affect the standard deduction. However, the amount of interest expense is limited so that lower income taxpayers receive the full subsidy.

Kimmel takes the position that double taxation of corporate earnings, once as earnings and again as dividends, has the effect of placing the corporate tax burden on stockholders. This effect discourages U.S. capital formation and production as it reduces saving and effectively benefits other countries. Taxes on income from capital drive a wedge between the gross rate of return on assets and the net rate of return received by households. Taxation of dividends is another line in the tax code that has the effect of encouraging relative capital formation to occur in more capital-friendly countries.

The influences of the personal income tax code encourage economic growth in other countries by discouraging U.S. production, work, and capital formation that effectively share U.S. wealth. This does not imply a zero-sum game in which the United States lost and other countries won, but rather an environment in which foreign companies benefit more than U.S. companies in creation of wealth because of U.S. policies. *This is the environment provided to other countries by a world leader.*

The U.S. federal personal tax code has encouraged growth in other countries since the 1940s and continues today except for the interest

TABLE 7.3
B.T. Returns Required at the Top Tax Rate to Yield 5% A.T.

	1950s	1965	1982	1988	1994
B.T.	55.6%	16.6%	10%	6.9%	8.3%
A.T.	5%	5%	5%	5%	5%

expense deduction. Table 7.3 illustrates the effect of U.S. personal tax-code changes over time on other countries. The higher the before-tax rate required to yield an after-tax return of 5 percent in the top marginal rate, the greater the efforts of the United States to share its wealth with other countries. This implies that the 1964 Kennedy tax-rate reduction reduced U.S. efforts to share wealth. Reagan tax-rate cuts in the 1980s had the effect of further slowing the U.S.'s effort to share wealth as the Soviet-containment strategy paid its dividend. President Clinton, however, decided to increase U.S. efforts to share wealth with other countries after the cold war had ended by hiking individual personal tax rates.

Figure 7.1 illustrates the effect of the top marginal statutory tax rate on an annual basis since 1913. High U.S. marginal personal income-tax rates result in fewer jobs, lower levels of both production and capital formation, and a lower work effort, which provides opposite effects in other countries and creates a more conducive environment for their economic growth. Those countries in turn export products into the United States that otherwise may have been produced in the United States.

When the Korean War started in 1950, the top individual marginal income-tax rate was increased from 82 percent to 91 percent, and an excess profits tax of 77 percent was implemented on business. Dwight Eisenhower was elected president in 1952 and chose not to support a bill that would have reduced individual income-tax rates by 30 percent, a key decision in helping the economic evolution and growth of U.S. allies in the Far East and Europe during the 1950s and early 1960s. The 91 percent top individual personal tax rate increased to 92 percent in 1952–53, then dropped back to 91 percent, and remained in effect until the 1964 tax-rate cut. The top marginal rate, however, is not always an accurate indicator of tax rates facing Americans, as both the top rate and income level to which it applies changed over time.

FIGURE 7.1
Top Statutory Individual Marginal Tax Rate

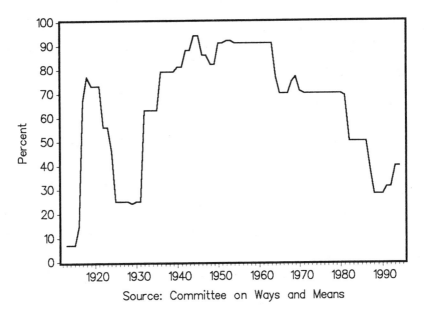

Source: Committee on Ways and Means

The 91 percent top rate in 1960 applied to taxable income in excess of $200,000. In 1965 the top rate of 70 percent applied to income over $100,000. After the Economic Recovery Tax Act of 1981, the top rate of 50 percent started at $106,000. (The $200,000 in 1960 is equivalent to $1 million in 1994 dollars, while the $106,000 in 1982 equates to $162,000 in 1994.) The top rate was much lower in 1982 than 1960, but many more taxpayers felt the adverse influence of the top rate in 1982 than in 1960. The 39.6 percent top marginal statutory rate in 1994 applied to incomes over $250,000. Another difficulty with top marginal tax rates is that the definition of taxable income changes over time. As the top tax rate was lowered, many deductions were reduced or eliminated. An objective of The Tax Reform Act of 1986 was to be revenue neutral. Individual and corporate tax rates were reduced, and, as an off-

FIGURE 7.2
Marginal Income Tax Rates at Income Levels

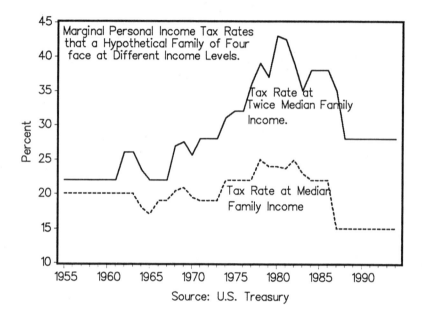

Source: U.S. Treasury

set, deductions were reduced or eliminated so that tax revenue generated from the tax-code revision would remain unchanged.

A somewhat different picture of marginal personal income-tax rates faced by taxpayers is to view a tax series constructed by the U.S. Treasury Department for different income levels for a four-person family—the median income (approximately $47,000 in 1994) and twice the median income. Income of these hypothetical families is assumed to come entirely from wages and/or salaries earned by one spouse. Figure 7.2 illustrates behavior of those tax rates.

The marginal rate faced by families having twice the median income increased from 1960 to 1980 when it peaked at 43 percent. The statutory marginal rate was lower in the 1970s than in 1950, but tax rates faced by taxpayers below that top rate increased rather sharply. Table

7.3 suggests U.S. personal tax policy shared less U.S. wealth with foreign countries in the 1960s, 1970s and 1980s (relative to the 1950s), while U.S. Treasury data illustrate the opposite—that efforts to share U.S. wealth with foreign countries *increased* during the 1960s and 1970s compared to the 1950s. Treasury data provide a realistic picture. Efforts to share wealth decreased with the sizeable personal income-tax-rate reductions in the early 1980s. The other point from figure 7.2 is that the federal income tax is progressive; that is, those at twice the median income pay a higher marginal tax rate than those at the median-income level. *A basic point of a tax code is tax what you don't want.* A system of high marginal income-tax rates evolved during World War II and continued until the rates started coming down in the early 1980s. That tax policy is U.S. production and capital formation unfriendly but friendly to production in other countries.

Capital is taxed multiple times in the United States, which also hinders capital formation. It is taxed once at the corporate level, whether retained or paid out as dividends, at 35% (larger corporations). So a dollar of earnings available for capital investment or dividends is reduced to sixty-five cents. From 1952 to 1963 the corporate tax rate was 52 percent. The amount available for earnings or dividends at a 52 percent tax rate was forty-eight cents. The Brookings study addresses adverse effects of a high corporate tax rate on business expansion and growth: "The present rate schedule for the corporate income tax is an adverse factor in decisions of small business concerning expansion."[14] The corporate income-tax rate in 1950 was 42 percent. That suggests companies in other countries in which the tax environment was more conducive to economic growth were able to expand production to supply goods to markets that U.S. companies might have. An alternative view is that incidence of the corporate income tax falls on customers in the form of higher prices and/or on employees of corporations disguised as lower wages and salaries or reduction in benefits—or even firings. In the 1980s and 1990s, the latter seems to be occurring—companies passing increased costs of doing business such as taxes and regulations backward to their employees, resulting in job losses, in order to remain competitive.

Capital is taxed again at the personal level when it is paid out as dividends, as pointed out above. The applicable top personal income tax rate in 1994 varied by income level—15 percent, 28 percent, 31 percent, 36 percent, and 39.6 percent. The top effective marginal rate climbed to 44.4 percent because of limits on itemized deductions and a phasing out of personal exemptions in the highest tax brackets. At the 36 percent rate that sixty-five cents of dividends paid to an individual is reduced to thirty-nine cents available for capital formation. An individual investing that capital is taxed on any gains. If a capital gain occurs, it is taxed at a 28 percent rate; that is, if an individual invested $10,000 in shares of a company in 1983 and sold those same shares for $14,500 in 1994, that taxpayer would pay at the 28 percent tax rate and be able to keep only 72 percent of the $4,500 gain (or $3,240) for a principle amount of $13,240.

But inflation increased 49 percent between 1983 and 1994. The investor would need $14,900 to have the same purchasing power in 1994 as in 1983. The capital gains tax does *not* allow an offset for the punishing effect of inflation. The investor, in this example, loses money by making the investment. The investor would have been better off spending the money in 1983 than in 1994 as purchasing power of his money was greater in 1983. This is another reason why the tax code is capital formation unfriendly. Many earners have more purchasing power if they don't invest their income but instead spend it when received. Capital is also effectively taxed through cost-recovery rules by not allowing the full cost of new equipment to be recovered. When a corporation retains capital and purchases a piece of new equipment for production, the cost-recovery rules are inadequate to allow for replacement. The tax code also encourages use of debt by business as interest expense is deductible. Businesses have an incentive to choose debt over equity to finance business growth as each dollar that a business borrows has an effective cost of sixty-five cents owing to interest-expense deductibility.

U.S. tax policies were and are production and capital formation unfriendly, while other counties such as Japan and West Germany developed capital-formation and economic-growth-friendly tax policies. This effectively implemented sharing of U.S. wealth with those countries. (How West Germany and Japan, through tax policy not only recovered from defeat but became in time strong economies as well is covered effectively in "Foreign Tax Policies and Economic Growth," a 1966 conference report of the National Bureau of Economic Research and Brookings Institution, and that report serves as the basis for the outline that follows of the development of the West German and Japanese economies.)[15]

Germany was split after the war, and in Western zones of occupation personal tax rates were increased along with corporate income taxes, inheritance taxes, and indirect taxes on items such as tobacco and beer. By early 1948 the German economy struggled with a tax code having marginal individual tax rates of 95 percent and 50 percent on incomes equivalent to over $15,000 and $600 respectively. These confiscatory tax rates were implemented after the war as part of the agreement among powers for dismantlement and reparations. Economic activity declined, as expected, but this conflicted with evolving U.S. policy of Soviet containment and directly contradicted Marshall Plan objectives for Western Europe. The three Western powers—the United States, Britain, and France—implemented new policies and revised tax laws for Germany that went into effect in June 1948.

Emphasis shifted to revitalization of the West German economy with currency reform, removal of price controls, tax rate reduction with emphasis on capital formation, and focus on rebuilding the economy for exports. Tax changes emphasized incentives for business to produce and labor to work by reduction of marginal income-tax rates and provided additional incentives to save and invest. Marginal rates were still hitting 50 percent for an income of $2250, but deductions were allowed for profits, investment, and savings. Exemptions were heavily weighted toward manufacturing industries, and in 1951 major tax incentives, such as allowing deduction of a percentage of income derived from exports from the corporate income tax, were introduced to funnel more investment into export industries. Tax incentives, such as making direct savings accounts partially deductible from taxable income in order to promote personal savings, were implemented. By 1955 the top personal income-tax rate in West Germany was reduced to 63 percent on incomes over $250,000, while the 50 percent bracket started at $42,000. By 1958 the top rate was down to 53 percent from 95 percent in 1948. In 1957 the top personal tax rate on dividend income was reduced from 30 percent to 15 percent. In 1948 it had been 65 percent. Germany in 1993 imposed no tax on capital gains and gave shareholders a credit against their individual taxes to offset taxes already paid on dividends at the corporate level. Other countries in Western Europe also moved to reduce tax rates in the 1950s. The Netherlands reduced personal tax rates in 1954 and 1955 with the idea that a "lightening of tax burdens would yield more revenue as a result of an accelerated expansion of production and income."[16]

Damage to the Japanese economy from World War II was extremely severe, and the subsequent reconstruction and recovery were lengthy. Post-World War II economic activity measures didn't reach their pre-war level until the first half of the 1950s, but the economy grew rapidly. Many concluded that Japan's rapid growth until that time was typical of strong growth in any recovering economy, but rapid growth continued in subsequent years. In a developing economy, which Japan effectively was at that time due to World War II damage, the rate of capital formation depends in large part on the supply of domestic capital available. Japan made the decision after World War II to exclude income from savings up to a specified amount from taxation. Between 1955 and 1957 interest income was entirely exempt. From 1957 to 1963 interest income was taxed at a maximum rate of 10 percent. The tax rate was cut to 5 percent in 1964, while interest income for small accounts continued to remain tax exempt. Dividend payments up to a specified limit were not subject to taxation. Withholding tax rates for dividends over that amount were reduced from 20 percent to 10 percent in 1955 and then to 5 percent in 1963. Capital gains on securities were tax exempt unless earned by "cornering stocks" or by "selling a business." Japan chose to reduce effective tax rates through use of exclusions and loopholes in order to promote savings and investment. Tax rates were cut by approximately 10 percent annually between 1950 and 1975. The saving exclusion helped make the Japanese economy powerful.

Japan and Germany are examples of foreign tax systems friendly to capital formation, which helped generate strong economies within the context of U.S. economic policies that were designed to encourage economic growth of market economies. Capital—plant, equipment, technology—is mobile and goes to less-punitive tax environments. U.S. multinationals made direct investments in such countries in order to be able to export products to the United States. Countries undertaking policies to achieve high levels of investment and orienting their economies to exports found a ready U.S. market for their output. These policies resulted in development of very strong market economies, which were resistant to radical social and/or economic moves away from democratic institutions.

Results of U.S. tax policy on the domestic economy were becoming evident in the latter 1950s and early 1960s, and John F. Kennedy was elected president on the theme of "getting the economy moving again."

President Kennedy, initially, wasn't thinking about reducing tax rates to encourage faster economic growth. Instead, he was interested in a public works and investment tax credit program, but those proposals didn't gain adequate support and were dropped. It wasn't until the middle of 1962 that President Kennedy promoted tax-rate cuts as a means of stimulating economic growth. The Committee for Economic Development (CED), consisting of 200 businesspeople and educators with a research staff that included such noted contributors as Paul Samuelson and Herbert Stein, helped generate support for Kennedy's program with the publication of their report, "Reducing Tax Rates for Production and Growth."[17] As a result, people from both political parties supported reducing tax rates in the 1960s as a method to get the economy moving.

The CED recommendations included (1) a maximum individual income-tax rate of 70 percent compared to the 91 percent that was in effect at that time; (2) an across-the-board reduction of all individual income-tax rates by 8 percent; and (3) reduction of the corporate profits tax rate by 5 percent, from 52 percent to 47 percent. This was essentially the program implemented by the Revenue Act of 1964—marginal personal rates for individuals that had ranged from 20 percent to 91 percent were reduced to 14 percent to 70 percent while the corporate tax rate was reduced to 48 percent from 52 percent. At the time President Johnson said of the Revenue Act, "This is a bill designed to increase our national income and Federal revenues, and to provide insurance against recession." Japan, as noted above, moved to offset the relative effects of the U.S. tax rate cut in 1964 by further reducing their tax on interest income from savings and the tax rate on dividends.

The CED recommended a part II of the economic program consisting of (1) restraint in federal government expenditures; (2) a further reduction of all individual income tax rates by 6 percent; (3) a ceiling on individual income tax rates of 60 percent; and (4) a further cut of the corporate profits tax rate by 5 percent. Part II was never enacted by the Johnson administration, and the top marginal personal income-tax rate remained at 70 percent until President Reagan was elected. The rationale for Parts I and II of the CED was a higher rate of U.S. private-capital investment would contribute to a higher economic growth rate and higher level of employment; a high rate of growth in capital formation was a necessary condition for higher economic growth; economic growth is a product of investment, education, technology, and research;

and the investment process increases the amount of capital per worker and incorporates new methods made available by technological advance. Reduction of individual and corporate income-tax rates would help reduce the cost of capital, encourage a higher rate of private investment, and encourage work in the United States. The CED proposal amounted to an attempt to slow the sharing of U.S. wealth with other countries.

8

The Creation—Building Bloc V, Oil

A low-cost energy source, oil, encouraged rapid development of market economies during the 1950s, 1960s, and early 1970s. Economies utilize a combination of inputs—such as labor, capital, technology, and energy—and an increase in efficiency to produce goods and services. When an input price is relatively cheap compared to other input prices, more of the less-expensive input is utilized. Japan, after World War II, had relatively cheap labor, which was an advantage for production in Japan. Japan also implemented tax policies to provide abundant capital. Those were advantages that Japan provided Japan. An input provided to all market economies after World War II was inexpensive oil. Oil competes with other fuels such as natural gas, coal, and electricity in industrial uses so that cheap oil places a ceiling on prices of other fuels as well.

World War II illustrated oil's importance as a factor in helping Allied forces defeat Axis powers. The Western hemisphere produced nearly 80 percent of the world's oil in 1941, while the United States was producing, alone, over 60 percent of world-total production. The United States supplied 6 billion out of 7 billion barrels of oil consumed by the Allies in World War II.[1] Meanwhile, Axis powers had little domestic production, so Germany spent considerable resources attempting to develop synthetic oil. The Roosevelt and Truman administrations were very concerned about oil since the United States had a relatively small proportion of the world's oil reserves—15 percent—even though the United States produced over 60 percent of the world's oil. That suggested to some as early as in the 1930s that the United States would become a net oil importer, creating a strategic concern about oil in the Roosevelt administration. The United States became a net oil importer in the latter 1940s.

Oil, as we know it, wasn't used in the United States until the 1860s. Lamps burned whale oil or coal oil until then. Col. A. C. Ferris of New York obtained small samples of rock oil from seeps and found that it could be distilled to make an improved lamp oil. He offered twenty dollars per barrel for rock oil, which induced E. L. Drake to drill his famous well, and the petroleum industry dates from Drake's well near Titusville, Pennsylvania. The well was completed on 27 August 1859 and produced about 2000 barrels of oil during the final months of 1859, which led to a search for oil in other parts of Pennsylvania, in other states, and in other countries. Oil production increased, and in 1860, 650,000 barrels were sold. In 1861 the price averaged fifty cents per barrel.

The Lucas gusher at Spindletop, Texas, in 1901; the Lakeview gusher in California in 1910; and large wells discovered in Oklahoma during this time period set the stage for major U.S. production. Oil was discovered in Mexico in 1901, Iran in 1908, and Venezuela in 1914. The Middle East produced only 10 percent as much oil as the United States in 1938. The key to low-cost Middle Eastern oil sources were large oil deposits found in Saudi Arabia and Kuwait in 1938. The United States in 1938 produced 61 percent of the world's 5.5 million barrels per day (mmbd) oil production at an average price of less than $1 for West Texas crude (that 1938 $1 equates to $10.50 in 1994), but U.S. oil wells were relatively small producers as well as high-cost compared to Middle Eastern fields.

U.S. concern about becoming a net oil importer shifted U.S. strategic interest to the Middle East in the late 1930s and early 1940s. Standard Oil Company of California (Socal) bought rights to a very large territory in Saudi Arabia in 1933 to explore for and produce oil in exchange for cash and a royalty rate of approximately ten cents per barrel. Socal brought what is now Texaco into the deal to manufacture and distribute crude oil. Crude production increased substantially in 1939 but fell in 1940, as attempts to supply Britain by tanker from the United States and other sources like the Middle East came under heavy attack by German U-boats. This distribution-chain disruption resulted in less oil being produced and exported from Saudi Arabia, creating a financial problem for Saudi Arabia. In 1941 President Roosevelt asked the British to assume 90 percent of the king's budget for the remainder of the war, though it was understood that the financial assistance would actually come from the United States through Britain. The slaughter of oil tankers en route primarily from the United States to Britain continued until the United States gained superiority over U-boats in April 1943.

The U.S. government, because of concern about its relative lack of oil reserves, attempted to purchase the Socal-Texaco Saudi Arabia concession in 1943 as well as concessions held by other oil companies (such as Gulf) in Kuwait. The Petroleum Reserves Corporation, a government-created entity, was to acquire ownership of oil reserves. There was also a concern that somehow the British might outmaneuver the U.S. government and gain access to Saudi oil, as the British were vitally interested in Middle East oil since World War II because of oil's strategic importance. Britain, at that point in World War II, however, was little threat to U.S. interests in the Middle East. Purchase of concessions by the Petroleum Reserves Corporation nearly occurred but was defeated in Congress as other oil companies marshalled congressional support to stop the buy out. The rationale for the attempted purchase of the Socal-Texaco concession was that oil companies wouldn't produce oil fast enough to meet postwar European demand. A major reason for the U.S. strategic-policy thrust in the Middle East was that a flow of cheap oil from the Middle East to Western Europe would hasten the European economic recovery. In addition, fewer barrels of U.S.-produced oil would need to go to Europe if ample Middle Eastern oil were available.

In February 1943 President Roosevelt decided to make Saudi Arabia eligible for lend-lease. Companies with Middle East concessions had lobbied State Department officials that the U.S. government needed to provide direct aid to Saudi Arabia to ensure a 100 percent U.S. interest would exist after the war, as well as protecting their own investment. Roosevelt was convinced by the military-strategic importance of that area and its resource to grant lend-lease. That same year the U.S. Navy estimated Middle East reserves of 56 billion barrels, according to Pollard,[2] who also uses a State Department quote that "the oil resources of [Saudi Arabia] constitute a stupendous source of strategic power, and one of the greatest material prizes in world history."[3]

The British government view was the possibility of too much cheap oil flooding markets after the war. Others wanted to encourage maximum production from the Middle East to conserve U.S. oil resources and promote European economic recovery. This latter was the U.S. State Department view. These views led to more discussions between Britain and the United States and in August 1944 an agreement between the two countries (called the Anglo-American Petroleum Agreement) was completed. This agreement was an attempt to manage oil supply with the objective of encouraging stability in the oil market which, after the war, was expected to be in oversupply. However, when the agreement appeared to be in violation of antitrust laws and it became clear that Congress was not going to approve it, President Roosevelt withdrew the proposal. Discussions between the United States and Britain continued and resulted in an informal understanding that the British postwar sphere of influence in the Middle East would be limited to Iran and Iraq with the United States predominant in the remainder of the Gulf.

U.S. State and Defense Departments continued to be concerned about adequacy of domestic oil reserves and strategic importance of Middle Eastern oil. Pollard quotes secretary of the navy James V. Forrestal in 1945 that he did not "care which American company or companies develop the Arabian reserves" as long as they were "American."[4] Forrestal attempted to revive the Anglo-American agreement in early 1946, but there was very limited congressional support as the strategic importance of the Middle East started to fade after the war. But the U.S. government did attempt to help U.S. oil companies strengthen their position in the Persian Gulf. State Department and Navy officials encouraged the Socal-Texaco concession, called Aramco, to expand and include Mobil and Standard Oil New Jersey with the idea to provide Aramco more capital as well as a larger distribution system so that Aramco could move more crude. In 1950 the State Department also encouraged Aramco partners to go along with the Saudi request for a 50 percent share of Aramco's overall profits. Taxes and royalties would be assessed so that Saudi Arabia's take would be equal to 50 percent of Aramco's net profits. The Saudi request was patterned after an agreement Venezuela had reached with Shell and Standard Oil New Jersey several years earlier, and the State Department reasoned that this would ensure that Saudi Arabia remain pleased with American companies and would have no need to turn toward the Soviets. Kuwait negotiated the same arrangement with Gulf Oil. The British, also, eventually went along with the same arrangement in their Middle Eastern companies.

The British and the United States orchestrated a coup in Iran when it appeared the Soviets were going to have a winner with Iran's Prime Minister Mossadegh. The Shah's prime minister had been assassinated and the opposition installed Mossadegh. The 1953 British and U.S. coup initially resulted in the Shah fleeing his country, but shortly thereafter Mossadegh was forced to leave and the Shah was put back in power. The U.S. State Department, in an attempt to strengthen the Shah's position, wanted to create a consortium of Western companies to operate in Iran as the United States wanted oil production increased so that the Shah would have a growing income base to use as a shield against Soviet influence.

A complicating factor in gaining a Western oil-companies agreement to operate in Iran was a criminal antitrust suit the Justice Department was pushing against oil companies. Cartel practices of U.S. oil companies operating in the Middle East were deemed to impact both domestic prices and business conditions and therefore were in violation of antitrust laws. State and Defense Departments rushed to aid oil companies, persuading President Truman to call off the Justice Department's criminal case in the national interest, and the national-security interest of Middle Eastern oil overrode the reach of Justice Department antitrust guidelines. Oil companies were, in effect, implementing foreign-policy interests of the U.S. by making oil plentiful and cheap. The Justice Department issued a guarantee in 1954 that companies producing oil in the Middle East were exempt from U.S. antitrust laws. The Eisenhower administration in April 1953, however, had filed a civil antitrust case against the downstream (manufacturing and disposal) operations of the oil companies, so the Justice Department guarantee in 1954 was interpreted as only applying to the upstream (exploration and production) portion of integrated oil companies.

Plentiful and cheap oil, made available by U.S. oil companies operating in the Middle East and watched over by Washington, was crucial to Soviet-containment policy. This is an excellent example of U.S. national planning that worked for twenty years. Private industry and government worked together to implement foreign policy to encourage a worldwide standard-of-living rise. Eventually seven oil companies formed the consortium to operate in Iran—four Aramco partners, Gulf Oil, Shell, and a French company. Aramco partners then proceeded to explain to the King of Saudi Arabia why they were entering the consortium; "They were doing this not because they wanted more petroleum because they didn't, but as a political matter at the request of our government," and, according to Yergin, Ibn Saud, Saudi's king, supposedly understood as he did not want

FIGURE 8.1
Real and Nominal Oil Prices

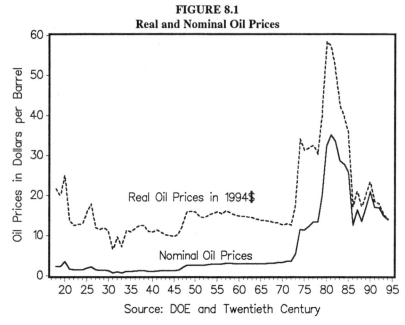

Source: DOE and Twentieth Century

FIGURE 8.2
World Crude Production and Middle East Market Share

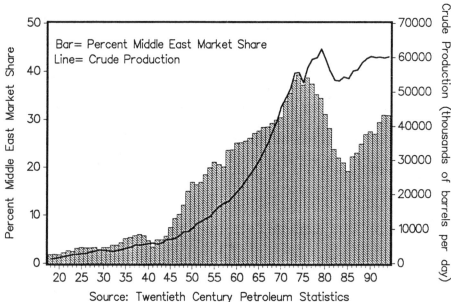

Source: Twentieth Century Petroleum Statistics

to see Iran go communist with its ramifications for Saudi Arabia.[5] During the 1950s and 1960s oil prices remained low—or until the 1973 oil embargo (figure 8.1). By 1956 Saudi Arabia produced 1 mmbd and the entire Middle East produced 3.5 mmbd. By 1973 Saudi produced 7.6 mmbd while the Middle East produced 21.2 mmbd. Middle East oil-market share went from 7.5 percent in 1945 to 35 percent in 1973—from .5 mmbd in 1945 to over 21 mmbd in 1973. Figure 8.2 shows changes in Middle East market share out of total world-crude production.

Oil companies did their job so well that it resulted in Middle East oil producers forming the Organization of Petroleum Companies (OPEC) in 1960. Standard Oil of New Jersey decided unilaterally to cut posted prices of Middle Eastern crude oil in August 1960 without consulting impacted producers.[6] This decision to reduce posted prices by approximately 7 percent or fourteen cents per barrel was a result of the steadily increasing surplus of crude oil. Production of oil as well as reserves of oil was increasing dramatically. Worldwide crude production increased by a factor of nearly three from approximately 7.5 mmbd in the middle 1940s to approximately 21 mmbd in 1960—a 7.1 percent annual increase. Major oil companies had more and more oil to move, and the method to move more was to lower prices, which stimulated economic activity, thus providing more oil demand.

The August 1960 price cut was a direct affront to the Middle Eastern producers. Iraq, acting on that major mistake by oil companies, convened a meeting in Baghdad and by 14 September 1960 reached an agreement on forming OPEC with the five major oil exporters of Iran, Iraq, Kuwait, Saudi Arabia, and Venezuela forming OPEC. Other countries joined later and OPEC envisioned themselves as a worldwide Texas Railroad Commission. Oil companies knew they had made a mistake as OPEC countries agreed among themselves to prohibit oil companies from decreasing posted prices of crude oil without permission. The OPEC staff studied the economics of oil production, transportation, refining, and marketing during the decade of the 1960s. OPEC attempted several times to raise prices above their production costs between 1960 and 1973, but they were not effective until October 1973. Among the reasons for their ineffectiveness were three distinct factors—oil in the ground belonged to oil companies according to contract, there was a relative surplus of oil production, and additional large fields of oil were being discovered around the world such as in Africa and South America.

In 1970 there were confrontations between Middle East oil-producing countries and Western oil companies. Oil producers threatened to withhold oil supplies and sought settlements that would be in the benefit of oil producers. That failed and OPEC's inability to increase prices resulted in a cheap energy input being available until 1973. But the series of confrontations between producers and the oil industry led many to conclude the balance of power was shifting from the oil industry and consuming countries to oil-producing countries. Oil producers wanted to maximize their government take from the market value of their oil by increasing its value through supply restrictions and obtain increasing control over oil operations. OPEC gained members: Qatar in 1961; Libya and Indonesia, 1962; United Arab Emirates, 1967; Algeria, 1969; Nigeria, 1971; Ecuador, 1973, and Gabon, 1975.

Meanwhile the oil industry wanted to maintain control of operations and produce enough to meet consumption, which was rising rapidly in response to the falling real oil prices. Oil consumption in market economies increased by a factor of 2.6 in thirteen years, from 18.3 mmbd in 1960 to 47 mmbd in 1973, as cheap oil led to more uses—and more intensive uses—in the industrial, transportation, and residential sectors of the global economy. But European countries and Japan started increasing oil prices at the consumer level through hiking taxes. The driving force for increased oil use was its price relative to other fuel prices and prices for capital and labor. Oil was cheap, so it was substituted for other fuels such as coal, labor, and capital. In addition, its price led to use of oil-intensive equipment as cheap oil encouraged use of manufacturing equipment built to utilize relatively larger amounts of oil as opposed to more efficient equipment which would use less oil. Japan's oil consumption increased by a spectacular 7.5 factor between 1960 and 1973, while the West German increase was a factor of 4.7. The combined increase in Britain, France, and Italy was a 3.5 factor. In comparison, the U.S. increase was a 1.8 factor.

The British government encouraged switching from coal to oil in the late 1940s. The price of oil made it more and more competitive with coal, but the 1946 Coal Industry Nationalization Act resulted in mandated difficulties in the coal industry and hastened the switch to oil. Nationalization of the coal industry effectively held the price of coal up and made oil more competitive in terms of energy delivered per dollar. Britain passed the Clean Air Act in 1957, which also had the effect of increasing oil use at expense of coal. The economies of oil compared to coal would have increased oil's importance, but British government actions hastened the process. A government official said, "Oil has become the lifeblood of the economy, as of all other industrialized countries, and it affects every part of it."[7] After the 1956 Suez crisis the British government did move forward with its nuclear-energy program to decrease reliance on oil. Movement from coal use to oil use occurred in other Western European countries.[8] In 1955, for instance, coal provided 75 percent of total energy use in Britain while petroleum accounted for 23 percent. By 1972 oil's use of total energy was 60 percent, and coal's proportion had fallen to 22 percent—"king coal" was king no more.

In Japan, the scenario was similar. In the early 1950s coal provided more than half of Japan's total energy while oil accounted for 7 percent—less than firewood.[9] By the end of the 1960s, oil accounted for 70 percent of total energy consumption. Oil demand in Japan grew at an 18 percent annual rate, while the economy grew at 11 percent in the second half of the 1960s. As Yergin points out, the Japanese auto boom helped fuel demand for gasoline.[10] Japan produced less than 70,000 cars in 1955. In 1968, Japan produced 4.1 million cars and 85 percent were sold in Japan. Quoting Alfred Chandler to the effect that "the German and Japanese miracles were based on improved institutional arrangements and cheap oil,"[11] Yergin adds, "In the boom years of the 1950s and the 1960s, economic growth throughout the industrial world was powered by cheap oil. In a mere two decades, a massive change in the underpinnings of industrial society had taken place. Coal, on a global basis, provided two-thirds of world energy in 1949. Oil and natural gas by 1971 provided two-thirds of world energy."[12]

Western oil companies effectively implemented the 1940s energy portion of U.S. government foreign policy over a two-decade span because it was in their self-interest. Oil companies also helped implement national policy at other times. During the Suez crisis in 1956–57, "Eisenhower similarly relied upon the oil corporations to execute national policy."[13] President Eisenhower in 1955 allowed oil-company interests to override free-trade objectives and antitrust considerations with restrictions on oil imports into the United States. Oil-producing states said imports were hurting their business. U.S. oil consumption went from 4.9 mmbd in 1946 to 17.3 mmbd in 1973—a 4.7 percent annual increase. In comparison, economic activity increased at a 3.5

FIGURE 8.3
Oil Consumption

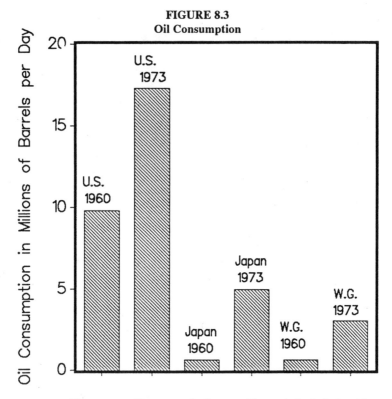

Source: Energy Information Administration

percent annual rate over that same time. Total U.S. oil consumption (figure 8.3) is much larger than in Japan or West Germany, but oil use in Japan and West Germany increased much more rapidly during the 1950s and 1960s. This rapid increase occurred as a result of many factors. One was the U.S. role of global leader. The United States through building blocs—Marshall Plan, open-door trade policy, a military umbrella, and tax policy—encouraged rapid economic growth and rising incomes in market economies. This encouraged oil use in manufacturing processes and in products produced. Accompanying job creation and rising incomes led to more and more houses, more appliances to go in them, more heating and air conditioning systems, more transportation systems, and more motor vehicles to facilitate movement of people and goods.

FIGURE 8.4
U.S. Annual Oil Consumed Per Capita

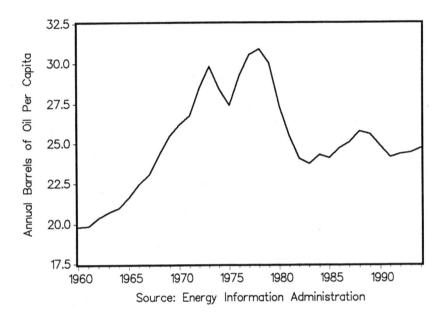

Source: Energy Information Administration

Saudi Arabian Light crude, often used as a market indicator at that time, was posted at $1.80 during the 1960s. Countries following a tax policy encouraging relatively high levels of saving and investment, such as Japan and West Germany, had not only relatively cheap capital but cheap energy as well. Inexpensive oil allowed the United States to follow a tax policy oriented toward making the cost of capital high relative to our trading partners which spurred their growth, in addition to having an improving standard of living in the United States. Oil was a cheap substitute for capital and it was utilized intensively relative to capital. Oil intensity (figure 8.4) increased in response to low prices, but intensity decreased after the sharp spike in oil prices during the 1970s. The oil price has fallen significantly since the 1980s and is back in line in real terms with prices in the 1950s and early 1960s.

A major reason for this price fall is that oil is in direct competition, since the 1980s, with another low-cost input—*the chip*—in the productive process. The chip is the world's answer to oil dependence. Chips are in many processes that use energy, ranging from motor vehicles, household appliances, and industrial equipment to manufacturing processes. Chips make such processes more energy efficient and are therefore in direct competition with energy. Producers of chips, such as Intel, are taking the place of oil producers as suppliers of low-cost inputs in the productive process.

9

British and American Golden Ages

U.S. building blocs in conjunction with cheap oil prior to 1974 created strong global economies. England assumed a somewhat similar role during the nineteenth century, and this role was transferred to the United States in the post-World War II years as England found herself tapped out. England had been losing relative economic strength for many decades prior to the power transfer.

British Golden Age (1815–1880)

In the nineteenth century and the early part of the twentieth, the world was under British hegemony. The British had the largest empire in history of the world in 1900, amounting to one-fifth of the world's land surface and a quarter of the globe's population. British military power was strong, in particular the Royal Navy, while London was the financial center. The navy was maintained at a level that was twice as powerful as the two next-most-powerful navies combined. England's registered shipping tonnage was more than the tonnage of the rest of the world combined in 1900. But England's dominant industrial and commercial base was eroding relative to others, and its economic base was that from which Britain drew her imperial strength.

British industrial production, according to Kennedy, grew at about 4 percent annually from 1820 to 1840, 3 percent between 1840 and 1870, and 1.5% annually between 1875 and 1894.[1] It was not that England's growth was declining, but her growth relative to growth in other countries was in relative decline. The British were losing relative share in newer and more important industries such as chemicals, machine tools, steel, and electrical goods. England had a nearly 23 percent share of world-manufacturing output in 1880, but by 1913

this had declined to less than 14 percent.[2] Both the United States and
Germany moved ahead of England in industrial strength. Some believe Britain's relative decline started before 1880; Kennedy, for instance, refers to a writer whose opinion was that the U.K. had a steady,
unbroken decline of 100 years starting in 1870.[3] Decline incorporated
a three-dimensional decline—economic, military, and political influence (and control) relative to other nations.

The British Empire was at the peak of its golden age as the Napoleonic
Wars ended in 1815, and their golden age continued for much of that
century. England, in 1815, had a large public debt but made the decision
to concentrate on economic growth by eliminating the income tax at
that time, which accounted for 20 percent of revenues. Demobilization
took place after the war, and operating costs were reduced, which led to
elimination of the income tax. It was decided to let economic growth
take care of the public-debt issue.

In retrospect, the British state pursued an "outward-looking" policy
from 1650 onward to help merchants and settlers in the struggle for the
New World.[4] This was not an official British doctrine, but it was, in
general, the policy followed, and one that put England's commercial
interests first. Wars with Holland, Spain, and France were fought for
control of the world economy and possession of the new territories.[5]
England, as with other governments in that time period, followed the
colonial system, which treated foreign acquisitions as foreign estates
designed to add directly to wealth and importance of the home country.
Taxation of their estates was heavy and trade controlled. England
emerged as the dominant force during that period with its only major
loss that of the American colonies. George Washington set 19 April 1783,
the anniversary of the Battle of Lexington, as the date of formal cessa-
tion of hostilities with England.

After the Battle of Waterloo in 1815, the British not only dominated
the world economy with its navy but also with its protected trade, colonies, and productivity. The British industrial boom took place after 1780
and continued during the Napoleonic wars. After those wars major
changes took place that included movement toward free trade and away
from colonial imperialism as well as toward a growth-oriented tax policy.
England took a major step toward financial stability with adoption of
the gold standard in 1821, which gave them a solid foundation for taking a world-leadership role. About fifty years later other countries such

as France, Germany, and the United States followed. This made gold the common monetary denominator and regulator of exchange rates and money supplies. As each country on the gold standard defined its monetary unit as a fixed quantity of gold, nations then undertook steps to keep its money at parity with the gold monetary unit. England, by tying its domestic currency to gold reserves, placed limits on domestic-currency expansion as issues of paper money needed to be backed by gold. Governments could still devalue their currency by changing the number of monetary units per fixed quantity of gold, but barring that, relatively stable money growth was assured, which had the effect of keeping government policy focused on maintaining a stable medium of exchange. Trade deficits, at that time, needed to be paid in gold. A persistent trade imbalance resulted in loss of gold reserves, which required domestic-money contraction reducing demand, lowering prices, and eventually restoring a balance.

England was on the gold standard from 1821 until its breakdown in 1914. John Maynard Keynes, a critic of the gold standard, has this to say:

> The remarkable feature of this long period was the relative stability of the price level. Approximately the same level of price ruled in or about the years 1826, 1841, 1855, 1862, 1867, 1871 and 1915. Prices were also level in the years 1844, 1881, and 1914. If we call the index number of these latter years 100, we find that for the period of close on a century from 1826 to the outbreak of war, the maximum fluctuation in either direction was 30 points, the index number never rising above 130 and never falling below 70. No wonder that we came to believe in the stability of money contracts over a long period.[6]

A gold standard calls for little governmental management of the monetary system, which is why it was and is opposed by many. But a gold standard has much to offer since it has the effect of removing the propensity of governments to inflate in order to decrease the value of outstanding debt.

Efficiency—or raising enough revenue for minimal state functions by not adversely altering economic growth—won out as the main rationale for raising tax revenue in the postwar period, not equity. Some in England had been arguing for a progressive tax system since the latter part of the eighteenth century. This was preferred, by some, to a consumption tax, which relied on consumption by the rich, to relate taxes to incomes. According to Webber, the highly influential Unitarian philosopher William Paley, in 1785, said, "I believe that a tax...ought to rise upon the different classes of the community, in a much higher ratio than the simple proportion of their incomes. The point...is not what men have, but what they can spare."[7] The French Declaration of the Rights of Man in 1789 had the same argument. The British economy boomed as a result of elimination of the income tax and adoption of the gold standard following the Napoleonic Wars, but the income tax was brought back in 1842, as income-tax revenues were utilized to replace revenue lost from dismantling of the Corn Laws, which had been passed in 1819. Corn Laws subsidized domestic agriculture in England as they kept out cheaper grain from abroad and discouraged use of capital-intensive equipment. Britain's personal income tax provided about 15 percent of total governmental revenues over the next thirty years.[8]

The trade debate in England was whether the Empire should be based on restricted trade with the colonies or on a free trade open to all the world. Free traders won with repeal of the Corn Laws, and England was the leader in the movement toward free trade. Continental Europe moved to tariff reduction of a reciprocal basis during the boom of the 1850s. England, in addition to the world leader in trade, was also the world banker and source of the industrial revolution. Supporters of England's free-trade policy argued on the basis that it was the cheapest policy to maintain British domination of the world economy. England had the lead in productivity and technology, so British goods should have had a competitive advantage in world markets. An expanding world economy led by the British allowed continued movement toward free trade. Both the movement to free trade and the personal income-tax code were the likely decisive economic events in what amounted to a beginning of the unraveling of the empire. The golden age of England started to fray shortly after nations such as France, Germany, Italy, Switzerland, the United States, and USSR increased their tariffs to protect their industries by shutting out British goods. Developing countries wishing to industrialize can gain an advantage if they protect their industries while the leader—in this case, Britain—does not. Such countries can industrialize very rapidly. Free-trade principles are fine if everyone plays by the same rules, but other nations don't always do that, particularly when they have their own internal imperatives. For instance, the United States followed its self-interest in increasing tariffs during the 1860s when incremental revenue was needed to fund the Civil War. Meanwhile, England clung to its free-trade policy. Such policies resulted in the British sharing wealth with other countries.

England's network of colonies began to require more and more monies, and concerns about German intentions created a call for a stronger military and corresponding funding in the 1870s. England remained the dominant economy, but income-tax rates were increased to help generate revenue. The aim of the income tax, up to this point, was to raise revenue, not redistribute income. Public spending on domestic services increased sharply after 1880, and income-tax rates increased to support that spending. Thus, the thrust of taxation shifted from encouraging resources to produce at their maximum to generating more revenue. After 1880 the notion was accepted that tax policy could be implemented to alter behavior and achieve particular actions and ends. The emphasis shifted toward redistribution of income as equity replaced efficiency as the rationale for levying taxes. Equity rests on the idea that high-income people should pay higher tax rates. The vehicle for doing this was the progressive income-tax system. The British, in the 1880s, hoped to implement the progressive income tax in a way that wouldn't interfere excessively with capital formation. A concern, in that time period, was that higher-income people were large savers, and by increasing tax rates, one might adversely impact capital formation and production. The British government, as well as other European nations, undertook responsibility for providing more and more public services to its citizens such as schools, roads, water supply, parks, and public-insurance programs like unemployment in addition to military needs. The fiscal theory developed that it wasn't necessary to have a tie between benefits received and taxes paid, which had been the idea in earlier times. Another important issue in Britain in the 1880s was whether taxes were paid by the original taxpayer or shifted to others.

Germany, during the 1880s, implemented compulsory sickness and accident insurance, funded by joint contributions from workers and employers. Germany also implemented the world's first social security system in 1889. The British followed by implementing a social security insurance system in the early 1900s, funded in part by a progressive tax system. Fiscal demands, however, were very limited in Western countries until World War I compared with modern-day revenue demands. Tax receipts were usually less than 10 percent of national income in most countries. Webber quotes a British public-finance specialist who,

TABLE 9.1
Relative Share of World Manufacturing Output (%)

	1880	1913	1938
Britain	22.9	13.6	10.7
US	14.7	32.0	31.4
Germany	8.5	14.8	12.7
France	7.8	6.1	4.4
Russia	7.6	8.2	9.0

Source: Kennedy

in summarizing informed opinion from several nations at the turn of this century, said: "If a government commands 5 percent of national income in taxes that represents a minimal demand. From 5 to 10 percent is moderate and reasonable. Taking more than 10 percent is too heavy a burden for the people to bear and when 15 or 16 percent is reached, it is impossible to increase it."[9] Most current-day developed-country governments take 40 percent or more of national income. The British economy continued growing but lost relative strength to the United States and other countries. In a few decades the United States moved from having a smaller share of world-manufacturing output than Britain to over twice as large as that of Britain (table 9.1).

Part of being a world leader is the willingness to share one's wealth with the rest of the world since that is what it means to be a world leader. Britain did that through several building blocks. One was through its open-door trade policy and gold standard. Britain kept their doors open, while trading partners didn't with the result that British exports were priced out and locked out of foreign markets by tariffs and quotas, while foreign imports penetrated British domestic markets. England, through its gold standard, maintained price-level stability, which complemented their open-door trade policy as it added stability.

A second building bloc was that as the British needed to finance and protect her colonies around the world, the U.K. maintained a massive navy and a network of bases to support it that served to keep world order. The rise of countries such as the United States in the Western Hemisphere and Germany on the mainland, as well as the USSR and China in their respective geographic areas, was viewed by England as challenges to the status quo. The British navy could more than meet any single rising power, but the number of perceived challengers to the status quo resulted in a continuing fragmentation of British power. That required more and more public spending to support the military buildup.

Another wealth-sharing process was that, as additional tax revenues were required, additional taxes were needed. As indicated, tax revenues required as a proportion of national income were modest around the turn of this century as compared to the present, but a progressive tax system increases the cost of capital and has a detrimental effect on capital formation and production relative to other countries.

Finally, the industrial revolution, which had its origins in England, no doubt played an important role in the rapid growth of the United States, hastened the relative decline of England. Other countries industrialized very rapidly aided by capital and machine tool exports from England. Communications, as well as financial and trading networks, were centered in London, allowing the dispersion of those services for world-economic needs.

Once the relative decline of England began—whether it started in the 1880s or the 1870s—its relative economic, political, and military decline continued, and there has been a steady erosion from the peak of the golden age to today. England went from being an absolute power militarily and economically to being dependent on the United States in World War II and after for economic aid and military protection. Yet, the British economy has not been in absolute decline. It continues to grow, but as other economies grow faster. Perhaps that was inevitable. A powerful nation and world leader has limitless demands placed on her economy, military, and political structure. The status quo can't be maintained and a world leader starts a relative decline, because other nations receive a partial free ride from the world leader. The productive capacity, financial resources, and subsequent military strength of other nations—with whom the world leader shared wealth—grow, and at some point those other nations grow faster than the world leader. Once relative decline begins, citizens of the world-leader country experience a changing environment. Their expectations can no longer be met by the private sector. Growth in wages and salaries doesn't meet expectations. Government responds and begins to provide more and more public-sector benefits to those whose expectations are not being met. In turn, this requires more tax revenue. Additional taxes may take the form of hikes in progressive income-tax rates, which not only alter savings, investment, and work incentives but also act to slow capital formation and production. In turn, these factors further limit the ability of the private sector to meet expectations of workers, which sets in motion demands for more government transfer programs. The process feeds upon itself. That process occurred in England as well as the U.S..

U.S. Golden Age (1945–1971)

The United States was the logical country to take over the world-leader role because of its dominant economic position after World War II. The United States returned to isolation after World War I. As indicated in earlier chapters, many factors coalesced after World War II resulting in the United States taking the world-leadership role when England was no longer capable of leadership. The United States responded by providing the signal that it was going to utilize its economic, political, and military might to shape global development, hopefully to achieve Soviet containment. The Soviets, of course, launched a countermove on their side with their resources, but the Soviet economic base, unlike the U.S. economic base, had suffered severe losses during World War II.

The United States was at the peak of its golden age at the end of World War II, as Britain was after the Napoleonic Wars, and the U.S. golden age continued for several decades after that. At the end of World War II, the United States enjoyed its greatest relative military, economic, and political influence and power over the rest of the world, as no other nation had the ability to challenge the United States on military or economic grounds. Other nations had been devastated by war with a bombed-out and worn-out capital base, an inability to produce adequate goods and service (as well as a lack of domestic customer purchasing power), and subsequent inability to support a strong military. Fear of both potential social unrest in Europe and Soviet expansion led to development of the Marshall Plan and the associated international financial system. Others building blocs followed, such as trade and military—a road much like Britain followed after 1815. The United States may have had a much longer golden age without the massive military and economic expenditures required to fight the cold war, which sapped both American and Soviet economic might at a rapid rate. The life cycle of a world leader was much shorter in the twentieth than in the nineteenth century.

FIGURE 9.1
Percent of Industrial Countries' GNP

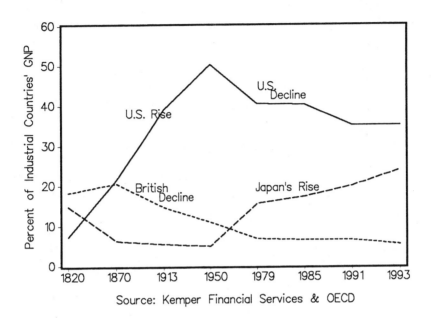

Source: Kemper Financial Services & OECD

The U.S. tax code and large military expenditures were the two building blocs that shortened the life cycle of the U.S. golden age. The Marshall Plan, while a large economic effort, did not sap the U.S. economy, as, indeed, it provided customers and markets for U.S. products and services. Access to U.S. markets, while U.S. companies didn't have equivalent access to foreign markets, was a factor influencing the demise of the golden age. U.S. trade policies, since World War II, have been favorable to our trading partners, but it could be argued that the concept of free trade, or at least movement in that direction, should have encouraged U.S. companies to become more competitive because of import competition. Competition is what drives a market economy. The basic purpose of a business is to create and maintain a customer. U.S. companies lost out to foreign producers that created customers for themselves in the U.S. markets. But the U.S. tax code worked to prevent free trade from functioning as it could have as the tax code helped foreign economies enjoy relatively faster growth than the U.S. economy (as explained in chapter 7).

When England was the world leader, an environment was created in which the U.S. economy, relative to other countries, grew somewhat faster (figure 9.1). After the United States became the world leader, the United States began to enter its relative decline. Britain, in the 1880s, attempted to levy personal income taxes so as not to interfere with savings and investment or alter incentives to work and to start businesses. That meant keeping marginal tax rates low, under 10 percent. The United States, with its very high marginal income-tax rates as well as double and triple taxation of corporate profits in the late 1940s and subsequent decades, without question, created the disincentives that Britain attempted to avoid. But U.S. policies achieved not only containment of the USSR but also the Soviet's economic and political defeat. Some policies were designed explicitly for that purpose, while others, such as the U.S. tax code, aimed at raising revenue during World War II, made an effective vehicle for wealth sharing after World War II and, as a result, were maintained. Marginal personal income-tax rates had been reduced after previous wars. The five building blocs, combined, amounted to an effective U.S. policy, and the United States had a dominating global influence in the 1945 to 1971 period.

The dollar cost to the United States of world leadership cannot be estimated. It includes some portion of the cumulative real $11.5 trillion cold war U.S. military burden from 1946 through 1992. But other costs, such as opportunity cost-of-defense dollars or relative decline of the United States through wealth sharing, cannot be estimated. U.S. policies also created many benefits, for example, not only rapid free-world growth and trade but also rapid spread and development of technology. The United States benefited from movement toward free trade but relatively much less than other market economies in the Far East and Europe, since the focus of such policies was to assist other countries. Measuring growth in real GDP, real GDP/man-hour, or real exports (table 9.2) leads to the same conclusion—a country that is a world leader has to pay for that role.

TABLE 9.2
Output and Export Growth, 1870–1987
(Average annual percent change)

	U.S.	Japan	W.G.	France	U.K.
Real GDP					
1870–1913	4.1	2.5	2.8	1.7	1.9
1913–1950	2.8	1.8	1.3	1.0	1.3
1950–1987	3.2	7.5	4.4	4.0	2.5
Real GDP/man-hour					
1870–1913	2.0	1.8	1.9	1.8	1.2
1913–1950	2.6	1.3	1.1	2.0	1.6
1950–1987	2.0	6.2	4.7	4.1	2.7
Real exports					
1870–1913	4.9	8.5	4.1	2.8	2.8
1913–1950	2.2	2.0	-2.8	1.1	0.0
1950–1987	5.2	12.4	9.3	6.5	3.8

Source: 1989 Economic Report of the President

10

Crumbling Foundation, 1971–1985

It may be that this process of a crumbling foundation, lean years, and broken promises is inevitable, and all world leaders, to varying degrees, go through the following five evolutionary stages. (1) A world leader needs a large and powerful central government playing a major role in the economy, taxing and spending in order to support its military structure and other building blocs. (2) Within that process the spinoff is a bureaucracy that becomes more and more involved in domestic affairs. Bureaucracies perpetuate themselves and one way to do that is through extension into the internal economy. That was easy for the United States as the Soviet-containment strategy required the United States to focus on an external threat rather than wealth creation. (3) Wealth sharing eventually means a huge gap between voters' expectations concerning increases in their standard of living and what the private economy can deliver as the relative decline sets in. That occurred in the post-1973 United States. (4) The entire political apparatus steps in to fill the gap with more and bigger government programs to appease citizens. In the United States both parties, at all levels of government, raced each other in an attempt to satisfy voters through redistribution of the economy's wealth. (5) That meant more taxes and government programs, which further burden the ability of the private economy to create wealth, leading to a further impairment of fundamental institutional parameters.

The building blocs of the United States golden age were successful in helping create economic powers in the Far East and Western Europe that, in many ways, were equal to the U.S. economy by the early 1970s. However, three major events in that same time period broke the news to the world that U.S. economic hegemony was over—Vietnam, Nixon's New Economic Policy (NEP), and the sharp rise in the price of oil in the early 1970s.

Vietnam cracked the U.S. military and political hegemony bubble. Concerns about creeping communism needing to be contained led to the Vietnam engagement. The United States pitted itself against a relatively small economic and military unit supplied by the Soviets and Chinese. Vietnam turned into a massive and costly intervention that reduced U.S. freedom of action, sucked in a significant portion of the defense budget, and placed strains on the U.S. economy and national psyche. All of which have been well documented.

U.S. defense spending climbed from $50 billion in 1965 to $79 billion in 1968. Much of this buildup was due to the Vietnam War as U.S. troops in Vietnam peaked at approximately 540,000 in 1969, and conventional arms flowed in. U.S. spending was going for conventional armaments, while Soviet spending was for strategic weapons. By the mid to late 1960s, the Soviets were nearly equivalent to the United States in areas such as ICBMs.[1] In other categories, such as bombers and submarine-launched missiles, the United States had major strategic advantages. However, Brzezinski indicates the Soviets gained in these areas, and the military balance was shifting from U.S. supremacy. Both sides had the capacity to destroy each other's societies and neither possessed a decisive first-strike capability.[2]

The Vietnam War was the first war that the United States decisively lost—and lost for everyone to see through daily television and press reports. The United States, with its vast technological, military, and economic advantage, lost the war to a much smaller economic competitor. It was not that the United States could not have won the war; it was that the United States chose to fight the war in Asia following the rules set by the enemy rather than establishing rules that could have utilized its advantage. U.S. firepower was made ineffective by fighting small-scale engagements in the jungle and rice paddy. The major battle, the Tet offensive, which the United States decisively won, was perceived instead as a loss and hastened the U.S. pullout. Vietnam broke the back of U.S. military hegemony, as it told the world that a much smaller country could defeat the United States.

U.S. economic hegemony was dealt a major blow in August 1971 when President Nixon outlined his New Economic Policy—two major parts were the decision to abandon the quasi-gold standard and a ninety-day freeze on wages, prices, and rents. Other items in his NEP included a tax on imports, an investment tax credit, and repealing excise taxes on automobiles. In the Gold Reserve Act of 1934, the official price of gold went to $35.00 from $20.67, and, importantly, U.S. citizens lost the right to convert currency into gold. The ability of citizens to exchange currency for gold is a key component of a gold standard. From 1934 to 1971, the United States was on a quasi-gold standard. Foreign governments had conversion rights, but that was lost in August 1971. The Federal Reserve rapidly expanded money in the time period before August 1971, adding to the world money supply. Foreigners, in turn, took that increase in money and converted it to gold. Up until that time, the gold standard provided financial stability for the international trading system, which helped implement the building-bloc strategy, and until August 1971, the United States was viewed as the world economic leader from the time of Bretton Woods.

The August 1971 announcement told the world, officially, that U.S. international monetary leadership was over. The Nixon administration argued that the United States shouldn't have to take the leadership role in international money flows, and exchange rates should be allowed to vary. Support for that argument was the point that the United States was successful in creating economic powers in Western Europe and the Far East. The European Community economy (combined) was over 90 percent as large as the U.S. economy by 1970, while Japan and other Far East countries were experiencing very rapid economic growth. The August 1971 announcement was a clear signal that the United States backed away from monetary leadership. Both the abdication of the gold standard and the rapid growth of money supply led to an environment in which OPEC oil-price increases, starting in 1973, were monetized into the price level.

OPEC struck the final and most decisive blow to U.S. world economic leadership, grabbing the world economic leadership position during the 1970s as oil became as good as gold. During the heyday of Bretton Woods, the dollar was as good as gold, but oil took the place of the dollar as a benchmark during the 1970s. OPEC (as indicated in chapter 8) attempted to increase posted prices during the 1960s but was ineffective. In 1970, OPEC governments demanded that oil companies increase posted prices of all crude oils. Lengthy negotiations between OPEC representatives and oil company officials ended in the Teheran Agreement in February 1971. The agreement amounted to increasing the posted price of Saudi light crude from $1.80 per barrel to $2.18 per

barrel, as well as setting a fixed schedule of price increases that reached
$3.23 in 1975. Oil companies thought they had bought four years of 16
percent annual increases in oil prices, which in the minds of oil company executives was relative stability.

This illusion did not last long as very soon most OPEC countries
demanded "participation" in their oil concessions. Further negotiations
ensued and in 1972 most OPEC countries signed agreements with companies operating in their country to "buy" a 25 percent interest in their
concession at a depreciated book value of installed equipment. Nothing
would be paid for the value of developed oil reserves, which, of course,
were resources of the respective oil-producing countries. The agreements
called for regular increases in the export countries' share of the concession until it would reach 51 percent in the early 1980s. By January 1973
Saudi light crude was posted at $2.59 per barrel, income tax rates were
55 percent, and the Saudi government had 25 percent of their crude,
which they sold back to oil companies at $1.85 per barrel.

In April 1973 James Akins, a State Department oil expert assigned to
the White House, was perceived as "crying wolf" about the potential for
an oil-supply crisis. In his scenario, a supply crisis could be created by
an oil exporter cutting off oil supplies.[3] He was not listened to, and Akins
gave his thoughts a public airing by publishing an article on the im-
pending oil crisis in *Foreign Affairs*.[4] Views about oil-supply disrup-
tions continued to be discussed up to October 1973. It is difficult to
create a governmental response to any issue when the threat does not
seem real and, in particular, when potential solutions are unpleasant.
Alternatives—other than raising the price of oil so that the marketplace
would utilize it less intensively—were limited. President Nixon, having
implemented wage-price controls in 1971, was concerned about inflation and had no interest in establishing a tariff on imported oil, as that
would have raised oil prices and added to upward general price-level
pressures. The secretary of labor, George Schultz, suggested a tariff earlier in Nixon's term to replace the Mandatory Oil Import Program that
had been in effect since 1959. The idea of the Oil Import Program was
to promote a "healthy domestic producing industry" by limiting petroleum imports to approximately 20 percent of U.S. consumption. President Nixon rejected the Schultz proposal and in 1973 abolished import
controls as imports had already reached approximately 35 percent of
consumption. A system of quotas to allocate existing oil supplies was

established, as Nixon's wage-price control scheme created a lack of incentives for companies to explore, drill, and produce domestic oil.

The United States needed more and more oil imports. Meanwhile, in the spring of 1973, according to Yergin, Anwar Sadat, the president of Egypt, received a promise of financial aid and use of the oil weapon from King Faisal of Saudi Arabia for the upcoming confrontation with Israel and the West.[5] In September 1973, OPEC members called for a new arrangement with oil companies, and a meeting between oil company representatives and OPEC representatives was scheduled on 8 October 1973 in Vienna. On 6 October, Yom Kippur, Egypt and Syria launched their offensive against Israel. The meeting between oil company and OPEC representatives went ahead as planned, and OPEC demanded a 100 percent increase in posted prices. Israel was in desperate need of munitions supply a few days into the war. The United States responded to the needs of Israel and lost her perceived role as a neutral broker. OPEC countries, in response, decided on monthly production cuts of 5 percent or more until their demands were met and to retaliate against the United States.[6] President Nixon then proposed a $2.2 billion military assistance package for Israel on 19 October 1973, and Saudi Arabia, in response, announced the next day they would cut 100 percent of all shipments to the United States—the dreaded embargo. The Netherlands was also included. The war ended a few days later, but the embargo remained in effect. The embargo was lifted on 18 March 1974 after the United States requested to have it lifted via Anwar Sadat. As U.S. peace efforts would not proceed until the embargo was lifted, it was in Sadat's self-interest to intervene with OPEC members.

Figure 10.1 illustrates net oil imports into the United States as well as oil imports as a percent of consumption. Net oil imports in 1973 were 6 mmbd, amounting to nearly 35 percent of U.S. oil consumption, but imports from Arab OPEC countries amounted to only slightly over 5 percent of total U.S. consumption. Yergin indicates oil available from Arab countries totalled 20.8 mmbd in early October.[7] Oil available from Arab countries fell to 15.8 mmbd in December, the most severe part of the embargo—a loss of 5 mmbd. Free-world consumption was running at approximately 51 mmbd in 1973, so this amounted to a 10 percent loss.[8] As oil is a global commodity, it doesn't matter what country is embargoed, the global market is impacted through higher prices if OPEC doesn't provide oil to the market, regardless of which country is embar-

FIGURE 10.1
U.S. Oil Imports as a Percent of Consumption

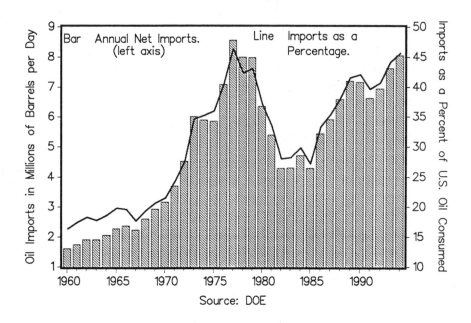

Source: DOE

goed. Oil prices went from $2.90 per barrel before the Yom Kippur war
to more than four times that price on the spot market after the oil embargo. The embargo would not have been effective or nearly as effective if the United States or other countries outside of OPEC had
significant spare capacity to produce incremental crude, but excess capacity didn't exist, so oil prices jumped.

Iran, at a Tehran meeting in late December 1973, argued for an increase in posted prices to $11.65 per barrel of Saudi light in January 1974.
OPEC members reluctantly agreed. Some members wanted more and some
less, so the $11.65 was a compromise. The Saudi light posted price had
gone from $1.80 in 1971 to $2.18 in 1971, then to $2.90 in the middle of
1973 , and ultimately to $11.65 in 1974. OPEC, for the remainder of the
1970s and into the early 1980s, was a world economic power. The United

States—because of Vietnam, abandonment of the gold standard, and the growing influence of Japan and Germany—lost its economic hegemony. OPEC's decision to embargo the United States was the fatal, as well as the most important factor, in permanently crippling U.S. global economic influence, though OPEC countries had combined economic activity that was less than 10 percent of the United States.

Vietnam, a much smaller economic power, placed a large crack in U.S. military hegemony, and Saudi Arabia, also much smaller than the United States, succeeded in bringing the United States to its knees with an economic weapon. Lines of motorists at gasoline pumps changed the perception of the United States from a country that was viewed as one of vast economic power to a country that was crippled. Impact on other countries, such as Japan and European countries, was as dramatic as in the United States (and perhaps more so), as many countries relied on imports for a larger proportion of their oil needs than did the United States. Many of these countries suffered shortages and severe damage during World War II, so it seemed to be understood that they were vulnerable. But the United States, in World War II, avoided that perception and came out of that war as the dominant economic power. Countries with small economies but having oil resources illustrated that the United States was as economically vulnerable as other countries.

Reaction to the oil crisis by the Nixon Administration included the establishment of an allocations system in addition to price controls that were in effect from Nixon's August 1971 wage-price control scheme. President Nixon also announced Project Independence, a plan intended to eliminate any need of foreign energy by 1980. The allocation system was the Emergency Petroleum Allocation Act of 1973, which established a two-tiered pricing system for domestic crude oil. "Old" oil, classified as crude from properties producing at or below their 1972 production levels, was subject to a price ceiling, while "new" oil, as well as stripper oil, was allowed to be sold at market prices. Imported oil also sold at market prices. Because of both the price disparity between old and new oil and the unequal impact on buyers of crude, additional regulatory programs were introduced such as the Entitlements Program and the Buy-Sell Program in an attempt to make the system fair. Growth in domestic exploration slowed as weighted domestic prices were significantly below those of imported. Oil companies increased exploration outside of the United States as oil prices told them to do that. Meanwhile, lower domestic oil prices gave U.S. oil consumers more incentive to consume oil, so oil demand increased rapidly along with imports. In 1977 the United States had net petroleum imports of 8.6 mmbd compared to 6.0 mmbd in 1973. U.S. inflation, which was running at 3.2 percent in 1972, climbed to 6.2 percent in 1973 and 11 percent in 1974. The U.S. economic pie had been expanding at a 5 percent rate in both 1972 and 1973, but in both 1974 and 1975, the economic pie got smaller as the recession hit.

More importantly U.S. productivity (figure 10.2), which had been expanding at 2.5 percent rate per year from 1947 to 1973, grew at approximately 0.5 percent rate per year between 1974 and 1981. The rate of productivity growth improved to 1.2 percent per year after the economy adjusted to higher oil prices, but that was still substantially below the pre-1973 embargo. OPEC cut the legs out from rapid improvements in productivity. OPEC, in addition, did something else—OPEC created an environment in which people's expectations of an improving standard of living in the United States were not met in the post-1973 era. This is exemplified by the trend in purchasing power for private-sector nonsupervisory jobs (figure 10.3), which represents over 80 percent of private-sector jobs.

Weekly wage trends increased until 1973. After that, purchasing power per job went downhill. Expectations of an increasing standard of living of the previous twenty-five years were not met. Workers asked their elected leaders for help, and politicians stepped in and developed more and bigger government programs for their constituencies to help fill the gap between people's expectations and what the private economy could deliver. Highly visible macroeconomic problems of inflation and unemployment during the 1970s acted as gasoline to fuel the need for more and bigger government economic and social programs. Government through tax policy had altered decisions on production and capital formation since World War II, and government economic and social programs, as it turned out, were just as effective at changing family and community values.

Prior to 1973 relatively low inflation, low unemployment, a rising standard of living, and the cold war covered over impacts of economic and social programs. OPEC jerked a key building bloc out from the Soviet-containment strategy and created an environment of severe macroeconomic problems. A growing economy utilizes combinations

FIGURE 10.2
Productivity Improvement

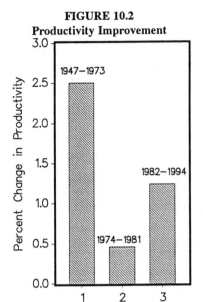

Economic Report of the President

FIGURE 10.3
Standard of Living per Job

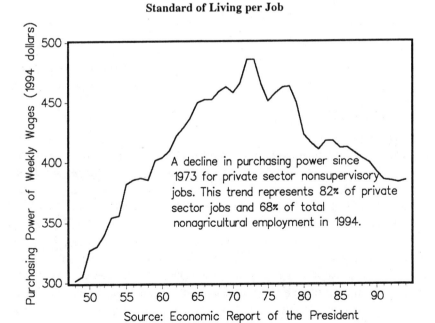

A decline in purchasing power since 1973 for private sector nonsupervisory jobs. This trend represents 82% of private sector jobs and 68% of total nonagricultural employment in 1994.

Source: Economic Report of the President

of inputs of capital, labor, energy, technology, and education. Before the 1973 embargo, the U.S. economy used these inputs and achieved growth in output per unit of input, enjoying substantial productivity gains. But U.S. policies resulted in relatively high capital and labor costs, while energy costs were cheap until 1973. Cheap oil was the U.S. advantage as the United States enjoyed rapid improvement in the standard of living per job. Business makes intensive use of the lowest-cost input in the production process. To many the United States became energy inefficient, but the United States made an economic decision to use large amounts of energy because of relative costs. Post-1973 energy costs remained relatively high through 1986. The United States kept other building blocs—trade, tax policy, and military dominance—in effect in the post-1973 period to contain the Soviets; thus, the U.S. economy faced not only high capital and labor costs but also high energy costs in the post-1973 period, resulting in slow growth as the rise in output per unit of input faltered.

OPEC grabbed the world economic leadership role from the United States. In its role as world leader, the United States shared its wealth with others, but OPEC, as world economic leader, took wealth from other countries into their coffers. OPEC held a negative leadership position. The Carter administration made an attempt to regain U.S. economic domestic strength by decontrolling industries such as air travel, trucking, and telecommunications. The Airline Deregulation Act of 1978, for instance, changed rules by which airlines were able to compete in the marketplace. Restrictions were removed on market entry, service routes, and prices, promoting increased competition. The Reagan administration kept the decontrol process rolling with the Petroleum Price and Allocation Decontrol Act in 1981. Decontrol of crude prices allowed domestic oil prices to rise to market-clearing prices. The oil-production sector responded to higher prices by increasing crude-oil exploration and production in the forty-eight coterminous states in the first half of the 1980s, and oil prices eventually crashed.

A major stab at lifting the domestic economy was made by the Reagan administration through lowering marginal personal tax rates in the early 1980s. Higher marginal personal income-tax rates (as outlined in chapter 7) equate to a higher cost of capital. Lowering tax rates was a step toward lowering the cost of capital to encourage faster growth of U.S. capital formation and productivity. The administration and Congress failed to restrain federal government expenditures, resulting in large federal budget deficits, which sucked up private-sector savings. That meant private-sector capital formation was inadequate for investment, requiring capital imports.

Macroeconomic numbers, such as economic growth, were strong in the 1980s, but there was a widespread feeling among U.S. citizens that something wasn't right in their country. But the United States remained the military leader, in particular after the relative increase in defense spending in the first half of the 1980s. Macroeconomic numbers were good and financial markets performed well, but citizens knew something was wrong—specifically, in areas of standard of living, education, and crime. In the 1970s the United States experienced high inflation and unemployment—the so-called misery index. Most people probably felt that if the United States could solve those problems, everything would again be okay—and the solutions seemed both obvious and attainable; namely, reduce inflation to a reasonable level such as 4 percent, create 20 million net jobs that would thereby reduce unemployment and put people to work, and regain stature as a world military leader. However, by the time the 1980s arrived, inflation in 1980 was 13.5 percent, unemployment in 1982 averaged 9.7 percent, and the United States was being kicked around by bullies like the Iranians in 1980. Many probably expected that the solution of those three problems would have again placed the United States in a strong domestic and international economic position.

Those problems were solved in the 1980s, yet something wasn't right, as the underlying fundamental problems present in the United States were laid bare for all to see. *The United States was in a relative decline.* Major macroeconomic problems focused everyone's attention on those issues in the 1970s and early 1980s. In the latter 1960s, Vietnam was the focus. The nation's attention was directed toward major issues while underneath change was occurring. It was not that underlying institutional problems were not there; it was that major issues such as Vietnam, oil, gasoline lines, high inflation, and high unemployment diverted attention from them.

The country went from high to low inflation, high unemployment to high employment, and from no improvement in productivity to faster productivity gains in the 1980s. This decade (the 1980s) will likely turn out to be the last decade in which the United States shored up its macroeconomic and military standing on a worldwide basis but failed to come to grips with crumbling family and community institutions. The cold war ended, removing the major outside threat, and allowed voters to focus on internal issues. George Bush lost and Bill Clinton won. President Bush was thought of as the foreign-policy president, while candidate Clinton was viewed as someone who would be a domestic-policy president and one who could perhaps fix what was wrong with the United States. Clinton made economic issues the centerpiece of his campaign and positioned himself as an agent of change, but the same underlying set of problems exists as before—only worse. When the economic numbers become better, it lays bare U.S. problems, for good macroeconomic numbers no longer mean a rising standard of living for many.

Part II

The Present—Broken Promises

11

The Lean Years, 1985 to...

Dating the beginning of the lean years will be an issue for debate by future historians. Some may argue that the lean years started in the 1970s when the United States went off the gold standard; others will say it was when OPEC took charge of the global economy, ending the days of U.S. economic hegemony, and still others may argue lean years started in the early 1980s with implementation of Reaganomics. President Reagan shared incremental U.S. wealth with U.S. allies through mounting a defense buildup to wear down the USSR, but the objective of Reagan's tax policy was to provide incentives for creating wealth in the United States.

A major reason for the success of Reagan's tax policies in creating wealth and job growth during the 1980s was the 1986 collapse in crude oil prices. OPEC in 1973, and again in the late 1970s, sharply increased crude prices. These price increases acted as large tax hikes and brought the United States to its knees. The late 1970s oil shock occurred as the religious leader Ayatollah Khomeini orchestrated the Iranian revolution beginning in late 1978; Iranian oil exports were halted in the latter part of December 1978. Iranian crude production was 6.1 million barrels per day (mmbd) in September 1978, but crude production decreased to only 700 thousand barrels per day in January 1979. Saudi Arabia increased production to help offset the Iranian shortfall in both 1979 and 1980, but a worldwide shortage remained. Oil prices rose to clear the market. Oil buyers fearing a repeat of 1973 bought oil for inventory, which resulted in the price increasing more than what it would have if inventory buying had not occurred. OPEC oil prices increased from approximately $13.50 per barrel in December 1978 to nearly $37 per barrel (FOB) by March 1981, before starting a downward drift (figure 11.1).

FIGURE 11.1
Monthly OPEC Crude Prices

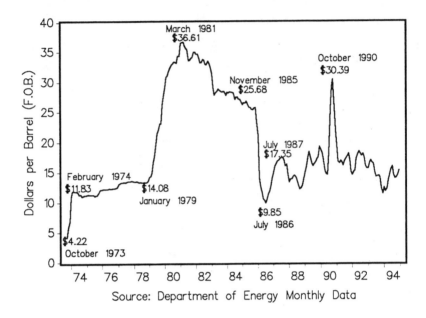

Source: Department of Energy Monthly Data

In 1986 the world community received a tax cut from OPEC. Oil prices fell sharply as Saudi Arabia made the decision to increase its market share by producing more. Saudi Arabia produced 10.4 mmbd of crude oil in August 1981, but by August 1985 their production was only 2.3 mmbd as production decreased to help prevent oil prices from falling. Saudi Arabia was rapidly becoming a marginal player in the world market as well as less important in Middle East politics. Saudi Arabia decreased production to hold the price of oil at the then agreed on benchmark of thirty-two dollars per barrel and then twenty-eight dollars. Saudi Arabia was afraid of the Ayatollah in that time frame, so they decreased production to appease the Iranians. Saudi Arabia, meanwhile, made noises that they were going to increase their market share. By 1985 Saudi Arabia knew they were rapidly approaching a situation in which they were going out of business; moreover, their fear of Iran was diminishing. Saudi Arabia sharply increased production and, thus, their market share. By December 1986 they were producing 5.1 mmbd of crude, and this production increase resulted in a sharp oil-price fall. Prices were under ten dollars per barrel in July 1986 but increased in latter 1986, as OPEC members came to an understanding on prices and market shares. However, the average OPEC oil price was nearly ten dollars a barrel lower, on average, in 1987 than what it was in 1985. This price fall acted as a tax cut for both businesses and consumers and propelled the U.S. and global economy forward.

In that same time frame, Congress passed the Tax Reform Act of 1986, which cut the top marginal personal tax rate to 28 percent in 1987 from 50 percent. The OPEC tax cut provided a major boost to the economy, but the administration's personal income-tax rate cut also helped. Together, the oil-price decrease and personal income-tax rate cut allowed the United States to act as if it remained an economic leader through the remainder of the 1980s. A major negative of the 1986 Tax Reform Act was the capital-gains tax-rate hike from 20 percent to 28 percent, which amounted to a 40 percent increase. This had the effect of reducing capital-gains tax revenue as well as locking up a large capital source. The Joint Economic Committee found that when the capital gains tax rate was 20 percent, capital-gains tax revenues rose from 1981 to 1985. By comparison, in the period from 1987 to 1991, the rate of realizations declined at the 28 percent capital-gains tax rate, and tax revenue was reduced in each of those years relatively to what it was before the 40 percent increase in the capital-gains tax rate.[1]

But lean years had already set in. A precise year for start of the lean years is perhaps not important. A country, once it steps into the friendly global-leadership role, is starting a process that eventually leads to lean years. The United States and Britain had their golden years. Other European countries such as Spain, France, Germany, Italy, and Holland went through similar processes. For any country, becoming a world leader means lean years, and broken promises are waiting somewhere down the road. Cracks in the economic foundation of the world leader, the United States, were obvious for many years. Measures of what a country puts back in itself are capital and knowledge formation relative to other countries around the globe (table 11.1).

TABLE 11.1
Capital Formation
(Investment as a Percent of GDP)

	1960s	1970s	1980s
Japan	34.9	34.5	29.6
Germany	26.5	23.4	20.3
U.S.	18.7	19.7	19.4

Source: International Monetary Fund

The United States deferred capital formation during the cold war to assist other countries in their capital formation and production. Deferred investment in any enterprise—whether it be a business, country, house or people—eventually takes its toll. Global leaders understand this process and knew what was occurring in the United States, which was sharing its wealth with European and Far East countries on the receiving end. Europeans had been preparing themselves for U.S. lean years for decades through a pooling of their economic strength. The European approach was allow the United States to share wealth with its Allies and when the U.S. taxpayer was tapped out, then attempt to take care of themselves. The European groundwork for this eventuality started in 1958 when the European Community (EC) was established with the goal of closer economic integration. Meaningful progress toward this goal was achieved in 1968 with both reduction of tariffs and quantitative restrictions on goods and services trade within the EC. The major movement came in 1985. Europe said officially that the United States as an economic world leader was tapped out, and Europe could no longer depend on U.S. economic assistance. U.S. economic leadership was over in the early 1970s, but the United States kept policies in effect as though it remained an economic leader; in other words, European and Far East nations continued to feed off the United States, even though it no longer had economic dominance.

President Reagan's 1981 Economic Recovery Tax Act changed the rules of the game from the European perspective. Reaganomics was an attempt to reverse decades of domestic deferred investment by changing the basic character of the U.S. tax system through shifting the burden of taxation away from capital, thus making the tax system more capital friendly. In addition, the reduction in marginal personal income-tax rates was expected to increase labor supply. The 1981 tax act was both capital and labor-supply friendly. That tax act in addition to years of U.S. federal deficits convinced Europeans that the U.S. free lunch was over. Western Europe's program for taking care of themselves was presented in the 1985 White Paper Report "Completing the Internal Market" and was subsequently incorporated into the EC Treaty via the Single European Act.

This program proposed almost 300 specific steps or directives designed to help create a single European market through elimination among member countries of technical barriers such as product, health, and safety standards; fiscal barriers like differing taxation rates, subsidies, and public procurement policies; and physical barriers such as customs and passport border controls. Integration is expected to be complete by the year 2000, but much of the integration had been at least partially achieved by implementation of Europe 1992, the EC plan also commonly known as "EC-1992." The idea of a single market is that elimination of technical, fiscal, and physical barriers lowers operating costs, boosts economic efficiency, and creates a larger and hopefully faster growing economic pie. The pluses and minuses of a single European market have been widely discussed, and the consensus view is that a single market has advantages over a fragmented market. The U.S. economy is a single market without technical, fiscal, and physical barriers. No one seriously argues that having a fragmented market within the United States would enhance efficiency of the U.S. economy. It is inconceivable that requiring inspections or passports to cross state borders would be beneficial for this economy. It is a similar situation for European economies. The concept of a single market for countries having somewhat similar costs, standard of living, and tax policy is a major plus.

The economic success of Europe going their own way depends in part on how Europe addresses its monolithic social-welfare state; how participants in the European single market abide by rules; how well Europe is able to integrate itself; and the route that the United States and Japan, as well as other economic powers, travel. But, Western Europe has been moving toward a trade block for quite some time. Figure 11.2 illustrates total Western European trade occurring within Western European countries as a percent of their total trade with the world and contrasts that with the percent of their total trade with the United States and Canada, with trade defined as the sum of reported merchandise exports and imports. Trade within Western European countries increased from approximately 40 percent of total trade in 1950 to approximately 70 percent in recent years. Trade with the United States after World War II was essential to rebuild the industrial capacity of Western Europe, which was destroyed during the war. However, while the U.S. share of European trade fell rapidly as Europe rebuilt, the intra-European trade increased rapidly, which was a Marshall Plan objective. European trade with the United States can be expected to decrease as a percent of total Western European trade in the future, a continuation of the longer-term trend. In the early 1980s there was a cyclical upturn, but trade patterns have since returned to their secular trend. As a result, European trade with the United States and Canada accounted for approximately only 7 percent of total Western European trade, and in the future, Western European countries will likely develop closer trading ties with Eastern Europe and Russia. (Data for Western European countries in figure 11.2 includes trade flows among Austria, Belgium, Britain, Denmark, Finland, France, Germany, Greece, Iceland, Ireland, Italy, Luxembourg, the Netherlands, Norway, Portugal, Spain, Sweden, and Switzerland.)

In 1985 Western Europe gave the official signal they were going their own way. Western Europe linked itself with the United States as long as support was provided and Western Europe faced the Soviet threat, but no more. It can be argued that Western Europe is really a grouping of similar states like the United States and trade data simply illustrates that Europe's states are trading with each other as the various states do within the United States, but countries within Western Europe are much too nationalistic for this point of view. At the same time, however, countries within Western Europe do give preference to trading with each other rather than other countries. While data in figure 11.2 measures country to country trade flows, it is not the country but firms and individuals within that country that make decisions to trade with other firms and individuals. However, governmental policies influence decisions firms and individuals make. U.S. success in ending the cold war diverted German attention from the workings of the single market in that they made a very expensive acquisition of East Germany, and Germany will follow fiscal and monetary policies aimed toward integration of the two. France, because of Germany's eastward tilt, may assume more of a Western European leadership role. Europeans expect the United States to have a continually decreasing economic and military influence on

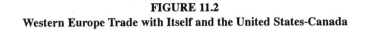

FIGURE 11.2
Western Europe Trade with Itself and the United States-Canada

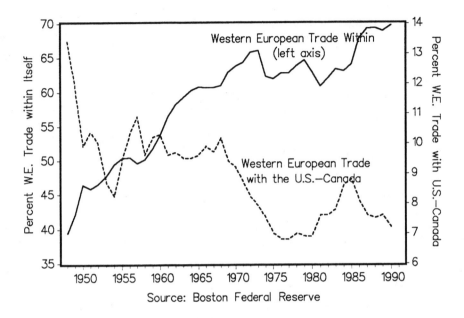

Source: Boston Federal Reserve

Europe. Most U.S. troops are out of Europe, and the French were successful in pushing through creation of Eurocorp—a European army outside NATO and U.S. control.

The United States and Canada, in comparison to Western Europe, do not show a similar relationship (figure 11.3). Canadian and U.S. trade as a percent of total Canadian and U.S. trade with the world has remained in the 30 percent range for the past forty years, as the United States, in fulfilling its role as world leader, moved to reduce trading barriers with countries in addition to Canada.

Western Europe classifies itself as a much more open economy than the United States as Western European countries trade much more with other countries (figure 11.4). If Western Europe would view itself as a market of states similar to the United States, then Western Europe is, in

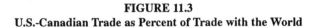

FIGURE 11.3
U.S.-Canadian Trade as Percent of Trade with the World

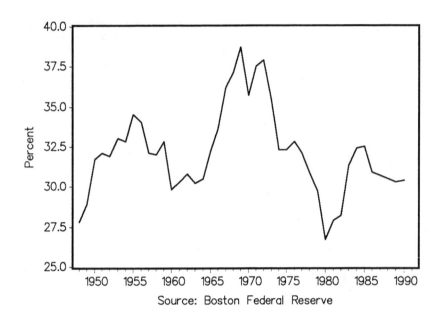

Source: Boston Federal Reserve

essence, trading with other states, and only that portion of trade that Western Europe conducts with countries other than within Western Europe is comparable to U.S. external trade. Utilizing this point of view, Western European economies and that of the United States can be thought of as having degrees of openness that are more similar.

In 1994 Japan was the U.S.'s second largest trading partner after Canada and before Mexico. Merchandise exports to Japan were approximately $53 billion compared to $114 billion for Canada and $51 billion for Mexico. Combined U.S. exports to the U.K., Germany, France, and Italy were $66 billion with the U.K. receiving the largest portion, but U.S. exports to Canada are larger by almost twice than U.S. exports to all of Western Europe. Japan's economic future is more closely tied to development of mainland China and other Far East economies than to

FIGURE 11.4
Western Europe and U.S.-Canada Trade

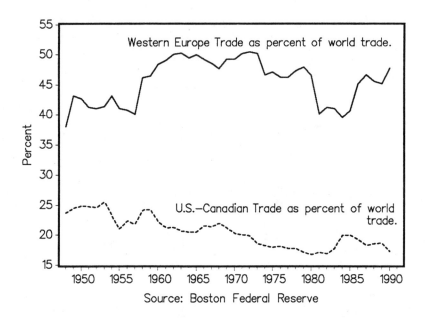

Source: Boston Federal Reserve

Western markets. Japan's growth over the past fifty 50 years has been directly linked to U.S. policies, but these policies will be modified to make the Japanese economy on more equal footing with the United States. Japan is taking steps in anticipation of this by developing economic strongholds in other Far East economies such as Korea, Vietnam, and China. The U.S. direction is likely to become much more centered on domestic issues such as crime, drugs, health and education, as well as on trade issues with its southern neighbors, than in decades past. The election of President Clinton in 1992 illustrates that.

In past decades U.S. self-interest was met by policies that led to wealth sharing and eventual ending of the cold war. Questions about U.S. ability to continue its wealth-sharing policies have been around for decades. The Reagan administration held the cold war constituency together during the 1980s, after candidate Reagan helped himself get elected by suggesting President Carter allowed himself to be misled by the Soviets. The East-West conflict was central in the Reagan administration and the American public perceived that as being in their self-interest. In the 1990s the East-West conflict is perceived to have ended. Japan is rated, in some surveys, as a major external threat to the U.S.economy, though China is likely to replace Japan in a few years if China continues growing at its current rate.

While the United States is no longer an economic superpower, it remains a military superpower. The Iraqi War demonstrated that. However, an economic superpower does not travel around hat-in-hand asking for donations to fight a significantly smaller economic and military power, which is what James Baker did as secretary of state. A political constituency can no longer be tied together to support the type of military and economic global-leadership role the United States took for the past fifty years. Perhaps, in the emerging model of global development, there may not be the need for the type of leadership role Great Britain took in the nineteenth century or the United States in the twentieth.

Pressures to fill the political and economic vacuum created by the departure of the USSR and the relative decline of the United States will be immense in the last years of the twentieth century and early years of the twenty-first century. Germany and Japan created great hegemonies in the Northern Hemisphere between the two world wars. World War II created great vacuums that were filled by the United States and the USSR—the two-superpowers model—within a few years after that war ended. The cold war ended with economic and political defeat of the Soviets and the American taxpayer being tapped out. As the Soviets discovered, a country's foreign policy is only as strong as its taxpayers. The U.S. military is the only superpower left but taxpayers may not fund that status. More hot wars will likely develop around the world that the United States will probably fail to extinguish. More and more countries are likely to want to alter their boundaries by force and will feel that without a superpower looking over their shoulder, they can do so.

The model of multipower economic centers is attempting to fill the large economic vacuum in the 1990s. Only time will tell if this model has the capability to do so. History is *not* on the side of multipower economic centers as military muscle is also needed to fill a large vacuum.

Multipower centers or free-trade zones are in place but are likely to be only an intermediate step as they may quickly become obsolete. Economic power centers are (1) a European center with 340 million people; (2) a North American center with 380 million people consisting of Canada-the United States-Mexico; (3) a Latin America trade area; (4) OPEC with its 700 billion barrels of oil reserves; (5) major independents such as Japan, whatever configuration the former Soviet Union takes, and mainland China and/or smaller independents around the globe. Smaller economic blocks—region states—are also developing, such as that of Hong Kong and southern China as well as that of southern Texas and Mexico. Region states develop out of economic relationships. Capital, information, and technology flow across political boundaries tying regions together. Region states develop in a method that makes sense economically and tend to be independent of the hands of politicians. As technology and information splice geographic areas of self-interest together, the region state concept is likely to be much more prevalent in coming years. A 1993 Federal Reserve study said data didn't support a de facto trading bloc in the Far East.[2]

The United States was the one center of economic power at the end of World War II. The glue in that old model, holding the United States, Western Europe, and Far East market economies together, was the common external Soviet Union threat as well as fear of U.S. dominance. The glue isn't so obvious in the multicenter economic model as there is no outside threat. Occasional threats from the Saddam Hussein's of the world will always be there, and his invasion of Kuwait brought a unified response as the economic well-being of the Western World was threatened. Kuwait has 100 billion barrels of oil reserves, while its neighbor, Saudi Arabia, has 250 billion barrels. It was in the economic self-interest of Western powers to respond in the manner they did. The tie binding economic blocks together is additional economic power enhanced by movement toward integration. Free-trade zones are geographic areas in which governments or countries explicitly collude to set policy. Part of that policy is elimination of internal barriers, which is expected to stimulate additional trade among member countries that does not displace third-country imports. Merged governments have enhanced economic power. For instance, EC-1992 is economically much stronger if the respective governments collude than if any individual country government acts on it own.

A major question concerns relationships among regions or between a region and another country. Explicit collusion among, for example, EC-1992 members can stifle trade with another region or individual country (as illustrated in figure 11.2). The increase in trade within Europe before EC-1992 suggests that intra-Western European trade will increase as a result of the free-trade agreement. One can make a counter argument that EC members demonstrated a willingness to sacrifice political sovereignty to obtain economic benefits of EC-1992; therefore, the same idea may lead to greater trade with other blocks rather than less. But self-interest of combined EC countries is likely to intervene in the market mechanism and dominate the possibility of more relative trade with the United States. EC countries can raise their national income at the expense of another country; for instance, EC 1992 members are likely to collude to limit Japanese imports as well as U.S. imports. If that can be accomplished without retaliation on Japan's or the U.S.'s part, then the EC has gained. Fear of retaliation is the implicit factor that may limit use of enhanced economic power of multicenter regions. Worldwide benefits of trading blocks can be achieved as long as individual regions do not attempt to influence their terms of trade favorably, but as seen in Western Europe, groups of countries are likely to influence their terms of trade favorably through other methods, such as political power and nontariff barriers. That, of course, raises the threat of economic warfare among economic power centers.

In the multipower economic-center framework, regions are tied together through economic, social, and political networks as well as mobility of capital, technology, and knowledge. Maintenance of world order also holds blocs together. Mobility of factors of production severely limits the ability of governments to erect trade barriers and may, therefore, act as the glue preventing regions from becoming too nationalistic. In addition, development of region states across political borders is likely to help hold subareas together, as technology and information flows appear to be very important in breaking down trade barriers.

Economic growth in the post-World War II period was measured by growth in income. In the multipower model era, more and more emphasis will be placed on the global ecosystem. Nations and trading blocks will focus on environmental issues in addition to growth in income. Environmental and health issues are part of the world-order issue, which holds regions together. Regions and most nations share a self-interest of a world order in which the spread of chemical and biological weapons is limited, and environmental interests are balanced with economic growth. Regional and business influences of cold war policies have been profound; likewise, the change to the multipower-center framework has already changed the face of business and will continue to do so.

As U.S. cold war policies impacted many aspects of economic development, defense companies and their suppliers were obviously effected. Benefits accrued to those geographic areas in which defense companies were located as well as regions and countries having military bases. Defense dollars in the research and development areas, including funds to universities and spinoffs such as space technology, were other benefits. An example of a defense related program having many nondefense effects was the National System of Interstate and Defense Highways, signed into law in June 1956 by President Eisenhower, who had been impressed during the war by Hitler's ability to utilize the autobahnen system and felt the United States could benefit substantially from such a system, as, if the need arose, cities could be evacuated more quickly and military equipment transported faster. Eisenhower's initial 1954 proposal was $5 billion a year for ten years to be financed by a Federal gasoline tax.[3] (The $5 billion amounted to 1.3 percent of 1954 GNP; in 1994 GNP, that percentage equated to nearly $90 billion.) That 1954 proposal was defeated and a modified bill passed two years later. The Eisenhower administration viewed construction of the interstate highway system as a public-works project in addition to its defense attributes. Cheap oil combined with the interstate highway system tilted public policy toward rapid U.S. decentralization. Western European countries also had access to cheap oil, but many governments chose the policy of placing high taxes on gasoline and build railways, which worked to inhibit decentralization relative to the United States.

U.S. public policy of decentralization also helped establish seeds of central-city problems. People were able to live at relatively remote locations and commute to work via highway systems. This propelled auto use and, in conjunction with cheap gasoline, made it feasible to establish low-density residential and commercial land use. Changing production methods and relative growth of the economy's service sector also worked together with transportation facilities and inexpensive oil to hasten decentralization. Another decentralization effect was that relatively higher-income people left the central cities, in many cases, to lower-income groups. Decentralization would have occurred eventually without the interstate highway project, but the highway project added a public subsidy in the name of national defense that significantly advanced the entire process. Impacts on consumers and business have been enormous and include the access to less-expensive land that led to larger relative single-family homes, low-density shopping-center and office-complex development, rapid growth of the fast-food and hotel-motel industries, and the far-reaching and low-density urban areas that developed. The information-technology production era encourages this trend as the information highway allows people to work at remote locations.

During the cold war the United States followed its strategy of Soviet containment and through sharing wealth created multipower economic centers. A rapidly growing standard of living in the United States up until 1973 turned into social contracts and promises between voters and their government. Those promises have been broken and are continuing to be broken. Economic growth and opportunity have been replaced with broken promises and entitlements.

12

Government Taxes and Outlays

President Clinton had it right during the 1992 campaign when he compared the economic environment under George Bush to the Herbert Hoover economy. A striking similarity existed between the economic times of the 1930s and that of the late 1980s and early 1990s, even though macroeconomic numbers in President Bush's term and, in particular, during the 1992 election year were much better than those in the 1930s. It is ironic that President Bush, the foreign-policy president, would lose the election because the American taxpayer was tapped out from serving as world leader, as voters wanted someone who would attempt to repair broken social contracts. Social contracts were broken in the 1930s, and FDR put together the New Deal to help in repair. FDR's success during the 1930s, together with success in World War II, helped fuel the idea that government can solve all problems. The operating premise that FDR left imbedded in society is that "the answer" is "more government." The model evolved, continually fed by politicians, that says, Don't worry, the government will take the initiative and responsibility to solve domestic as well as international problems. The United States as a nation drifted from the individual taking responsibility for his well-being and actions to one where taxpayers, through higher taxes, funded a larger and larger bureaucracy to take that responsibility.

President Bush fed the federal bureaucracy while state and local governments were increasing their take, so that total government outlays climbed as a proportion of national income (figure 12.1). President Bush, having grown up during the 1930s and a pilot during World War II, had experienced positive impacts of government involvement in domestic and international affairs. In the post-World War II period, he became a participant in developing and implementing foreign policy. This wealth-sharing effort turned into a huge success as it prevented a hot war from

147

FIGURE 12.1
Government Takes Over 40 Percent of Your Income

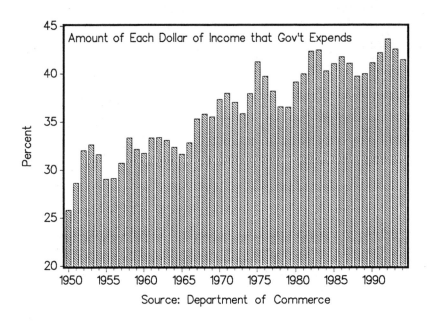

Source: Department of Commerce

developing, and the *USSR* finally disintegrated. It is easy to understand why President Bush, due to his life experiences, reversed Reagan administration tax and spending policies and never understood that he was following in footsteps of Herbert Hoover. American voters, knowing something was wrong with the model of bigger and bigger government, had elected President Reagan to two terms on the theme of encouraging wealth creation.

U.S. voters had a sense that government bureaucracy is responsible for at least a portion of the problems as they were willing to give Reagan eight years to attempt to place a damper on government activities. Macroeconomic numbers improved, but underlying issues were not resolved. President Bush hiked relative government outlays and marginal income-tax rates and then saw macroeconomic numbers worsen. His decision to hike personal income-tax rates was a step backward toward cold war tax policy and Soviet containment. Candidate Clinton ran as a new Democrat in that he was going to do things differently and better. Economic programs he signed off on, such as higher personal and corporate income-tax rates, were an even bigger step backward to cold war policies of the 1950s, 1960s and 1970s.

That was an interesting policy decision by President Clinton. Voters wanted a president that would focus on and put in place policies to help repair broken promises at home. Higher marginal personal and corporate-income tax rates have the effect of deferring domestic capital investment in segments such as start-up businesses and central cities. These sectors are hit the hardest, as they are on the receiving end of the highest-cost capital because they are the highest risk. This hits younger people and poor people the hardest. Higher marginal tax rates have the effect of hurting President Clinton's core constituency as they make it more difficult for the young and the poor to be upwardly mobile and prevent groups and sectors most in need of capital from obtaining capital to improve their lot in life, which means these groups need more and bigger entitlements. The basic issue confronting the United States—broken promises—can't be solved by increasing tax rates and creating bigger and better entitlements. An increased burden on taxpayers acts to enlarge the gap of broken promises—the chasm between what the private economy can provide and that of peoples' expectations. People attempting to pick their way through a life filled with broken promises grab whatever government programs they can and hang on.

Governments at the federal, state, and local level are busy taking a larger cut of national income as these entities continue encroaching on backs of taxpayers. In 1950, government expenditures captured approximately 25 percent of national income; in 1994 the figure approached 42 percent. Government expenditures grow faster than income as politicians and voters attempt to alleviate voter concerns about broken promises with wealth redistribution (figure 12.2 illustrates per capita taxes necessary to fund government spending shown in figure 12.1). Each man, woman, and child in the United States forks over $8100 to fund the check-writing frenzy of government. To put it another way, a three-person household pays over $24,000 in taxes. Is this—a government that takes over 40 percent of national income and redistributes it—what voters want? After World War II voters were confident about the future

FIGURE 12.2

Soak the Taxpayer

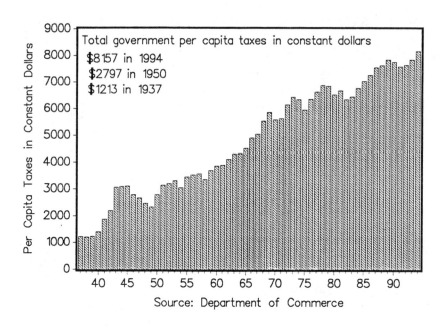

and taxpayers funded the U.S. world-leadership role. The United States was strong and delivered more than what many expected. A rapidly improving standard of living continued, and citizens came to expect that if they acquired a good education and worked hard, they could expect to do well. Taxes are only one part of the wealth-sharing picture but are a primary mechanism of a country to share wealth with other countries and to redistribute wealth domestically.

The other side of the coin is per capita government expenditures (figure 12.3). Americans in all income classes have queued up to obtain their entitlements at the government trough. Per capita expenditures amounted to nearly $8700 in 1994, a figure up by a factor of three from 1950 in constant dollars. Many Americans are asking, Am I getting my fair share of this government pie? A list of general entitlements people line up for

FIGURE 12.3
Americans with Both Hands in the Trough

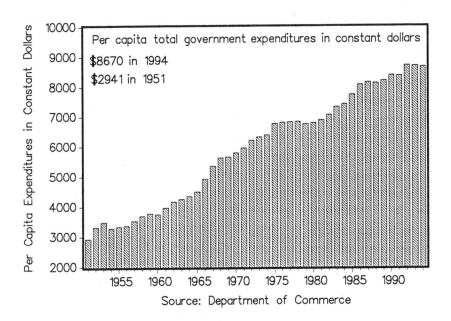

Source: Department of Commerce

include Social Security, good education, a decent job, retirement programs, quality health care, good housing, ample food, safety, home-mortgage deduction, good highways, and a strong national defense. These are some general parameters many feel the United States owes them as the U.S. economy did deliver that list in the 1950s and 1960s.

People growing up during the 1950s and 1960s, such as the baby boomers, expected the same to be delivered to them and their children in the 1970s, 1980s and 1990s. People like President Clinton, growing up during the 1950s and 1960s, experienced an environment in which a good education and hard work allowed upward mobility and a rapidly rising standard of living. It is ironic that somehow many came to associate the golden age with government tax policy and programs, but it was not government programs as they do not create wealth. Rather, it was a healthy, strong, and vibrant U.S. economy that was not destroyed during World War II—together with cheap oil—that created wealth and led to rising expectations. It is not only the elderly or poor but also many others who feel that they are entitled to a long list of benefits in the United States that the private economy can no longer deliver. As the standard-of-living improvement faltered, bureaucracies expanded on the backs of taxpayers, while entitlements ended up having perverse impacts on incentives of those receiving them.

The cold war created its external entitlements through Soviet containment. Market economies surrounding the USSR were entitled to defense protection. In addition, the United States welcomed their products. The direct tax that U.S. taxpayers felt was defense spending (figure 12.4). In 1994 defense spending amounted to over $1100 per capita. Can other nations afford to pay more of this burden? Yes. Will they? Perhaps. National defense spending was not placing a larger burden on the average American in 1994 than it has for most of the past forty years. The cold war created an environment in which U.S. allies grew accustomed to the U.S. providing national defense and security. Can the tapped-out U.S. taxpayer do that in the post-cold war? Or can the United States afford the world-watchdog role in the latter half of this decade and beyond? Events suggest the United States is not going to provide the world-leadership role that it did during the cold war. The United States won't provide the major leadership role unless there is a direct threat to the economic interests of this country, such as was the case in the Gulf War when the United States had to take the leadership role.

U.S. open-door trade policy is another external entitlement expected by other nations. During the cold war countries around the globe that aligned themselves with the United States had open-door access to U.S. customers, and this country never demanded equal access to their markets. The cold war is over. The United States has negotiated equal access to the Canadian and Mexican economies, but does not have equal access to the European, Far East, and South American markets, yet those areas have ready access to the U.S. market. This open access is expected by other countries because that is what they had for the past fifty years. However, Europeans, for instance, are not about to provide the United States equal access to their markets, though they have negotiated a free-trade agreement among themselves to help take care of themselves. Japan will only very grudgingly move toward equal access with the United States,

FIGURE 12.4
A Good Buy

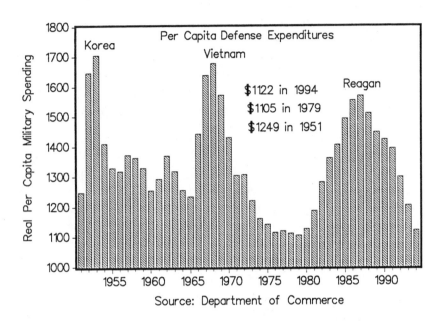

Source: Department of Commerce

as it is not in Japan's self-interest to do so, though for nearly fifty years, Japan, as well as other Far East countries, received special treatment—an open-door policy to U.S. customers. The United States may, over time, gain equal access to their markets, but not having equal access to Far East or European markets is another tax on this economy. It is an indirect tax as Americans don't see it on their W-2 forms, yet it is there.

Economic problems in the 1990s are much different than in the decades between the 1930s and 1980s. In earlier decades the United States had the economic capacity to be a world leader and enjoy a rising standard of living. In the 1990s the United States doesn't have the economic capacity to be a world economic leader. That is clear. U.S. trade and tax policies, however, remain those of a world leader, while Americans understand that the U.S. can no longer be the world economic leader. In addition, they have come to grips with the fact that the U.S. economy is unable to deliver an improving standard of living for many, which explains entitlement growth. A high-school education for many does not provide the foundation necessary to succeed in either college or a job. Decent jobs continue to disappear. More and more neighborhoods are unsafe. The security of retirement—in particular, Social Security—is a major question. Broken promises and promises yet-to-be-broken make this time period different from earlier decades.

In the 1990s the U.S. taxpayer is burdened by high direct and indirect tax rates. That means the model that worked in the 1930s, as well as in the 1950s and 1960s, won't work in the 1990s. The economic picture is completely changed as taxpayers are tapped out and the entitlement model is breaking down (as discussed in following chapters). In 1935 when real per capita government expenditures were 23 percent of income, per capita government expenditures were $1120. Respective figures in 1994, adjusted for inflation, were 42 percent and nearly $8700. The United States could be the world leader in the 1950s and 1960s as well as provide for its citizens. A country creating wealth can share wealth. A country can't share what it doesn't create.

An example of an entitlement that focuses on wealth sharing is the near-$3700 per capita expenditure payments to other people (figure 12.5). Increasing the size of government relative to income is *not* a method to create wealth. For an average family of three, expenditures on payments to other people amount to $11,000 per year. Transfer payments to persons include programs such as Social Security, Medicare, Medicaid, welfare, unemployment insurance, and federal employee retirement among others. The real per capita cost of programs such as Social Security, Medicare and federal employee retirement increased by a factor of 7.2 from $510 in 1952 to $3671 in 1994. The increase since 1973 was a factor of 1.8. In comparison, real weekly earnings of U.S. workers increased by a factor of 1.2 from $327 in 1950 to $385 in 1994. Real weekly earnings have decreased since 1973. The burden of transfer programs to persons is much greater on the average American worker in the 1990s than in prior decades. Transfer-payment-to-person programs are necessary in society. That is not the question. Instead the question is, How many and how big can these programs become? Could programs be developed that encourage people to help themselves and, as a result,

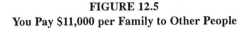

FIGURE 12.5
You Pay $11,000 per Family to Other People

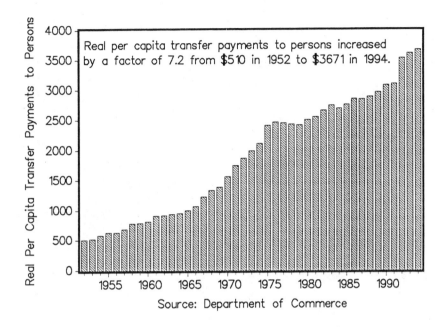

Real per capita transfer payments to persons increased by a factor of 7.2 from $510 in 1952 to $3671 in 1994.

Source: Department of Commerce

not have more and more people dependent on the government? Examples include making capital available, making it easier to start and grow businesses, and eliminating the federal personal income tax.

Another sizeable government expenditure is education (figure 12.6). Taxpayers have responded to a call to improve education by increasing educational spending in real terms by a factor of 4.5 over the past forty years. Weekly incomes, in comparison, increased by a 1.2 factor. Per capita education spending is a much larger burden on the average American family in the 1990s than in earlier decades, and the quality of education at the primary and secondary level has declined (see chapter 16).

Taxpayers responded to public-safety concerns by increasing major real per capita safety spending by a factor of 4.9 over the past forty

FIGURE 12.6
Education Expenditures Up, Quality Down

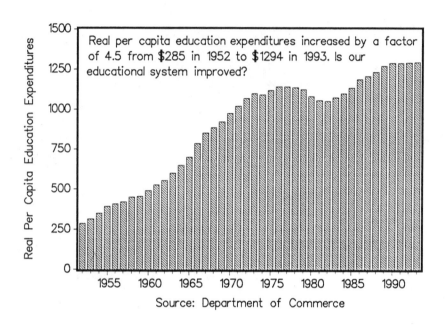

Source: Department of Commerce

years (figure 12.7). This occurred while weekly income increased by a factor of 1.2. What happened to crime? The premise that there is a connection between massive increases in per capita government spending and their effect on perceived problems is highly questionable. Most people feel that public-safety concerns have increased several times over the past forty years while governmental spending in an attempt to solve that problem increased by nearly a factor of 5 (chapters 17 and 18 are on safety).

Governmental expenditures on transportation are illustrated in figure 12.8. Many highway facilities were constructed during the 1950s and 1960s, and a greater and greater dollar allocation goes for maintenance as the system constructed back-then ages. In the 1950s and 1960s the

FIGURE 12.7
Less Safe but Spending More

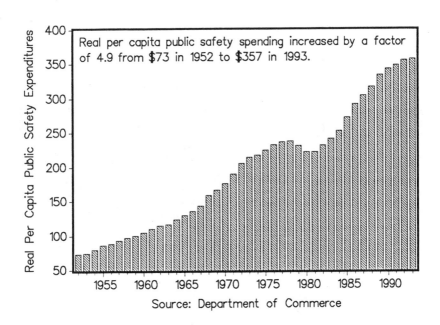

Real per capita public safety spending increased by a factor of 4.9 from $73 in 1952 to $357 in 1993.

Source: Department of Commerce

lion's share of total dollars—70 percent to 80 percent—went for high-ways. In the 1980s the majority of total dollars—over 50 percent—continued to be allocated to highways, but a growing proportion goes for airports, transit, and waterway expenditures. The dollar allocation on conventional transportation—highways, airports, transit, and water-ways—may be adequate, but in the future incremental transportation dollars may go toward technology highways to move information instead of people and goods.

Figure 12.9 illustrates another growth area in government spending—government bureaucracy, which includes central administration, tax collection, and legislative and judicial activities. Each sector grabs roughly one-third of the total. *Efficiency* and *customers* are

FIGURE 12.8
Transportation—Getting What We Pay For

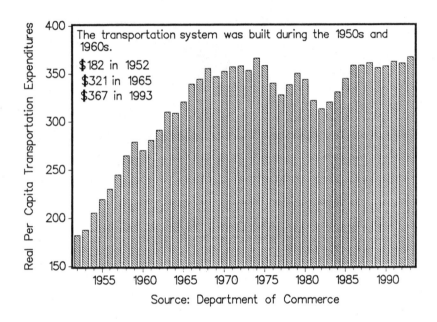

The transportation system was built during the 1950s and 1960s.

$182 in 1952
$321 in 1965
$367 in 1993

Source: Department of Commerce

foreign words to government bureaucracy, whose costs march upward regardless of quality of product and economic conditions. Business, in comparison, has a bottom line and has made a major effort over the past ten to fifteen years to downsize, reengineer, move closer to the customer, and cut bureaucracy. Government bureaucracies are doomed to failure. Success for a program like Social Security is the number of people receiving monthly checks. The more people receiving monthly checks, the larger the Social Security Administration needs to be to cope with recipients and the more money it receives. This further burdens the taxpayer. Likewise, criteria for success in Medicare, Medicaid and welfare are the number of people signing up since that creates a larger bureaucracy, and more people

FIGURE 12.9
This Bureaucracy is Breaking the U.S.

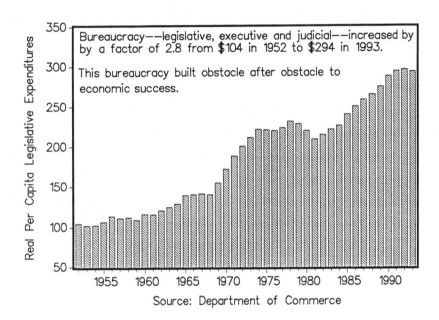

Bureaucracy——legislative, executive and judicial——increased by
by a factor of 2.8 from $104 in 1952 to $294 in 1993.

This bureaucracy built obstacle after obstacle to
economic success.

Source: Department of Commerce

are needed to administer programs. Costs increase; taxes and spending are hiked.

Since 1961 the federal government has had a balanced budget in one
year, 1969. Entitlement spending raced ahead of a rapidly increasing
tax burden for decades, and Congress and voters chose to finance this
difference by selling bonds. (The combined cost of above categories of
spending in terms of interest on the outstanding federal debt is shown in
figure 12.10.) Broken promises result in people turning to government
for help, but government can't recreate those promises through higher
outlays and taxes. The private sector can't generate enough incremental
wealth to shore up broken social promises as government taxes production as well as physical and human capital formation.

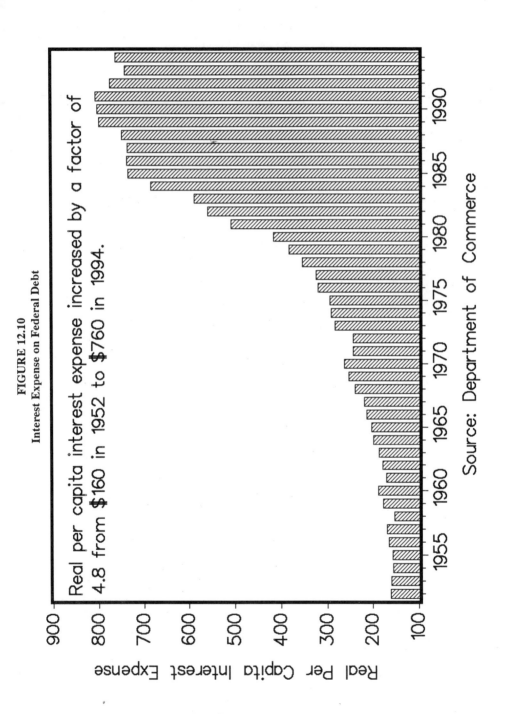

FIGURE 12.10
Interest Expense on Federal Debt

Real per capita interest expense increased by a factor of 4.8 from $160 in 1952 to $760 in 1994.

Real Per Capita Interest Expense

Source: Department of Commerce

13

Purchasing Power Broken Promise

The United States, by any measure of purchasing power, experienced a boom from the end of World War II until the 1973 OPEC oil embargo. Purchasing power—whether one refers to weekly wages, hourly wages, family income, or household income—raced ahead, and for many purchasing-power gains very likely exceeded expectations. People had been through hard times in the 1930s and in the war years, and, all of a sudden, real wages increased and labor saving devices became available for the home as well as other amenities, such as air conditioning. Leisure time increased, interstate highway system construction started, auto sales increased, mobility increased, and more people attended college. The decades of the 1950s and 1960s, in economic terms, stood in sharp contrast to the previous two decades, when many people learned to expect that the future held adverse conditions. The 1950s and 1960s were anything but adverse as the standard of living for many rapidly improved. Advancement, opportunity, and upward mobility for many were rapid. Significant progress was made in civil rights, and there was expansion of the safety net for the needy. Opportunities created by an economy generating wealth were many, but the 1950s and 1960s also had their share of difficulties with Korea, Vietnam, cold war tensions, and social problems.

But the U.S. success story popped when oil prices (as illustrated in figure 11.1) shot up. Oil was added to the list of high-cost inputs (described in chapter 7), and the standard of living declined for the majority of private-sector jobs (as illustrated in figure 10.3). During the golden years, 1945–1971, weekly purchasing power steadily improved for private-sector-production and nonsupervisory workers. After 1973 the standard of living per job went the other way. For 77 million nonagricultural private-sector jobs in 1994, the average weekly purchasing power had declined to the 1956 level.

Other economies, in particular ones like Japan that relied on a larger percentage of oil imports, bounced back better than the United States from the oil-price shocks as Japan's economy utilized inputs like capital that had a lower relative cost (as described in chapter 7). The United States substituted low cost energy for high-cost capital and labor during the 1950s and 1960s, and the post-1973 U.S. economy didn't have access to a cheap input for a number of years to substitute for capital and labor, resulting in all inputs being high cost. The result was an economy that didn't generate enough incremental wealth to allow for an improving standard of living for many Americans, but the U.S. economy attempted to turn a problem—high-cost inputs—into an opportunity as high-cost oil sent two messages. First, energy-using technology was told to use oil more efficiently, and secondly, economies were told to develop a nonenergy-using technology. That new technology was the chip, which is building the knowledge-based economy—the second message of higher oil prices was one OPEC didn't anticipate.

People involved in segments of this new economy, such as knowledge and information-based activities, are rewarded with an improving standard of living, as illustrated by the higher of two lines in figure 13.1 (see note to figure 13.1 in sources). There are people in this economy that do relatively well while others don't. Post-1973 the economy moved into a two-tier standard of living. People engaged in the tier based on a cheap input—energy—found that the post-1973 economy could no longer provide them with an improving standard of living. This tier amounted to the majority of private-sector jobs—77 million non-supervisory ones.

But the standard of living improved for people engaged in activities of the new economy. Inputs becoming high-cost created incentives for people to invent and develop the new economy—the information-age economy. The microprocessor developed, over time, as the cheap input allowing the global economy to grow and generate incremental wealth. Oil, when it was discovered, created an entirely new economy—the motorized transportation industry and also the many spinoff and related industries. The microprocessor created the information society, as the chip was the vehicle to store and process information. The microprocessor and microcomputer allowed people to rearrange and analyze information, which became the economic tier for adding value and capturing wealth. The information segment of the economy evolved into the *knowl-*

FIGURE 13.1
Purchasing Power Trends in Real Dollars

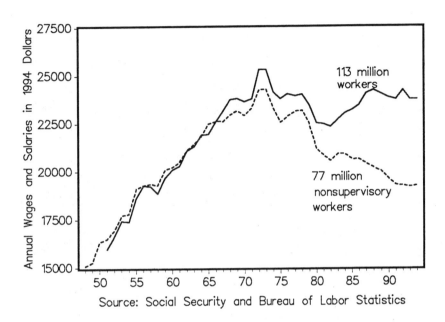

Source: Social Security and Bureau of Labor Statistics

edge segment of the new economy during the 1980s. Income and wealth flow to people involved in knowledge production. Related industries and spinoff industries are being created and will continue to be created into the next century. This shift to the knowledge economy is much like the shift that occurred early in this century to the auto-truck-airplane oil-using technology and away from the horse-train-water technology that was fueled by grain, coal, and water. Cheap oil facilitated that transition. Microprocessors are facilitators of the current shift.

An adverse aspect of this transition to a new technology is that people's expectations are formed, in part, by past experiences. Pre-1973 represented an era of improving standard of living for many, while post-1973 provides an improved standard of living for only a portion of the population. That meant many people's expectations for an improving standard of living were not being met post-1973. Many middle-class families found it necessary to restructure—for example, perhaps more people worked per family and/or decreased their personal-savings rate to make ends meet as purchasing power per job fell. This made it harder to save for retirement—voters wanted middle-class entitlements expanded. Social Security and Medicare are examples of large middle-class entitlements that helped compensate for declining purchasing power.

In the 1950s and 1960s, the United States was doing well and voters wanted to help those less fortunate. That was the trigger, along with the civil rights movement, to expand the size of the social safety net—it was the right thing to do. The United States expanded lower-income entitlements as well as implementing minority entitlements. Post-1973, middle-class voters, in a stagnant standard of living environment, demanded bigger and new entitlements for themselves, which meant higher taxes and a larger and larger burden for workers to carry on their back. Payroll taxes are ultimately shifted onto the backs of employees through lower salaries. Initially, as payroll taxes increase, companies continue paying workers the same salary and attempt to obtain more productivity from workers to compensate for the increased payroll tax. Increases in the tax burden, in addition to incremental regulatory burdens, meant that companies found themselves in a position of becoming uncompetitive.

Disappearance of low-cost oil meant that it was difficult for many companies to be competitive. As with the payroll taxes, the higher oil-cost increases made it necessary to shift costs onto the backs of their workers. As soon as oil prices jumped, the purchasing power for the average of nonsupervisory jobs started its downhill slide. Companies passed increased costs of doing business either backward to employees and/or forward to customers. The other alternative is to pass costs along to owners of the business—a last resort. By 1980 many companies found attempts to shift costs to employees and/or to customers were inadequate, and companies began to alter their way of doing business. That meant utilizing the chip, the low-cost input to the economy. Companies started to rationalize, restructure, cut costs, and shed employees to remain competitive. Businesses found that the microprocessor and its uses in information and knowledge facilitated rationalization of their businesses. Chips, because of their low cost and uses, are utilized intensively on a global scale. In the 1950s and 1960s, oil a cheap commodity, was also utilized intensively by business on a global scale. The United States came in for much criticism as being wasteful of energy after the 1973 embargo, but pre-1973, it was cheap, so, why not use it? The world economy has another cheap commodity, the chip, and *companies have to use it more and more intensively*. Some criticize business for restructuring and rationalizing, but business is doing what the marketplace tells it to—use the cheapest input intensively, which means using knowledge to produce goods and services. The old economy is gradually being revitalized through application of what is produced and distributed by the knowledge economy. Productivity gains in the old economy rested on cheap oil; productivity gains in the modern economy rest on use of the microprocessor.

The old manufacturing-service-government segment of the economy, in which the majority of people are employed, doesn't receive as much incremental wealth as the knowledge segment since they aren't adding as much value. The knowledge segment—a sector that wasn't there twenty years ago—receives the lion's share of the incremental wealth. Examples range from biogenetics, software, and artificial intelligence to telecommunications—areas in which intellectual capital and its ability to add value are made possible by the chip. This segment of the economy will continue to capture the lion's share of the value added in the global economy and to create a tier of people that do very well. Companies in the old segment of this economy are attempting to renew and revitalize themselves by application of the knowledge tier, and there is a shopping list of terms for this movement, terms that include restructuring, reengineering, total quality management, rightsizing, downsizing, renewal, joint venturing, mergers, divesture, and on and on. Revitalization is part of a global stampede as companies push forward to capture knowledge applications.

Government is in this old segment of the economy because of the way it is organized—a bureaucracy. Government maintains the status quo and loads cost after cost onto the backs of business and workers. The bureaucracy surrounding warfare development was essential because of large-scale battles that took place, and it took a large pyramid organization to accomplish the mission. As recently as the Gulf War, this was the case. The military-bureaucracy concept was transferred to corporations and government after World War II, but as businesses renew themselves, the quasi-military bureaucracy is disappearing, as applications of the chip makes the chain of command obsolete, people

redundant, and the pyramid organization obsolete. Business is attempting this renewal—moving from one technology to another. Competitors that renew themselves will displace businesses that don't. Businesses
change as their working environment and available technologies change.

Government at all levels adopted the military-bureaucracy pyramid
scheme, but government bureaucracy has no bottom line other than to
perpetuate itself. Congress grades itself on output measures, such as
amount of legislation passed under the guise of helping its citizens. This
legislation is turned over to government bureaucracy to implement.
Implementation means more guidelines, mandates, and regulations.
Business passes those increased costs of doing business onto employees and/or on to customers. Cheap oil in the 1950s and 1960s allowed
business to enjoy economies of scale and created a chain of command
environment. The military pyramid organization, in that environment,
worked well. Government with its military organization passes and
implements legislation via the pyramid organization. Congress and its
bureaucracies go against the chip by attempting to centralize, organize,
and plan for production, distribution, and consumption. In history, there
has never before been a greater mismatch than the one between the direction in which the private sector needs to go and the direction government is attempting to force the private sector. Government—not only in
Washington, D.C., but also at the state and local levels—is attempting
to enforce a rigid economy while the knowledge segment attempts to
decentralize and disperse the economy. Regulations, mandates, and taxes
encourage a rigid economy, while microprocessor applications encourage flexibility, revitalization, and growth.

Government and microprocessors are locked in combat. Government,
through its policies and regulatory apparatus, is still fighting the cold war,
which hamstrings the economy and keeps real wages declining. A movement toward a more fluid economy would allow people to start businesses,
obtain funding, hire people, and advance. Government policies are winning as the standard of living for the majority continues to slide. President
Reagan attempted to create a more fluid economy by breaking the cycle
of steadily increasing relative taxes, spending, and regulations that had
become the standard. His idea was that by reducing tax rates, he might be
able to convince Congress to slow the growth rate of expenditures. It
didn't work. Tax rates were reduced, and rapid economic growth resulted
in tax revenues continuing to grow, but Congress increased outlays at a

faster rate than tax revenues grew. In his eight years, President Reagan had success in reducing federal tax rates but met with limited success in slowing spending, the result of which was a massive increase in outstanding federal debt and in interest payments. President Bush, in less than four years, reversed eight years of Reaganomics .

President Bush never understood voters' concern about the domestic economy. Their concern was what candidate Clinton talked about—the worst economy since the days of Hoover. President Bush, on his behalf, had a gigantic foreign-policy image to shine and show off in his reelection bid—the defeat of Iraq. In perspective, President Carter campaigned for reelection in 1980 when the economic pie was shrinking and inflation was screaming ahead at 13.5 percent rate, yet almost won reelection in the midst of a terrible economy and the Iranian hostage situation. Something more than surface macroeconomic conditions disturbed voters in 1992. It was—and *is*—broken promises. Candidate Clinton understood the problem, as FDR had in the 1930s. President Clinton—through examples such as his Omnibus Budget Reconciliation Act of 1993 and the proposed Health Security Act of 1993—attempted to emulate FDR's approach. What worked in the 1930s won't work in the 1990s, as the key nonhuman input to economic growth is the microprocessor, not oil, and the November 1994 election results suggest citizens understand that the old big government model is obsolete.

Families attempt to compensate for losses in weekly purchasing power by methods such as more relative people working in each family and multiple jobs. The loss of purchasing power per job was an incentive that helped propel the growing percentage of women in the labor force (figure 13.2). While increasing participation of women is a secular trend, the loss of purchasing power turned a choice into a necessity for many families. Many women enter the labor force because they choose to have a career, and labor-saving devices for the house allowed that option. But a twenty-year decline in average purchasing power for private-sector nonsupervisory jobs suggests a substantial proportion of women find it a necessity to enter the job market, not a choice.

Another method to offset loss in purchasing power from one's primary job is to work in a second job. In 1994, multiple-job holders were a fairly small proportion of total job holders—varying between 4.5 percent to 6.4 percent of total job holders over the past twenty years. A total of 7.3 million workers held multiple jobs, which amounts to 6.4

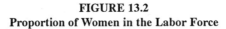

FIGURE 13.2
Proportion of Women in the Labor Force

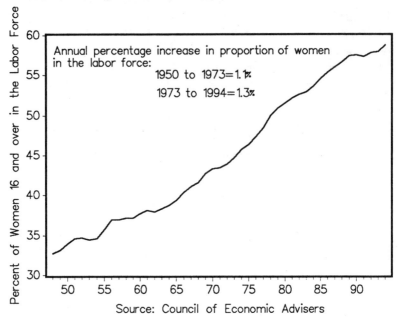

percent of total nonagricultural workers. The managerial and professional jobholder classification had the largest percent of multiple-job
holders at 7.3 percent, while the skilled blue collar category had a smaller
percentage at nearly 4.0 percent. Meeting regular household expenses
was the primary reason listed for holding an additional job.

   The result of having two or more breadwinners per family is illustrated in the figure 13.3, which plots average and median family income
from 1967 to 1993 (families are defined as two or more persons related
by blood, marriage, or adoption). There were 68 million families in 1993.
Median family income is the midpoint—half of families are above that
number while the other half fall below. Average family income is above
the median, which implies high-income families pull the average above
the median. High-income families pulling the average up has been an

FIGURE 13.3
Real Family Average and Median Income

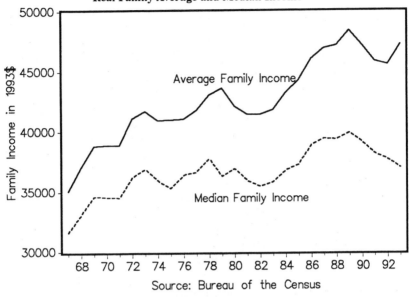

Source: Bureau of the Census

FIGURE 13.4
Average Family minus Median Family Income

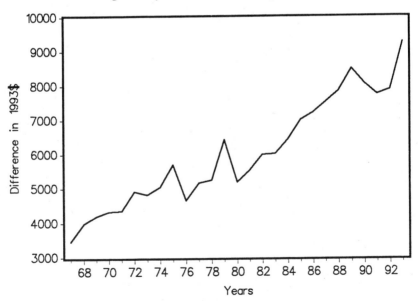

Years

ongoing trend (figure 13.4), which plots average family income minus median family income. The average has been pulled up by high income families relative to the median over the years shown.

Income redistribution has been a key theme since the late 1960s, as illustrated in figure 13.5. Wages and salaries are in a secular decline as a percent of total personal income, while government transfer payments to persons excluding interest income to persons, are in a secular increase. Wages and salaries, as a proportion of total personal income, turned up on a temporary basis during part of the 1980s, suggesting the temporary upturn was due to changes in the tax code. Government transfer payments to persons, excluding interest payments, are in a secular rise but stabilized on a temporary basis in the 1980s. The basic thrust of U.S. tax and expenditure policies is income redistribution as the portion of government transfer payments are in a long-term upward secular trend. Figure 13.5 is illustrative of a major change occurring in U.S. society—movement from a fluid to a rigid society. In short, tax policy, government regulations, and a poor-quality primary and secondary public-education system make it more difficult for many to obtain capital, start and grow businesses, hire workers, and contribute to wealth creation. Capital is taxed multiple times, and growth of regulations and mandates makes for a much more rigid society. Many students getting out of high school are neither qualified to enter college, obtain a decent job, nor start a business. Congress is creating—through policies—a class-oriented society.

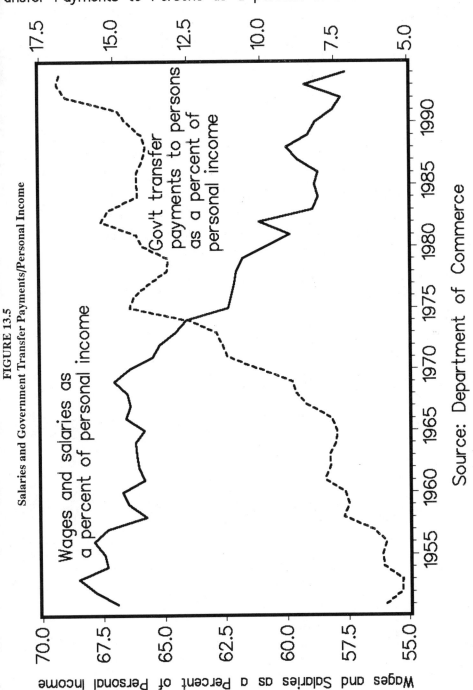

FIGURE 13.5

Salaries and Government Transfer Payments/Personal Income

14

Loss of High Paying Jobs—A Broken Promise

The United States shared the wealth of its consumers, taxpayers, and workers with its allies, which resulted in broken promises for consumers, workers, and taxpayers, but the corporate sector remains healthy. The corporate sector keeps its promises of paying bills and returns to stockholders. Societies function as long as broken promises are limited to consumers, taxpayers, and workers but become dysfunctional when the corporate sector can't pay its bills or pay adequate returns to stockholders.

Most politicians understand this difference, which is why taxes, regulations, and mandates placed on business are ones that can be passed on to customers and employees. The corporate sector represents a market economy and is the "golden goose" for everyone. Harm it and voters— and Washington D.C.—harm themselves. A command economy such as that of the former Soviet Union illustrates a situation in which politicians killed a golden goose through decades of poor policies. The country shut down when the command economy could no longer pay its bills, hire people, or provide returns. The Soviets, as the end neared, liberalized their political system before their economic system and found that sequence didn't work well. The Chinese chose first to liberalize their command economy but to maintain their political system.

The United States through its selection of policies inflicted broken promises on consumers, employees, and taxpayers but not on the production sector. Broken promises were not the intent but nonetheless resulted from policies implemented. That sometimes occurs. The former Soviet Union is an extreme case in which broken promises spilled over to production, but there are varying degrees of harming the golden goose. South American and Central American countries such as Brazil, Argentina, and Mexico are examples of politicians stepping too far away from market economies and crippling their production sectors with bad policies. In the 1980s and 1990s, these countries began to work their way back toward more of a market economy concept, as it was obvious to everyone that they had moved too far away. These countries are examples of politicians breaking consumer, worker, and taxpayer promises, but when their production sectors broke promises, their societies began to shut down. In comparison, corporations in the United States continue to spinoff cash flow approximately equal to what it was in decades past (figure 14.1), and the average return for the past several decades has been roughly 10 percent of national income. Economic activity, on average—and, in particular cash flow—has been increasing faster than the U.S. population (figure 14.2).

Many assume that if consumers, taxpayers, and workers suffer broken promises, corporate America must also experience broken promises. U.S. voters and politicians, to date, have been too clever to allow the golden goose to break promises as that could mean no jobs. The political apparatus gets away with being able to break promises to voters by making a sizeable segment of the population dependent on government and providing goodies. But broken promises to business would mean political parties would be skating on very thin ice, which is why most politicians want corporate America to remain healthy.

A steady decline in the purchasing power of the majority of jobs in the United States is indicative of a relative loss of high-paying jobs resulting from the Soviet-containment policies. Two trends occur; first, fewer high-quality and high-paying jobs are created in the developing portion of the U.S. economy—the knowledge-producing portion—and secondly, more relative jobs are lost from the old service-manufacturing economy—the energy-technology portion. The net result is a decline in job purchasing power for many, which necessitates more people working per family or holding multiple jobs. Corporate America remains healthy in this process by shifting costs forward to customers in the form of higher-priced goods and services and backward to employees, resulting in fewer employees and lower-paid employees. Alternatively, the U.S. economy, as we know it, will begin its shutdown if the political apparatus should decide to force corporate America to swallow increased costs.

Low-cost oil induced the auto-truck-airplane energy technology era to replace the horse-train-waterway technology in the early part of this

FIGURE 14.1
Corporate Cash Flow Divided by National Income

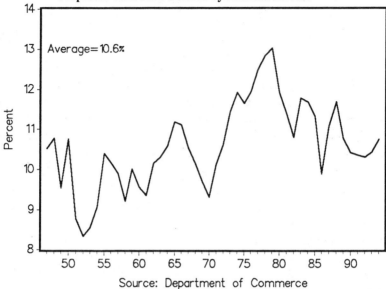

Source: Department of Commerce

FIGURE 14.2
Corporate Cash Flow per Person

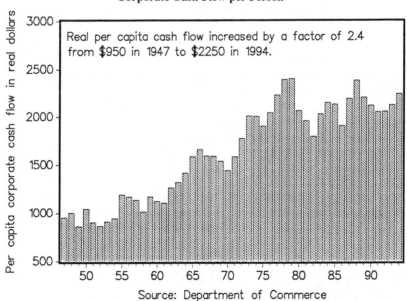

Source: Department of Commerce

century. World War II and its aftermath saw the goods-producing stage fade away to become service producing. High-cost oil ended up creating uses for the microprocessor, and over time the knowledge era replaced the energy era. The growth and value-added portion of the U.S. economy shifted from goods producing in the early part of this century to service producing to information producing to knowledge producing. Figure 14.3 illustrates employment trends of three groups—goods, service, and government producing. Concerns about relative loss of U.S. manufacturing employment (goods producing) are dismissed by many as they say developed economies are not manufacturing but service economies. That misses the point, as part of manufacturing—the part that grows in mature economies—is knowledge-producing manufacturing. It may not be important whether the United States fabricates soda pop cans, but it is important whether the United States is able to have a strong knowledge-producing manufacturing base of such products as computers, scientific instruments, medicines and communication equipment, etc. In recent years knowledge-producing manufacturing made up roughly 30 percent of total manufacturing output compared to 20 percent in 1980, according to a Federal Reserve study.[1] Total manufacturing output, in comparison, as a percent of U.S. gross domestic product has been approximately constant over the past decade. That means non-knowledge-producing manufacturing is declining rapidly in the United States.

The manufacturing goods-producing era is being replaced by manufacturing knowledge-producing era. (Information on knowledge-producing that follows is derived from publications of the Federal Reserve Bank of St. Louis and CIA.)[2] Industries classified as knowledge producing have the following characteristics: (1) a strong research and development (R and D) effort defined by R and D expenditures relative to production costs; (2) high-risk and large capital investments; and (3) strategic importance. Manufacturing industries meeting these characteristics include aerospace, office machines and computers, electronics and components, drugs and medicine, scientific instruments, electrical machinery, communication equipment, and machine tools.

Knowledge-producing industries are important because of provision of unique benefits—that is, *innovation*—not necessarily present in other manufacturing industries. Innovation takes an invention and transforms it into a product or process that can be utilized or sold. The innovation

FIGURE 14.3
Proportion of Producing Emloyment

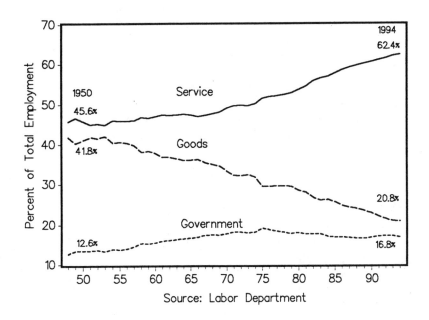

process typically results from research and development expenditures; thus, the proportion of R and D expenditures is key in defining knowledge-producing industries. R&D expenditures go to basic research, applied research, and development. Basic research does not necessarily have commercial objectives but does have scientific objectives, while applied research is application of new knowledge in order to meet a specific need. Development research is use of knowledge geared toward the design or production process.

Innovation resulting from R and D expenditures can be subdivided into three types: (1) process innovation; (2) intermediate product innovation; and (3) final product innovation. The first, process innovation, improves production techniques. An example from past decades is use of an assembly line to mass-produce a product. The second type, intermediate product innovation, is development of a new product that another company could utilize to produce a product more efficiently for the final consumer. An example is development of a machine tool that can be utilized in manufacturing a computer that replaces a less efficient machine. The third type, final product innovation, introduces an improved variation of the same product or a new product for final customers, such as replacement of the adding machine by the hand-held calculator.

Companies invest in R and D if they expect an above-average rate of return on the resulting innovation, but in many cases, an innovation that may result from R and D spending is highly uncertain. Companies, therefore, expect an above-average rate of return to compensate them on those R and D expenses that do not lead to innovation. Benefits to society may be much greater than the return to the company. For instance, if a researcher at a company develops a cure for Alzheimer's disease or addiction to drugs, the company will benefit by providing the drug, but society will benefit much more as people will not be nearly as much of a burden on society. Because of this characteristic, countries implement policies—through government programs such as tax credits, through patent and copyright protection, or through public funds—that encourage innovation. As an example, it is estimated that the United States publicly financed over 40 percent of all R and D spending in 1991. Defense-related R and D expenditures accounted for nearly 30 percent of total R and D spending during the late 1980s, though defense expenditures declining on a relative basis suggests that R and D aggregate spending may suffer in the 1990s. This raises a question about countries such as Japan that allocate their R and D spending to commercial efforts as opposed to the military, which is, Does this make Japan more competitive in commercial activities? This may suggest aggregate R and D spending in the United States is very misleading when compared to R and D spending by Japan. Another very important method countries follow to encourage a successful R and D program in their country is through having a quality primary and secondary educational system, as well as that on the university level. Primary and secondary education is a weak link in the United States, as the quality of high-school graduates, as measured by SAT scores, declined relative to the 1960s (described in chapter 17).

Benefits of innovation flow across international boundaries so that all countries receive some benefit of knowledge-producing industries. But countries engaging in innovation and manufacturing have larger gains

FIGURE 14.4
Manufacturing Average Hourly Purchasing Power

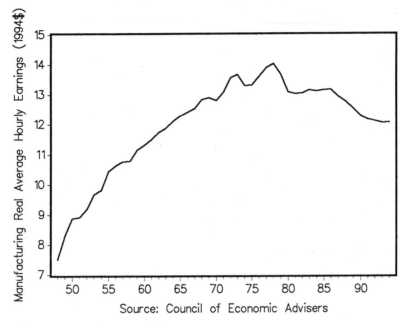

Source: Council of Economic Advisers

than countries that only import the product or import the technology in hopes of producing the product, because countries involved in innovation and manufacturing in knowledge industries have a larger proportion of high-wage jobs since innovation and manufacturing account for a sizeable chunk of value added. Figure 14.4 illustrates the trend in U.S. manufacturing purchasing power hourly wages rates since 1948. Manufacturing wages in real purchasing power increased until the latter 1970s, before falling in 1994 to a 1964 purchasing-power level. This occurs, in part, because U.S. knowledge-producing manufacturing employment is inadequate relative to our major trading partners. As indicated, U.S. knowledge-producing manufacturing increased its share of total manufacturing output from 20 percent to over 30 percent in ten years, but that increase was not enough to halt the purchasing power decline.

TABLE 14.1
OECD Market Shares (Percent) of Knowledge-producing
Industries by Country

	1980	1990
Drugs and Medicine		
U.S.	29.6	29.2
Japan	21.2	20.3
Germany	13.1	10.9
Communication Equipment		
U.S.	36.6	30.6
Japan	26.4	42.0
Germany	12.0	10.0
Office Machines & Computers		
U.S.	50.0	34.8
Japan	22.0	37.5
Germany	6.5	5.4
Scientific Instruments		
U.S.	49.1	53.4
Japan	17.6	15.4
Germany	11.4	11.1
Aircraft		
U.S.	57.6	55.9
Japan	2.2	3.6
Germany	4.8	4.8
Machine Tools & Robotics		
U.S.	14.1	13.1
Japan	11.3	21.8
Germany	25.8	20.2

Source: Federal Reserve and CIA

In industries such as drugs and medicine, aircraft, and scientific instruments, the United States held or increased its global market position. In other industries, such as office and computing machinery as well as communications equipment, the United States lost market position among OECD countries (table 14.1).

Companies in manufacturing can utilize industrial robots, which are considered reprogrammable multifunctional manipulators designed to move materials, parts, tools, or specialized devices through variable

TABLE 14.2
Installed Industrial Robots per 10,000 Persons in Manufacturing

	1981	1991
U.S.	3.2	24.7
Japan	19.9	296.4
Germany	3.2	48.0

Source: CIA

programmed motions for the performance of a variety of tasks. Japan is far ahead in use of installed industrial robots (table 14.2), Japanese companies apparently feel this makes them more competitive. Part of the reason for this may be that robots are much more effective for Japanese companies as Japan doesn't have the available labor supply that the U.S. does. In absolute terms Japanese companies had approximately 350,000 industrial robots installed in 1992, compared to 47,000 in the United States, and 39,000 in Germany.

In some areas of knowledge-producing manufacturing the United States does well, while in others the United States is positioned poorly. This is to be expected—doing well in some industries and not in others. However, for manufacturing wages to reverse their decline, the United States needs to have more rapid growth in knowledge-producing manufacturing. U.S. machine-tool production is an area in which the United States lost its competitive position. This relative loss is even more striking when comparing export and import data for various countries. Figure 14.5 shows Germany and Japan each export about five times the U.S. dollar volume of machine tools. The United States exports approximately the same dollar amount of machine tools as Taiwan. U.S. imports of machine tools (figure 14.6) are relatively high as countries such as Japan and Germany export to the United States. Germany's skill in industries such as technology is a tradition that has existed in Germany over a long time period.[3]

The United States needs major growth in the knowledge area to offset relative losses in conventional manufacturing areas. U.S. auto production, a conventional goods-producing industry, has a large proportion of high-paying jobs and has not fared well over the past couple decades (table 14.3) and that may be one reason manufacturing wages, in purchasing-power terms, are in decline. Some of the so-called "good" auto-production jobs, those needed to build autos marketed around the world,

FIGURE 14.5
Exports of Machine Tools by Select Country

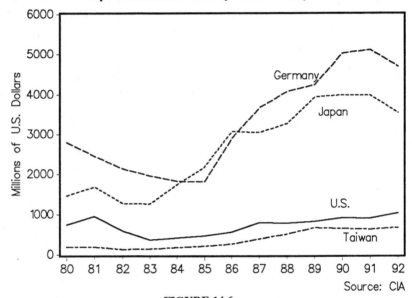

Source: CIA

FIGURE 14.6
Imports of Machine Tools by Select Country

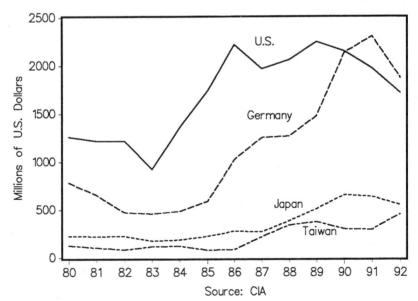

Source: CIA

TABLE 14.3
Global Market Share of Auto Production (%)

	1970	1980	1993
U.S.	37.2	29.6	22.4
Japan	18.1	32.6	32.8
Germany	20.6	16.7	14.8
South Korea	NA	0.3	5.8
Mexico	0.8	1.5	3.2

Source: CIA

are occurring for companies of other countries such as those of Japan, South Korea, and Mexico. U.S. market share of global auto production started to recover in recent years. The absolute number of autos produced on a global scale was 17.6 million, 21.6 million, and 26.5 million units respectively in 1970, 1980, and 1993.

More light and heavy truck production is, however, taking place in U.S. companies (table 14.4), reflecting both customer needs and import restrictions on light trucks coming from Japan. U.S. truck production is an area of conventional manufacturing that is a positive force for the purchasing power of manufacturing. The absolute number of trucks produced on a global basis was 5.5 million in 1970, 8.3 million in 1980, and 10.9 million in 1993.

Another useful indicator of the U.S. relative loss in jobs and purchasing power is decline of the dollar relative to yen and mark (figure 14.7). Before President Nixon severed the gold standard in 1971, one dollar would buy 360 yen and 4 marks. One dollar, in 1994, purchased an average of 102 yen and 1.62 marks, a dramatic decline in dollar purchasing power. That decline is a proxy for U.S. relative economic strength compared to Japan and Germany. It says that U.S. wealth-sharing policies were very successful as Japan and Germany are large economic powers. A cheaper dollar is suggestive of U.S. weakness, not strength. Dollar weakness or strength is an avenue global investors utilize to inform the United States what they think, as global investors vote with their monies. A country that devotes relatively more resources to R and D for commercial uses, has a relatively higher rate of capital formation, and a relatively stronger educational system can expect over time to create more new jobs and more better paying jobs. A country like Japan

TABLE 14.4
Global Market Share of Light & Heavy Truck Production (%)

	1970	1980	1993
U.S.	31.0	20.0	43.7
Japan	39.0	48.2	25.0
Germany	6.3	5.1	2.5
Canada	4.3	6.4	7.8

Source: CIA

that limits imports can also expect to have relatively fewer jobs destroyed. In comparison, the United States encourages imports, which means jobs are destroyed relatively faster. Combine that with a low rate of capital formation and a less than adequate primary and secondary educational system, and an economy in relative decline is created.

FIGURE 14.7
Devaluation of the Dollar

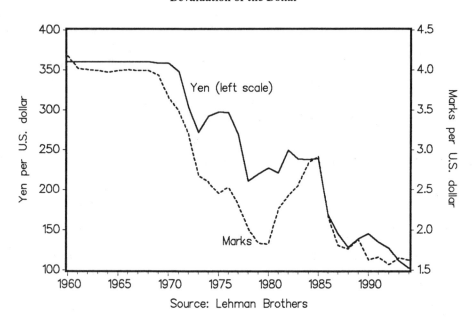

Source: Lehman Brothers

15

Creation of Jobs—A Broken Promise

Opportunity in the United States has meant being able to obtain a good education and subsequently find a decent job with a small or large business or perhaps start a business, but in contemporary times, roadblocks and obstacles to this opportunity have been set up, and the road of opportunity has become impeded. For many the idea of even obtaining a good education is not able to be realized (as the next chapter illustrates). Finding a decent job if one obtained a good education was something taken for granted in recent decades, but then a realization hit people who were living the American dream—both those in white and blue-collar positions—that this assumption was no longer a given. Corporate staff positions—white-collar jobs—suffered one million to two million permanent staff cuts from 1988 to 1994 as restructuring was taking place throughout the 1980s and 1990s, and permanent staff cuts will likely continue as technology makes new business structures possible. Blue-collar jobs have also been downgraded and eliminated, and decent high-paying jobs disappear (as indicated in the previous chapter) with lower-paying jobs taking their place.

In 1994 U.S. manufacturing jobs totaled roughly 18 million in absolute terms, which is about the same as in the late 1960s. It is not that the United States is losing manufacturing jobs absolutely, but that lower-paying manufacturing jobs are not only replacing higher-paying manufacturing jobs, which are going overseas, but also that the U.S. economy has roughly doubled in size (in real terms) since the 1960s, while manufacturing jobs have been added in other countries to supply U.S. needs. The United States was a world economic leader and through its policies provided both manufacturing jobs that would have been created in this country to other countries and U.S. high-paying manufacturing jobs, ones already existing is this country, to other countries. For many years there were few complaints as the U.S. economy grew; manufacturing jobs lost to other countries were replaced with service jobs and white-collar staff jobs in bureaucracies, while service-sector jobs in the "professions," such as lawyers and accountants, were regulated into existence by government.

Staff people are needed in a pyramid organizational structure—resulting in a bureaucracy. Many staff people were surplus to manufacturing, distribution, and marketing functions that were necessary to move the product or service to customers, but a bureaucracy needs them. A top-heavy staff structure can be supported in a rapidly growing global economy as long as corporations as a group play by the same rules. This entitlement of a decent white or blue-collar job for life was broken in the 1970s and 1980s. The concept of corporate pyramids and bureaucracies went out the corner-office window as OPEC's tax increases hit users of energy and the purchasing-power decline set in. That decline started the unwinding of the high cost of doing business, as businesses fought to maintain relative margins. Pressure on selling-prices from a declining standard of living meant companies worked to reduce their cost structure. This meant doing away with jobs not essential to getting the product or service to customers. The corporate pyramid and bureaucracy that had developed was due in large part to the World War II military influence.

Many World War II soldiers learned the value of teamwork, taking orders, and a pyramid organization. They utilized the GI bill after the war and moved into the private sector with a college degree. They advanced and implemented the pyramid-organization concept learned in the military. This organization structure worked well for people of that age group and created many relatively high-paying white-collar jobs in various professions. That age group—those who fought in World War II—eventually started hiring leading-edge baby boomers. The baby boomers did not have the teamwork or taking-orders experience of World War II, but they did have excellent educational backgrounds (many holding advanced degrees such as MBAs) and advanced rapidly in the latter 1960s and 1970s.

Questions were asked by baby boomers about the value and usefulness of the pyramid organization, and when OPEC implemented tax increases, the two came together. OPEC provided the incentive for businesses to think in terms of a slimmed-down organization, and baby boomers provided skills and know-how for getting it done and for developing alternative structures for running a business. Baby boomers advanced in organizations, and, as a result, by the 1980s they had major influences on strategy and organization, particularly in the financial area. This combined with the Reagan administration decision in 1982 to issue relaxed merger rules that Justice would use in deciding which mergers to challenge, increasing global competition, and tax laws favoring debt over equity—that all worked together to create an environment for increased takeovers and buyouts.

Baby boomers at the senior-management level and relaxed merger guidelines were new in the 1980s. Competition and a tax system favoring debt over equity were not. Revised merger guidelines didn't question vertical and conglomerate mergers and only challenged horizontal mergers if there was a large increase in concentration in excess of guidelines. This resulted in waves of horizontal mergers across industry segments, involving, for example, airline, oil, food, and tobacco companies, among others. Mergers and buyouts resulted in substitution of debt for equity. World War II holdovers in organizations had an adverse orientation toward debt as a result of their experience during the 1930s when many of their parents who were leveraged lost possessions. Baby boomers, in comparison, had no such aversion to debt; in addition, they had financial skills acquired in MBA programs. MBA students grew up following the Modigliani-Miller financial theory, which suggests that the financial structure of a firm expressed as the sum of its debt and equity securities has no impact on its value. In other words, debt levels are irrelevant to firm value. The Modigliani-Miller concept may hold for any one firm, but a penalty is paid when nonfinancial business debt of the entire sector increases substantially in excess of economic growth. Baby boomers utilized their skills and theories to put deals together, which rapidly increased the aggregate debt burden of the business sector during the 1980s (figure 15.1).

Increasing interest payments required cost savings, as many businesses failed to generate adequate cash flow for their existing operations when burdened with relative large incremental interest payments. Corporate savings were obtained through restructuring, downsizing, and rightsizing—the process of chopping away at the pyramid organization going by a number of names in the 1970s and early 1980s. Many of World War II vintage, as well as the demographic group following along behind the World War II segment, were placed in early

FIGURE 15.1
Business Debt

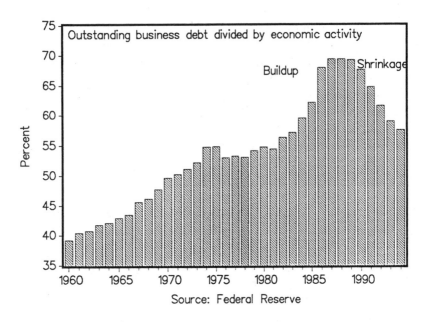

Source: Federal Reserve

retirement. Chopping meant a lot of good white-collar jobs disappearing, jobs that were not replaced. A pyramid structure works well when
each management layer follows orders, assuming that the right order
has been given. Following orders came naturally for those of World
War II vintage, but for baby boomers, it didn't. Baby boomers established new organizational structures to their liking. Baby boomers like
task forces, as that moves them away from taking and giving direct
orders, so instead of a smaller pyramid, alternative structures developed in which information flows are central. Structure was central in
World War II pyramid organizations. Information flows and their use
are key in the 1990s, and structure is secondary to information flows.
Debt requirements per dollar of economic activity started to shrink in
this new 1990s operating environment.

This shift to information from structure occurred in the 1980s. Prior to this, restructuring involved slimming-down the pyramid. Restructuring, after the shift, involved fundamentally altering businesses to take advantage of information and ability to process information. The personal computer and its applications allowed for information flows to alter business structures in order to serve the customer better. The PC was the great facilitator for baby boomers in establishing information flows for decision making. The environment moved from taking and giving orders to altering a business in order to utilize information flows to create and keep customers. In an environment of information flows and PCs, there are relatively fewer traditional high-paying corporate jobs. Business is being conducted in an environment in which the focus is on the quality of information in order to provide a better product or service to the customer. As recently as 1980 the focus, in many corporations, remained organizational structure, not the customer. The focus of IBM as recently as 1992 was structure, not customers.

This alternative information flow organization means many, many jobs have been lost forever, but in time new jobs can be expected to more-than-replace jobs that are lost. That is the way "creative destruction" is expected to work—jobs that the computer replaces should be more than replaced by new jobs that the computer creates. Computer, technology, and related created jobs need to be in the United States for creative destruction to work for Americans. The U.S. economy has doubled in size since the middle 1960s, but the number of manufacturing jobs has remained roughly constant. A market economy creates jobs, and transportation in the twentieth century provides an excellent example of the way creative destruction is expected to work. The automobile and airplane created competition for the then-conventional transportation industries that ranged from the horse-and-buggy trade to railroads and water transport. Jobs were permanently lost by the millions in industries that the automobile, truck, and airplane replaced (table 15.1). For example, the Dallas Federal Reserve reports that more than 2 million Americans worked for the railroads in 1920 compared to just over 200,000 in the early 1990s, and that in 1910 there were 238,000 blacksmiths.[1] The automobile and truck created many new occupations such as manufacturers, designers, mechanics, and drivers, as well as spillover industries such as the oil and travel business. Many more new jobs were created than lost.

TABLE 15.1
Creative Destruction at Work

	People Employed	
Destruction	**Today**	**Yesterday**
Railroad employees	231,000	2.1 million (1920)
Carriage and harness makers	*	109,000 (1900)
Telegraph operators	8,000	75,000 (1920)
Boilermakers	*	74,000 (1920)
Milliners	*	100,000 (1910)
Cobblers	25,000	102,000 (1900)
Blacksmiths	*	238,000 (1910)
Watchmakers	*	101,000 (1920)
Switchboard operators	213,000	421,000 (1970)
Farm Workers	851,000	11.5 million (1910)
Creation		
Airline pilots & mechanics	232,000	0 (1900)
Medical technicians	1.4 million	0 (1910)
Engineers	1.8 million	38,000 (1900)
Computer programmers/operators	1.3 million	* (1960)
Fax machine workers	699,000	0 (1900)
Auto Mechanics	864,000	0 (1900)
Truck, Bus & Taxi Drivers	3.3 million	0 (1900)
Professional athletes	77,000	* (1920)
TV & Radio Announcers	60,000	* (1930)
Electricians/electronic repairers	711,000	51,000 (1900)
Optometrists	62,000	* (1910)

*Less than 5,000
Source: Dallas Federal Reserve.

Technological advances create new industries and jobs but make obsolete old ones. The old needs to be replaced with the new, though this
replacement process can be a very unpleasant experience for people
having their jobs destroyed. Creative destruction illustrates the futility
of a government attempting to maintain the status quo. Societies can't
advance and achieve economic evolution when governments attempt to
do so. Society can help ease the transition from one technology to the
next—the evolution of an economy—by having in place four major
conditions. These are (1) a well-educated and trained labor force that

can readily adapt to the new technology; (2) a climate in which citizens are encouraged to start and grow new businesses that, in turn, allow more jobs to be created; (3) an environment that allows businesses and industries to go out of business as technology and customer-needs change and as competition provides better or less-expensive products and services; and (4) policies that encourage job creation in its own country to produce and achieve high rates of human and capital investment. However, creative destruction, which worked well in the past, seems beset with near fatal flaws in current times, as roadblocks are set up in the path of each of the above four major conditions that could help ease the transition from one technology to the next.

As to the first point—having a well-educated and trained labor force—the U.S. elementary and secondary educational system is mediocre. Business needs people that can utilize information and technology rather than being an obstacle to people who do not have necessary skills to adapt to these advances. Many coming out of the U.S. public high-school system face major hurdles in obtaining good jobs and/or attending college. Without a strong educational background, it is difficult to gain skills and utilize information. This suggests that many will be relegated to relatively low-paying jobs for much of their life. The old portion of the economy, energy technology, utilizes information as does the new segment, knowledge production, but this new segment needs higher-qualified people, demanding a college degree or perhaps a postgraduate degree. People with a quality high-school degree and some college (or perhaps on-the-job training) can participate in information utilization, but not knowledge production, while people without a quality high-school degree are faced with major roadblocks that make society rigid for them—that is, they are unable to advance. People with a college degree or postgraduate degree find society much more fluid.

While technology, information flows, and knowledge production provide tremendous opportunities, they also present a barrier to those not having needed skills. This is an example of technology creating both opportunities and barriers in an economy. Opportunities, if people have skills or the ability to acquire them, make society and income levels very fluid. Roadblocks, if people do not have skills or the ability to acquire them, make society and income levels very rigid. People without skills or the ability to acquire them have found it difficult to participate in manufacturing jobs in the old portion of the economy as even they now utilize information technology; an example of this is auto manufacturing. Mediocrity in the primary and secondary educational system does not bode well for creative destruction. The R and D effort for knowledge-production industries may be ample, but the quality of workers to produce products may not be. The United States develops its share of knowledge-producing industries, but because of wealth sharing and inadequate education at the production level, knowledge-producing manufacturing jobs may shift to other countries.

The roadblock to the second major condition is that government policies discourage workers from starting and growing businesses with high tax rates, perhaps the most cruelest roadblock of all. In a fluid society government lowers obstacles so that people can be mobile, advance, and move to higher-income levels. High tax rates make that process difficult, since the more money people make, the more government takes. Income people earn as wages, salaries, interest income, and dividends was taxed at statutory personal income-tax rates of up to 39.6 percent in 1994. The top effective rate was 44.5 percent. Income earned as a capital gain was taxed at a rate of 28 percent. Marginal federal tax rates influence decisions to work and to risk capital to start and grow businesses. High marginal tax rates are perhaps the one single biggest roadblock. People in states with state personal income taxes face higher effective combined marginal tax rates, as state and local governments levy taxes that increase total taxes paid.

If one drives around neighborhoods in midsummer, he or she may see young children operating lemonade stands. The number of lemonade stands will decrease if parents tell them any profit is going to be taxed at a 40 percent rate. Production of lemonade will decrease if a marginal personal income tax rate is implemented. Change that lemonade stand to any business and the result will be the same—the higher the marginal personal income-tax rate, the fewer goods and services produced. Less production means fewer workers hired, lower total wages and salaries paid, less total savings, and less total taxes paid.

There are many other government impediments to starting and operating a business, such as the Social Security tax mandate. The 1994 Social Security tax rate was 15.3 percent (2.9 percent of that is for the Hospital Trust Fund) with the employee paying half and business paying half up to $60,600—a total Social Security tax bill per person of nearly $9300 at that income level ($4636 per both employee and em-

ployer). People earning over $60,600 pay 1.45 percent of their income—
and their employer pays an equivalent tax rate—into Part A of the Medicare trust fund (Hospital Trust Fund). Let's say the lemonade stand (or
any business) is successful and you tentatively decide to hire someone
at $60,600, which is the approximate value the person would add to
your business. Then you find out that if you do hire someone at that
salary, you must pay an additional $4636 in Social Security taxes. You
don't think the employee can add $65,236 in value to your business.
The way to solve the problem is offer $60,600 minus your portion of
Social Security cost which is nearly $4600. The job offer is then made
at approximately $56,000. The employee is this case (which is a typical
one) pays the total Social Security cost. Businesses pass the cost of doing business (in this example, their portion of Social Security taxes)
backward on their employees. Other alternatives to this step are to increase the selling price of lemonade (which hurts one's competitive
position) or alternatively to reduce profit margins. Reduction of margins or passing costs through to customers is not an option that businesses care to take.

Shifting costs backward on employees or forward to customers holds
for other mandates, laws, and programs that Congress forces on businesses. Some federal laws impose burdensome compliance costs on
businesses. An August 1994 editorial in the *Wall Street Journal* by
Clark S. Judge compiles laws that apply to businesses when their number of employees exceeds a set number ranging from 4 to 100 and
include the Civil Rights Act of 1964 (Title VII), Age Discrimination
Employment Act of 1967, Employee Retirement Income Security Act
of 1974 (ERISA), Occupational Safety and Health Act of 1970 (OSHA),
Omnibus Reconciliation Act of 1986, Worker Adjustment and Retrain-
ing Notification Act of 1988 (WARN), Emergency Planning and Community Right to Know Act of 1986, Americans With Disabilities Act
of 1990, Civil Rights Act Amendments of 1991, Older Workers Benefit Protection Act of 1990, Family Medical Leave Act of 1993, and
Clean Air Act Amendments of 1990.[2] Each of these laws is well-
intentioned and was passed with the idea of helping people. Judge
uses the Civil Rights Act of 1964 as an example of how the outcome
often is different from the intention. The Equal Employment Opportunity Commission enforces Title VII, and the Commission, in recent
years, has been suing businesses that employ mostly minority em-

ployees on grounds that the mix of minority employees does not represent the same percentage of minorities as live in the community. One would think that in the years since the 1960s compliance with Title VII would be very clear to businesses. Judge suggests the opposite is the case as discrimination law suits increased by a factor of twenty between 1970 and 1989. Title VII applies to companies with fifteen or more employees. If a business owner thinks he or she may be sued if they hire fifteen as opposed to fourteen workers, the owner won't hire the fifteenth worker. Such laws act as roadblocks both for people growing businesses and for people looking for work, because these laws add to the cost of doing business and are shifted backward to employees. Another impediment to capital formation is the capital-gains tax (as explained in chapter 7), since it is a tax on capital formation as well as a tax on the illusory gains due to inflation.

The roadblock to the third major condition is that government policies discourage businesses from growing and if the need is there, also from shutting their doors. Businesses have to be able to shut their doors. Government wades in with mandates requiring that businesses give their workers so many days notification of plant closure and suggesting that businesses pay their workers for a certain time period. A Cleveland Federal Reserve study suggests businesses slowed hirings in recent years because of employment costs associated with hiring and firing workers.[3]

The fourth and final major condition a society can follow to ease the transition from one technology to the next—policies to encourage job creation and capital formation—is straightforward. A high-quality educational system at the primary and secondary public school level as well as the university level is essential. Another essential policy would be to remove or reduce barriers to growing business, such as high tax rates. Everyone knows the obstacles. High tax rates, during the cold war, were instrumental in defeating the Soviets. The cold war is over and the need for such tax policies is past.

The destruction of jobs process proceeds too rapidly in the United States because of wealth-sharing policies, while the job creation process doesn't work well enough owing to problems outlined above. Problems were disguised, in part, during the 1950s, 1960s, and 1970s as growth of pyramid structures and growth of mandates created good jobs for many people coming out of professional schools. The pyramid is out and many professionals are out of the "decent" job they expected or felt they were entitled to for life. These professionals may become vocal in their concerns. They have the know-how to form constituencies in an attempt to have their needs met. Blue-collar workers, such as displaced auto workers, aren't nearly as vocal and may not possess skills necessary to organize and to lobby for their needs as do professionals.

Underemployment and unemployment are becoming a way of life for many. University graduates are taking jobs that once were once held by high-school graduates, according to a *Wall Street Journal* article on the auto industry.[4] Underemployment or unemployment by blue-collar workers is an issue that has plagued blue-collar workers for decades. Their efforts at organizing through unions, while helping produce protectionism in select industries, have been largely ineffective. Professional organizations like the National Educational Association are having much more success for their members. The educational system and wealth-sharing policies of the United States are creating a three-tier salary and wage structure. Baby boomers with skills are rewarded with relatively high salaries, while other baby boomers, also with skills, stall at a level that is significantly under their counterparts. Others end up working for a business via a temporary help agency that only offers reduced benefits.

Chief executives at the nation's 200 largest companies had an average income in recent years of $2.8 million, including stock options. That was nearly 160 times the average worker's pay of $17,430, according to compensation expert Graef Crystal.[5] Professionals and, in particular,both athletes and entertainers who reach the top or are near the top of their fields are paid extremely well. Some may argue that these people are being compensated for their value added, which for some is probably correct, but for many, it is case in which market imperfections, lack of competition, and entry barriers allow huge salary spreads to exist. Market imperfections include a very complex tax code and high priced lawyers as well as other professionals who develop complex compensation schemes that allow themselves and their clients to profit handsomely. Meanwhile, people lower on the totem pole are in a different playing field. The problem with this large differential is that people lower on the pole feel that something isn't quite right and politicians feed those feelings with soak-the-rich campaigns. This is nothing new. Politicians have been feeding envy for centuries.

People having only a high school diploma are on the third salary tier, not possessing skills to participate in knowledge-producing industries (there are many exceptions). Such people may be locked in a near-minimum wage for the rest of their lives in the fast-food, lodging, health, or other service-producing industry not facing foreign competition. Those facing foreign competition in low-tech industries may see their jobs disappear.

The computer and associated technological revolution, in addition to the deteriorating quality of high school education, changed that relationship. The income gap of high school relative to a college education is expected to widen further. The trend in annual income since the early 1970s reflects the same trend as other salary data in terms of the peak occurring in the early 1970s. The United States has a domestic economy that can no longer provide enough decent jobs. Job creation—or, at least, "decent" job creation—is a broken promise for many. Technological change is sweeping not only the United States but the rest of the world and handicaps those without the ability and skills to participate in production and utilization of new technology.

Many have addressed the issue of unequal distribution of income in the 1980s in terms of the haves and have-nots. The haves are college graduates and have-nots are ones with a high school diploma or less. Figure 15.2 illustrates the percentage difference between the two groups or the percentage in annual median real income that male college graduates receive over the median annual income of male high school graduates. Before 1980 the percentage difference remained roughly constant. After 1980 the gap steadily widened, and many attributed the gap to trickle-down economics or Reaganomics. However, Ronald Reagan is not the one to blame for the widening income gap. A better person to attribute it to would be Steven Jobs, as the computer and computer-related industries rapidly phased out the value of a high school diploma. Prior to 1980 the deteriorating quality of the high school diploma was not as crucial as technology changed more slowly and high school graduates and their employers adjusted. Steven Jobs and people that came after him (Bill Gates, for example) changed that. The mix of rapidly changing technology with its distribution and application means a high school diploma is of limited value in the marketplace. With rapidly changing technology, employers found that college graduates added much more value.

FIGURE 15.2

A College Degree vs. a High School Diploma

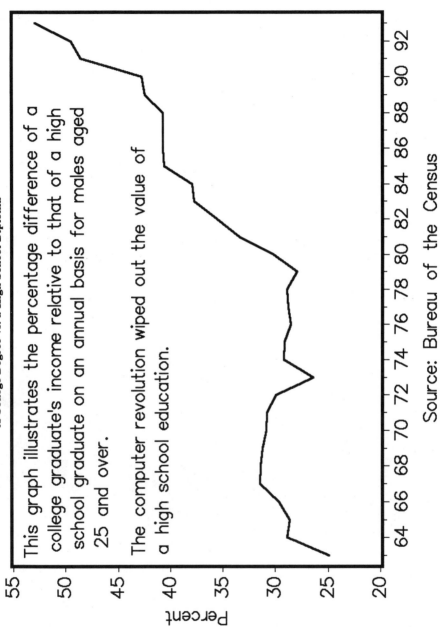

This graph illustrates the percentage difference of a college graduate's income relative to that of a high school graduate on an annual basis for males aged 25 and over.

The computer revolution wiped out the value of a high school education.

Source: Bureau of the Census

16

Public Education—A Broken Promise

High school graduates in 1900 made up 6.4 percent of the seventeen-year-old population, and this percentage reached nearly 17 percent by 1920. During that period many people worked for railroads (2.1 million in 1920) and on farms as laborers (11.5 million in 1910.) The major technology in use at that time was horse-drawn equipment and trains, which didn't require a high school diploma to produce or operate, but the trend toward more education was underway. The Great Depression of the 1930s created a sense among people that they needed something that couldn't be taken away, and education met that criterion. Jobs were lost along with property in the 1930s, but an education couldn't be taken away. Parents encouraged their children to finish high school. High school graduates, as a percent of the seventeen-year-old population, jumped from 29 percent in 1930 to nearly 51 percent in 1940. Technology had changed to the internal-combustion engine, but a high school diploma was still not required to work in manufacturing or to operate equipment. However, workers found that more education made society more fluid—more education made it easier to move from one job to another and perhaps advance in doing so. All of these factors—along with increasing urbanization and recognition of the value of education—dramatically increased incentives for high school and college degrees.

The perception developed during and after World War II that people with more education were at least partially responsible for U.S. success. This helped create the sense of value of an education, as it made society and income levels more fluid for Americans. Soon an implicit promise developed between government and people: Obtain a good education and you will be able to find a decent job for life and enjoy an improving standard of living. That became a basic premise of life in the United States. The GI bill added to that promise as many veterans, who otherwise might not have had the opportunity, attended college. The GI bill was signed into law 22 June 1944 and financed education and training for 7.8 million World War II veterans. The generation of Americans born between 1901 and 1924 was three times as likely to attend college as the generation born between 1883 and 1900. Subsequent GI bills educated over 10 million veterans of the Korean and Vietnam wars. Peter Drucker, in talking about the GI bill, said "It was probably the most important piece of legislation of the last 50 years."[1] That promise— obtain a good education, work hard, and have an improving standard of living—lasted until the early 1970s; that is, until Saudi Arabia placed an embargo on oil.

The embargo removed cheap oil from the economic-growth equation and U.S. taxpayers were left paying taxes for Soviet containment, while facing a falling standard of living for the majority of private-sector jobs (figure 10.3). The proportion of high-school graduates stopped increasing, started to decline, and then stabilized (figure 16.1) about the time that the standard of living per job tapered off, eliciting more questions about education. Scholastic Aptitude Test (SAT) scores were reported in 1975 to have declined for the previous twelve years.[2] Questions about quality of the U.S. primary and secondary educational system had been around for some time. In the early 1950s people felt the educational system provided the foundation needed to secure the future they wanted, but Sputnik in 1957 sparked questions about U.S. education.

The objective of placing a man on the moon involved both technology and dollars and was a national response to Sputnik. Taxpayers voted with their feet to increase expenditures per pupil for primary and secondary education in anticipation of a quality increase. The 1970s became alarming for many as declining purchasing power made people feel less comfortable about the future. Quality problems in local elementary and secondary public educational systems made the future even more alarming. Increases in spending to increase quality of education no longer worked, but taxpayers continued relative funding increases for public schools in the face of a purchasing-power decline and quality of education decline (figure 16.2). Per pupil total expenditure raced ahead during the 1970s at a pace exceeding the inflation increase, as taxpayers became convinced that spending money was the solution to the educational shortfall. World War I, recovery from the Great Depression, World War II, the space program, and construction of highways were examples

FIGURE 16.1
Proportion of High School Graduates vs. Standard of Living

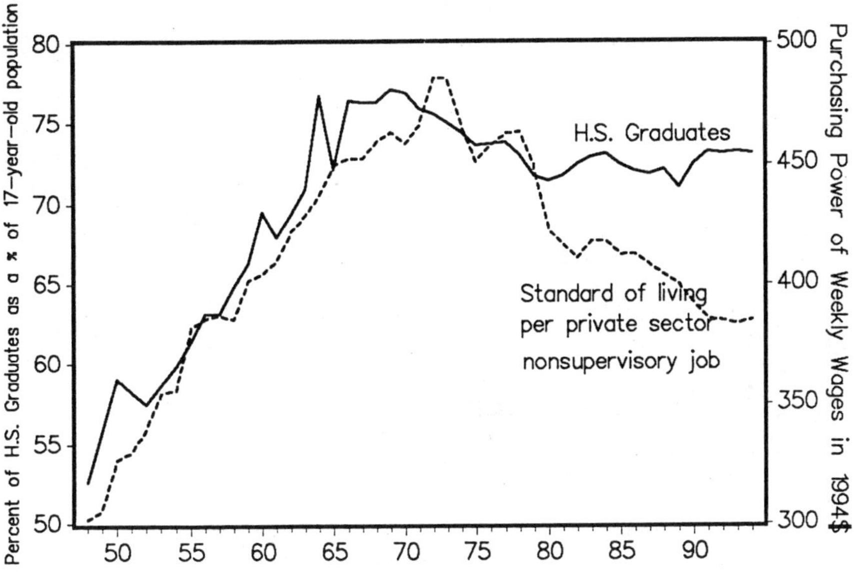

Source: Digest of Educational Statistics

telling taxpayers that spending more relative dollars was the method to improve or solve U.S. problems.

More relative spending per pupil failed to improve educational score results (figure 16.3). The promise of improving education by spending more relative dollars was broken. Taxpayers funded the educational system by digging into their pockets at the time purchasing power of nearly four-fifths of U.S. private-sector jobs was in decline. SAT scores are for college-bound high-school seniors. There is no national test that all high-school seniors must take.

The aggregate quality decline in SAT scores has been attributed to many factors including (1) less parental involvement in their local school system relative to earlier periods; (2) excessive time spent watching television; (3) violence in schools; (4) not enough quality teachers, or

FIGURE 16.2
Expenditures per Pupil in Constant Dollars vs. Standard of Living

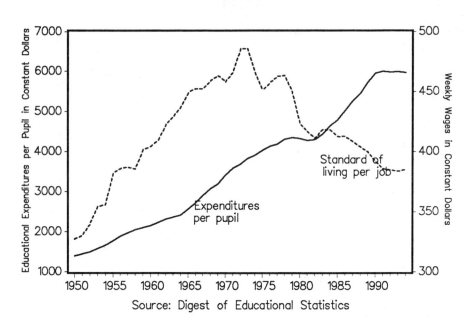

Source: Digest of Educational Statistics

underpaid teachers; (5) more working mothers relative to twenty or thirty years ago, resulting in less supervision; (6) inadequate standardized tests or not testing what students learn—or the counter-argument that they actually show inflated results relative to what students learn; (7) a more diverse student population; and (8) the educational-system bureaucracy.

Each factor listed no doubt contributes. Students from other countries cope with the standardized test issue. The educational bureaucracy is a major culprit, but schools can't replace a level of parental involvement and community values. Parental involvement includes parents involving themselves in school activities and encouraging children to minimize time watching television, spend time studying, attend school, and behave in school. A single or dual-parent home has this minimum responsibility to shoulder, one that can't be loaded on backs of school

FIGURE 16.3
SAT Scores for College-Bound Seniors vs. Expenditures per Pupil

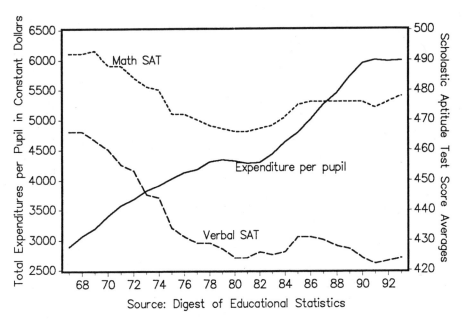

Source: Digest of Educational Statistics

systems. Additional parental involvement is needed both *at-home* and *at-school* to attempt to limit the influence of labor unions in the educational system and to generate across-the-board improvement in educational quality. However, some improvement in components of aggregate SAT scores is taking place (figure 16.4).

Math SAT scores of black Americans demonstrated modest improvement and are approximately 10 percent higher than in 1976, while Mexican-American scores are about 4 percent above their 1976 level. Scores for white Americans declined in the latter 1970s, but then increased and are back at approximate levels obtained in the 1975–76 school year, while Asian-American scores are slightly above their 1976 level. The absolute Asian-American SAT math score is 8 percent above white-American math scores while white-American scores are approximately

FIGURE 16.4
Math SAT Scores by Ethnic Group

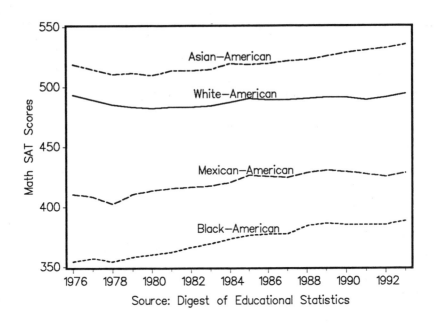

Source: Digest of Educational Statistics

15 percent greater than Mexican-American scores and nearly 27 percent greater than black-American scores. The gap among ethnic groups closed rather substantially over this period. In 1976 white-Americans scores were nearly 40 percent above black-American scores, but by 1993 the percentage difference had been reduced to 27 percent by an elevation of black-American scores. The Mexican-American group also made relative improvement. In math, the educational system is generating relative improvement in scores of two major ethnic groups.

White-American verbal scores are slightly lower in the 1990s than in 1976, while scores of Mexican-Americans and Asian-Americans are unchanged (figure 16.5). Black Americans show a 6 percent improvement over the time period, and the gap between black Americans and white Americans fell from 36 percent in 1976 to 26 percent by 1993.

FIGURE 16.5
Verbal SAT Scores by Ethnic Group

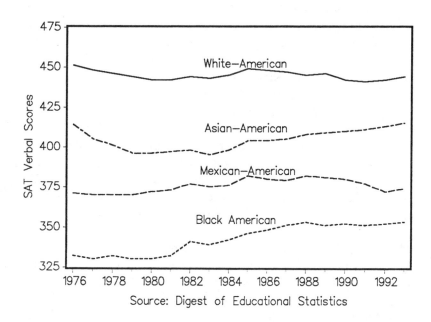

Source: Digest of Educational Statistics

White-American verbal scores were higher than the Asian-American, Mexican-American, and black-American segments in 1993 by respectively 7 percent, 19 percent, and 26 percent. One might expect that the vast amount of dollars expended on public education would have resulted in not only more substantial improvements overall but in higher scores of all ethnic groups as well. Blacks were the primary ethnic group showing meaningful improvement in both verbal and math scores, and black Americans started closing the gap relative to white Americans since no improvement occurred for white Americans.

Problems with the educational system can be split into two major segments, at-home and at-school. As described above, the at-home difficulty revolves around degree of parental involvement. A 1994 *Digest of Educational Statistics* survey of teacher perceptions of serious problems in schools cites lack of parental involvement as the most often mentioned problem, with thirty percent of teachers indicating it as a serious problem.[3] Student apathy (at 24 percent) was perceived by teachers to be the next most serious problem. When results were separated by public and private schools, five percent of private school teachers listed lack of parental involvement as a serious item, this perceived problem having the highest percentage among problems listed by private school teachers. Issues of racial tension and cultural conflict were perceived by both public and private-school teachers to be relatively minor. Other sizeable problems listed by public school teachers included student tardiness, absenteeism, cutting class and student disrespect for teachers. Many of these problems reflect home and community values. Drug and alcohol abuse were listed as problems by public school teachers at 7 percent and 14 percent respectively. Less than 1 percent of private school teachers listed drug abuse as a problem, while the percentage for alcohol was less than 2 percent. Physical abuse of teachers was mentioned by less than 2 percent of public school teachers.

Teacher perceptions of problems facing local public schools are in sharp contrast with that of the general public. Items most frequently listed by the general public, according to a Gallup Poll referenced in *Digest of Educational Statistics* are (1) use of drugs; (2) lack of financial support; and (3) lack of discipline.[4] Each of these three problems was mentioned between 15 and 20 percent of the time. Lack of parental involvement was mentioned by only 4 percent of the general public. This survey, conducted annually, cites use of drugs, lack of discipline, and inadequate financial support to be usually perceived as the largest problems in each year since 1970. Teachers didn't mention lack of financial support as a problem but did perceive poverty to be a serious issue.

This difference in perception between parents and teachers over local public school problems is astounding. Items perceived by the general public to be major problems—such as drugs, alcohol, violence, racism, cultural problems, and lack of financial support—are perceived by teachers to be much smaller problems or are not even mentioned as problems. Teacher perceptions are likely much closer to reality than those of the general public. The general public's perceptions are strongly influenced by media reports, which focus on drugs, alcohol, violence, and financial conditions as those are newsworthy items. The media likely report in large part what is provided to them by the National Education Association (NEA). Drugs, alcohol, and violence sell with the public, while stories on lack of parental involvement and on student apathy may not sell. Other issues—such as disrespect for teachers, tardiness, and absenteeism—also reflect, in part, on parents. A large perceived general-public issue is inadequate financial support of local school systems, which is surprising since the general public pays the tab. Figure 16.3 illustrates financial support is increasing rapidly with little effect on overall quality. However, the general public knows quality of education is a major problem and apparently perceives a positive relationship between increasing spending and increasing quality.

Another survey on teacher perception about school conditions and teaching tends to support teacher perceptions of problems.[5] In this survey over 90 percent of public school teachers said they agreed with the statement: "I usually look forward to each working day at this school." That doesn't sound as though teachers are afraid to attend school because of violence. Over 90 percent of teachers also agreed with the statement: "For me, the job of teaching has more advantages than disadvantages." Only 31 percent of public school teachers agreed with the statement: "If I had the chance to exchange my job as a teacher for another kind of job, I would." Public school teachers, on average, seem pleased with their profession. If the teachers are correct, more funding is *not* the answer. Teacher perceptions suggest many problems originate at home, though when students are at school, their results show up as an at-school problem. Test-score difficulties appear to be based, in large part, on at-home difficulties that carry over to the school day.

But, there are also many other difficulties when students arrive at school. These problems are due, in part, to the NEA, which has over 2 million members. Of those, 1.5 million are teachers. According to Toch, the NEA is one of strongest political forces in the United States, as it is the dominant teachers' union in all states except New York with three-fourths of the nation's public school teachers members.[6] The NEA has 52 state-level affiliates and 13,000 local-level affiliates.[7] When teachers join the local education association, they automatically become members of the state affiliate and national organization. The NEA was formed in 1857 as the National Teachers Association, but its rapid growth in membership, budget, and political influence didn't occur until the 1960s and, in particular, the 1970s under leadership of Terry Herndon, the executive director from 1973 to 1983. The NEA decided to become a labor union for teachers in 1960s and 1970s, and as their membership rose, so did revenues and influence of the NEA. Total dues collected in 1993–94 were estimated in the $750 million to $800 million range. The NEA has been a major backer of Democratic presidential candidates since 1976, when it played a leading role in the Carter campaign, and perhaps it should not be surprising that following the election President Carter created the federal Department of Education.[8] The NEA endorsed candidate Clinton in July 1992 but had opposed him in Arkansas when Governor Clinton supported a campaign to require a test for teachers in that state. According to Toch, the NEA developed a powerful political network, and NEA members have been the single largest block of delegates at every Democratic convention since 1980.[9]

In the early 1980s the NEA denied that there were major problems in public education. Finally, it acknowledged there was a problem and that problem was lack of funding, in particular, salaries of teachers—its customers. The NEA opposed virtually all major teacher reforms, including those, for instance, that would have raised standards for teachers, rewarded performance within teaching, advocated teacher testing, recommended peer review, and attempted to strengthen preparation of new teachers in academic subjects.[10] Preparation of teachers in education courses is notoriously weak and would-be teachers tend to avoid more rigorous courses.[11]

Toch indicates that even though the NEA is opposed to teacher reforms, it spends millions of dollars to run a public relations campaign designed to convince the general public that it is committed to reform of teaching and public schools.[12] This explains why the public perceives the education problem differently from teachers—the public hears a Madison Avenue version of what the NEA wants them to hear. Toch pointedly characterizes the messages the NEA uses in its public relations advertising as "flagrant misrepresentations of fact designed to mask the NEA's opposition to reform."[13] However, significant teacher reform has been made in some areas—such as teacher testing, peer review, and developing teaching into more of profession—in spite of the NEA opposition.[14]

The NEA also is strongly opposed to school choice, supports spending increases by local school systems, and promotes employment growth through curriculum modifications.[15] Large increases in employment of

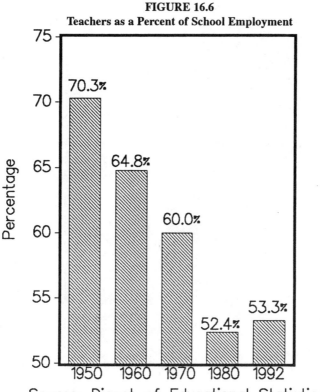

FIGURE 16.6
Teachers as a Percent of School Employment

Source: Digest of Educational Statistics

nonteachers relative to teachers in elementary and secondary public school systems are illustrated in figure 16.6. In 1950 there were 914,000 teachers in public school systems and 386,000 nonteachers. In 1992 there were 2.5 million teachers and 2.2 million nonteachers, figures revealing a system approaching a one for one ratio of one nonteacher for each teacher. The numbers of teachers increased by 170 percent since 1950, while the number of nonteachers increased by 457 percent.

Meanwhile, students enrolled in elementary and secondary public schools increased from 25.1 million in 1950 to 42.7 million in 1992 for a 70 percent increase. The number of teachers increased 2.4 times faster than the number of students, while nonteachers increased 6.5 times faster than students. Massive employment increases occurred, and taxpayers picked up the tab while educational quality decreased.

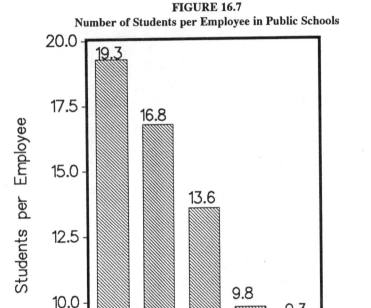

FIGURE 16.7
Number of Students per Employee in Public Schools

Source: Digest of Educational Statistics

The trend in students per employee (both teachers and nonteachers) in elementary and secondary public school systems is illustrated in figure 16.7. In 1950 there was one public school employee for every nineteen students, but by 1992 there was one employee for every nine students. Not only did relative teachers and nonteachers increase, but so also did relative spending per pupil, while quality of education declined. This implies problems other than financial ones. Lack of parental involvement and the NEA are the culprits. The rise in power of the NEA and the lack of parental involvement coincide with cost increases and quality deterioration of local public schools. Lieberman argues that cost and quality of public education, as long as it remains a government monopoly, are as bad as costs and quality are under socialism.[16]

Taxpayers paid through the teeth in the expectation that more spending per student would improve educational quality. Instead, increased spending turned into a jobs program, a method for school districts to provide jobs to more people. More relative teachers and nonteachers were hired to spend taxpayer money with the result being another broken promise and another broken social contract between taxpayers and their expectations of the elementary and secondary public educational system, but the general public doesn't perceive it that way. That perception and explosion in growth of public school employees are driven by the NEA, which needs more employees to ensure NEA-driven mandates are met with compliance.

School choice, which the NEA strongly opposes, has been discussed for years. Nobel Prize-winning economist Milton Friedman promoted school choice via a voucher system as early as the 1960s, speaking of public education as an inherently inefficient governmental or "nationalized" monopoly.[17] Competition is an aspect that serves the market economy and consumers well. Competition encourages firms to provide value-added products and services to their customers. If they don't, they eventually go out of business. U.S. automobile manufacturers when faced with higher quality imports produced better-quality cars. Deregulation of long-distance phone service resulted in lower costs, more alternatives, and better products. The idea of school choice is to allow students to attend the school of their choice. If students go to the better schools, soon other schools will improve their quality to compete for students, become more efficient, and offer a better education. The U.S. university system is based on that premise and is chosen by students from around the world. While school choice is not a panacea for all educational system ills, it is a major step in the right direction. Pay-for-performance would be another meaningful step in the right direction in that it also encourages competition.[18]

The NEA is the main opposition to school choice, the reason being that their constituency is comprised of union members, not students or parents. Their self-interest is to have more dues-paying members, who are obtained by maintaining a monopoly and promoting a bureaucracy that needs more teachers and nonteachers. Monopolies and the NEA are at the opposite end of the spectrum from school choice. The NEA, to date, has been very successful in preserving the monopoly as it not only keeps the general public misinformed about problems in public schools via its Madison Avenue public relations program, but it also financially supports politicians like President Clinton, who opposes school choice even though he attended a private school in Arkansas and sends his daughter to private school.

SATs are taken by slightly more than 1 million students each year in a universe of over 2.4 million high-school seniors—approximately 43 percent. (While some high-school juniors or even sophomores may take SATs as a "rehearsal," it is not believed that the number doing so would greatly alter the approximate percentage.) Those who take SAT exams are in general the best and the brightest. The NEA opposes a national test for all high school seniors; thus, there is no standardized test. Were such a test available, it may well show a marked decline over the years, in particular for the 57 percent of students who do not take the SAT. The standardized test high school students without a college degree face is the job market. They *fail* this test (figure 16.8), as real median income for male high school graduates without college is in a steep decline. This tells us that the job market thinks the high school degree is of diminishing value. Over 80 percent of persons age twenty-five and over have a high school diploma, while nearly 22 percent of those over twenty-five have a bachelor's degree or higher.

School choice can be modelled after the U.S. university system in which universities compete with each other for students. This encourages universities to improve the quality of their offerings. Competition among businesses encourages more and better products and services. No competition among elementary and secondary public schools is a major factor preventing quality improvements. The results of SAT ethnic-group scores suggest the educational system is geared toward mediocrity by lifting scores on the bottom. Segments with the highest scores show no improvement, while groups with lower absolute scores have a slight rise. An implication can therefore be drawn that the educational system is geared toward bringing scores of ethnic groups together—by increasing scores of lower groups while reducing or holding steady scores of higher groups—instead of improving the quality of all. This movement toward mediocrity is driven by the NEA as well as state and federal regulations. The educational system appears to be unintentionally designed to fail by focusing on improving scores of lower-performing college-bound groups. Another method to increase SAT scores for all ethnic groups is to recenter SAT scores,which is what occurred in the

FIGURE 16.8
Real Income of Male High School Graduates

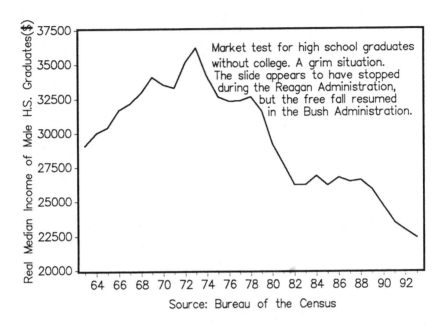

Market test for high school graduates
without college. A grim situation.
The slide appears to have stopped
during the Reagan Administration,
but the free fall resumed
in the Bush Administration.

Source: Bureau of the Census

fall of 1994. The College Board, sponsor of the SAT, defined *recentering* as meaning that yesterday's student who scored a 424 verbal and a 478 math (national averages before recentering) would henceforth obtain a 500 verbal and 500 math for identical test performance. It is a cosmetic change made to improve SAT scores, as the NEA and lack of parental involvement prevent the educational process from turning out students with improving scores.

Private education is a method to bypass quality problems of public school systems. Relatively high outlays required by all taxpayers for funding public school systems mean that mainly only higher-income families can afford to send their children to private schools. Private school enrollment in proportion to public school enrollment decreased in the 1980s (figure 16.9) but appears to be stabilizing in the 1990s. Private

FIGURE 16.9
Percent Private Elementary and Secondary Enrollment

Source: Digest of Educational Statistics

education is a choice, but it is a realistic choice for only a relatively small proportion of the population as incomes are squeezed because of rising costs of private education and the decline in purchasing power per job. Many students and parents, given a choice, would probably prefer a private school. Since that is out of reach for most parents, the next best alternative is to allow students to attend the public school of their choice, which means schools wanting to compete would need to upgrade their offerings. Choice is a method that can be utilized to start improving quality of public schools.

One point is clear. The solution lies not in increasing relative spending. History tells us that. Table 16.1 illustrates dollars spent per student in select states with their SAT ranking as well as eighth-grade National Assessment of Educational Progress (NAEP) math scores, according to Manno.[19]

TABLE 16.1
Average per Pupil Expenditure and Rank

State	Average per pupil Expenditure	SAT Rank	NAEP Rank
New Jersey	$9,159	39	14
New York	8,500	42	22
Connecticut	7,914	35	11
Pennsylvania	6,534	45	14
Massachusetts	6,351	33	12
Wisconsin	5,946	7	6
Maine	5,894	41	4
Vermont	5,740	36	N.A.
Ohio	5,639	24	18
Florida	5,154	40	31
Illinois	5,062	10	N.A.
Kansas	5,009	6	N.A.
Georgia	4,860	50	31
Iowa	4,839	1	1
California	4,826	34	29
Nebraska	4,381	8	6
South Carolina	4,327	51	29
Texas	4,238	46	25
South Dakota	3,730	5	N.A.
North Dakota	3,685	2	1
Arkansas	3,334	17	38
Mississippi	3,322	12	41
Utah	2,993	4	8

Source: Manno

There appears to be relatively little relation between average per pupil expenditure on education and SAT scores. In many cases states with lower average expenditures have higher test scores while states with higher average expenditures have lower SAT scores. The NAEP ranking appears to correlate somewhat better with spending, but it is very difficult to make a case that the problem with the U.S. public education system is inadequate funding. An international comparison of average expenditures per student leads to the same conclusion (table 16.2). Three countries—the United States, Switzerland, and Sweden—spend a relatively high amount per student, while other developed nations spend

TABLE 16.2
Expenditure per Student by Select Country

Country	Expenditure per student (1989)
Switzerland	$4,845
U.S.	$4,083
Sweden	4,040
Canada	3,730
Austria	3,613
Norway	3,336
United Kingdom	2,897
France	2,483
W.Germany	2,487
Netherlands	2,413
Japan	2,243

Source: Digest of Educational Statistics

considerably less. Anecdotal evidence suggests that countries such as Japan, Netherlands, and Germany that do spend relatively less produce well-educated students.

The two major primary and secondary education problems in the United States, as indicated, appear to be (1) the NEA and their misrepresentation of issues facing local systems along with their opposition to most actions that would improve educational quality, and (2) lack of parental involvement both at-home and at-school. While school choice can help solve at-school difficulties created by the NEA, it can't solve at-home problems. At-home problems may be addressed by the proposal of Joe Gorman who suggests that each child be entitled to an advocate.[19] The advocate would be a concerned adult who would see that the child is learning, completing homework, and being tutored. Public sector spending can't overcome a situation when the parent(s) are not involved or interested.

17

Public Safety—A Broken Promise

During the 1950s and early 1960s people in the United States could feel relatively safe in this country—safe to walk in their neighborhoods, safe to travel around town or to other cities, safe to live in their apartments or houses, safe to go shopping, and safe to go to work. Many people probably felt they could even leave their doors unlocked at night. A social contract or promise had evolved between government and taxpayer—government provided protection, and its citizens felt relatively safe to carry on day-to-day activities. Taxpayers provided a level of public funding for police and a criminal justice system that controlled property and violent crime, which in turn allowed this degree of relative safety.

Criminals (or potential criminals) back then evaluated not only expected benefits but also the costs of committing a crime. A level of crime was produced—the tradeoff between criminal activity and tax dollars spent for public safety. The resulting level of crime in the 1950s and early 1960s allowed much of the population to feel safe—this was, in effect, the social contract. Criminals implicitly agreed to a contract with law enforcement, the court system, and penitentiaries that left many Americans feeling safe. Criminals, in calculating costs and benefits, take into consideration the likelihood of being caught, the court system, probability of jail time, and length of jail time. Nobel-prize winning economist Gary Becker applied economic analysis to crime and punishment in the 1960s and concluded that criminals and potential criminals evaluate economic tradeoffs.[1] People make an economic decision in selecting a criminal profession relative to other professions, which resulted in relative safety for law-abiding citizens in the 1950s and early 1960s. Around the middle 1960s a dramatic change in the benefit/cost ratio estimated by criminals or potential criminals occurred (figure 17.1). Charles Murray

FIGURE 17.1
Frequency of Violent and Property Crimes

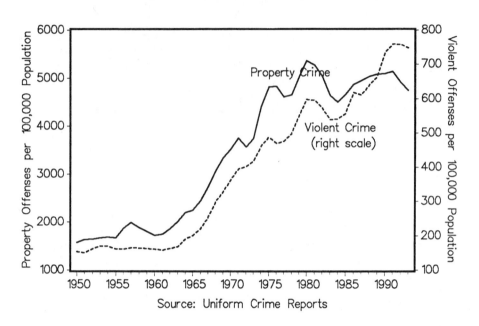

Source: Uniform Crime Reports

suggests the year 1964 as the year the crime rate started climbing steeply for both property and violent crime.[2]

Many more people have chosen the criminal life-style since 1964, resulting in many more victims. Many factors influenced this, but certainty of capture, imprisonment, and length of imprisonment must have been perceived as becoming less likely during the 1960s. It seems obvious that if all criminals committing crimes were sentenced to jail, the crime rate would fall dramatically. Since the crime rate went the other way after 1964, it is clear criminals felt relatively safer. In other words, if criminals had continued to perceive benefits and costs as remaining the same as in the 1950s and early 1960s, the level of crime per 100,000 people would very likely be in the same ballpark today as back then, though an adjustment would be necessary for demographics. The incidence of crime would have been somewhat higher, other things equal, starting in the middle 1960s, with the adjustment for demographics. For example, people in the broad age group of thirteen to thirty-four accounted for 74 percent of persons arrested in 1992, while that age group represented only 33 percent of U.S. population. In the middle 1960s the post-World War II baby boom was moving into this age group, but demographics can't begin to explain the rapid increase of crime reported to police (figure 17.1). The President's Crime Commission in 1967 found that the increase in reported crimes was substantially larger than the increase in crime-prone age groups of the population. Something else was going on.[3]

In particular, criminals decided benefits relative to costs of that life-style were much greater than before. This change has resulted in a level of criminal activity that, for many, means it is no longer safe, without precautions, to walk in their neighborhood, live in their homes, go shopping, or go to work—and people certainly don't leave their doors unlocked. Relatively more people choose the criminal life-style because they feel crime does pay. The result is a large relative increase in violent as well as property crime over the past thirty years. Violent crimes are offenses of murder, rape, robbery, and aggravated assault, while property crimes are offenses of burglary, larceny, and motor-vehicle theft. But economic analysis can only be pushed so far; there are those who commit crimes whatever the costs and risks, and for some, the greater the risk, the greater the thrill. At the other end of the spectrum, everyone is capable of violating the law and most people do, provided they believe the benefit/cost ratio is in their favor, as they do, for example, in exceeding a speed limit, minor cheating on income taxes, using the office phone for personal calls, or calling in sick just to have the day off. These are not morally reprehensible crimes and chances of getting caught are slim. If, however, every time someone exceeded a speed limit he or she were caught, the benefit/cost ratio would be tilted with the likely result being that they would soon mend their ways.

Relatively more people made a conscious decision to choose the criminal life-style as the benefit/cost ratio of breaking the law appealed to them. A slightly different way of saying this is that with the breakdown of both family and community values and that of the educational system, the United States is producing more and more people who fail to comprehend right from wrong and cannot understand the cost portion of the benefit/cost ratio. People grasp the immediate benefit side, while the cost side, which may never affect them because only a small percentage go to jail, is not given much weight. The benefit/cost ratio is obviously perceived by the criminal as tilted in his favor, and consequently many or most law-abiding citizens must modify their life-style to account for this change. In particular, more and more citizens pay twice for their own protection.

Thirty years ago citizens paid taxes to support a police, legal, and incarceration system that provided for *public safety*. This public safety shield allowed most citizens ample degrees of freedom to live their daily lives without fear of violence. Monumental change has occurred, as citizens pay sharply higher taxes for public protection in addition to the sums a growing number of citizens pay for their own protection. Lifestyles of typical U.S. citizens have been altered by the level and fear of crime—the social contract between government and the people has been broken (figure 17.2). People pay more and more taxes, yet violent crime continues to increase. Citizens know they can't depend on government for protection, as they did in the past, and are attempting to reassert control over the public process. An example of that is *three strikes and you're out* laws at the state level with California and Alabama among the first states to implement specific versions of this legislation. Repeat offenders commit the majority of crimes, and voters in these states want repeat offenders off the street.

Citizens find it necessary to pony up additional dollars for private security items such as security systems for houses, apartments, and cars to prevent their life-styles from being altered more. Citizens also purchase items such as Mace and/or other weapons for protection. In the 1950s and early 1960s crime control was viewed as the job of police, not citizens. That is what citizens paid taxes for—the social contract. The average American came to believe crime prevention and control was the job of the legal system, but that is changing. Individuals are paying for more of their own protection because they realize tax dollars do not adequately protect them.

The United States has always been relatively individualistic rather than group oriented. Cowboys and settlers in the Old West were viewed as highly individualistic, but they banded together for protection from the criminal element. Individuals in the Old West had responsibility for their own protection as well as that of their family and used weapons in

FIGURE 17.2
Public Safety Expenditures vs. Violent Crime

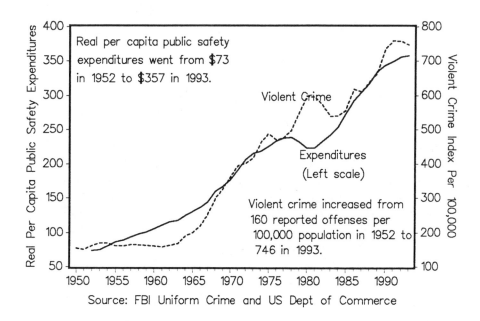

Source: FBI Uniform Crime and US Dept of Commerce

their defense. They were also concerned about their horses being stolen, and western lore has it that horse stealing was an offense punished by hanging. Penalties for crimes were probably well understood on both sides, and justice was swift. Criminals back then also evaluated the benefit/cost ratio of choosing that profession. They understood that the victim might resist and fight with an equivalent weapon; they understood justice would be swift and certain. Homicide rates in 1960 were one-fifth to one-seventh of their 1860 level.[4]

The 1990s is reverting to certain Old West ways. People are using a variety of means to protect themselves, their houses, and cars. In the Old West, people were concerned about being killed for their horse; in modern times, people are concerned about carjacking. In the Old West, people would build houses with portholes for weapons; in modern times, people install security systems in their houses. In the Old West, citizens carried guns with them at all times for protection; in modern times more and more people carry guns, mace and/or some electronic device for protection. The Old West had forts with walls around them; some houses or housing developments today are surrounded by brick walls and a monitored gate. The fort of the Old West had soldiers patrolling the perimeter; in modern times it is a private-security force. Or one can go back to olden days in England where people banded together for protection in castles with moats. Some modern-day housing developments resemble these fortresses.

In the Old West, citizens started levying taxes to pay for a sheriff, who provided protection as towns and cities developed. Citizens continued paying for their own protection (i.e., weapons) but were willing to begin funding public protection. Public protection worked well, and citizens became less concerned about providing for their own protection and soon left it to law-enforcement officials. Taxpayer-supported public protection replaced private protection by the turn of the century, and a social protection contract evolved between the public sector and taxpayers. Starting in the middle 1960s, violent crime escalated along with increased taxpayer support for protection. It may appear from figure 17.2 that more taxpayer funding of public protection results in faster rises in violent crime; however, other factors—such as the legal system, criminal rights, and a breakdown of family and community values—are at work allowing crime rates to rise. One example in which the modern-day legal system is not like that of the Old West is that justice today is not swift. A modern-day criminal is unlikely to be caught, and if caught, the process of conviction is arduous. Jail time may or may not be meted out to someone committing a violent crime. If the criminal does spend time in jail, the sentence is likely to be reduced, perhaps even substantially. In the Old West the time from capture to court to jail was probably brief compared to present day.

Citizens take it upon themselves to provide private protection—reverting to the Old West in privatizing security. Spending on security systems services is over $3 billion annually. This percentage, 3.3 percent, is small relative to the $92 billion taxpayers provide federal, state, and local government to spend for civilian safety, but it will likely continue to grow rapidly. Growth in spending on safety doesn't include a dollar amount assigned to modification of life-styles or to fear, but the cost is large in terms of reduction in freedom. Criminals disrupt life-styles in addition to inflicting major damage on victims, their families, and property. *Business Week*, in a 13 December 1993 article estimated that crime costs U.S. citizens $425 billion each year.[5] This includes direct and indirect costs of both violent and property crimes, hospital costs, private security as well as income lost by victims over their lifetimes. That number, of course, doesn't include costs of fear and life-style changes.

The amount allocated to private security is an attempt by citizens to gain control and feel safer as well as to protect property. The majority of spending for private security systems is probably undertaken by those at or above the median income level. Many more may wish to have security devices but financial constraints don't allow it, and, instead, citizens resort to modification of life-style. Property crime rates may be responding to massive public and private-spending efforts in that crime rates might be leveling off (figure 17.1), but people have seen public spending on crime increase dramatically with little apparent influence on violent crime (figure 17.2).

Within the violent-crime grouping, murder remains below its peak rate in 1980, while rape is trending upward (figure 17.3). Homicide rates shot up rapidly after mid-1960s. Murder rates also increased in some European countries.[6] That could suggest that a changing age structure was a major contributing factor since homicide-rate increases were widespread; however, Wilson makes reference to an MIT study that concluded the murder-rate increase in the United States during the 1960s was more than ten times greater than one would have expected from a changing age structure of the population alone.[7]

Murray looks at the increase in homicide rates by race and writes, "It was much more dangerous to be black in 1972 than it was in 1965."[8] This homicide difference by race also suggests something other than a changing age structure (figure 17.4). White-male homicide rates increased by more than a factor of three from the middle 1950s to their peak in 1980 and are only modestly lower now. Homicide rates for blacks didn't increase nearly as rapidly as those for whites but remained sharply higher than those for whites over the entire time period. Black-American homicide rates in 1980 were higher by a factor of over six relative to white-American. The black homicide rate by the 1990s was higher than white homicides by a factor of 7.7 as black homicide rates headed up in the latter 1980s.

FIGURE 17.3
Murders and Rapes

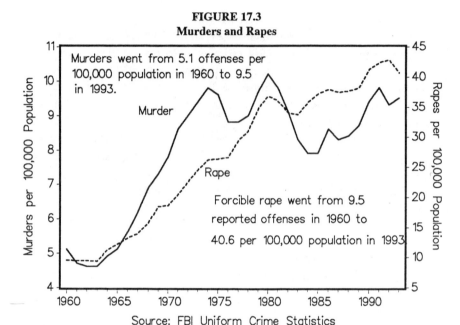

Murders went from 5.1 offenses per 100,000 population in 1960 to 9.5 in 1993.

Murder

Rape

Forcible rape went from 9.5 reported offenses in 1960 to 40.6 per 100,000 population in 1993

Source: FBI Uniform Crime Statistics

Other violent crimes such as robberies and assaults continue to rise (figure 17.5). Wilson suggests that "robbery is perhaps the most feared crime, inasmuch as it so often occurs among strangers, without warning, and involves the use or threat of force."[9]

Public and private spending is having limited impact on violent crime, although the homicide rate for white-Americans may be in decline. Is another $100 billion or $300 billion of taxpayer money going to do it? Money pours in with little result, and the idea develops that as with education, more public spending might not be the answer. Real per capita spending on public protection has been increasing for several decades, and neighborhoods and streets are less safe. The *why* is in the benefit/cost ratio and the breakdown in both family and community values. People have difficulty in distinguishing right from wrong. Benefits must be reduced and/or costs increased so that relatively fewer people choose the criminal life-style.

There are two major aspects to the U.S. crime problem: (1) costs relative to perceived benefits are not high enough to deter criminals and would-be criminals, and (2) for any given benefit/cost ratio, the breakdown of family and community values means that the level of deter-

FIGURE 17.4
Male Homicide Rate by Race

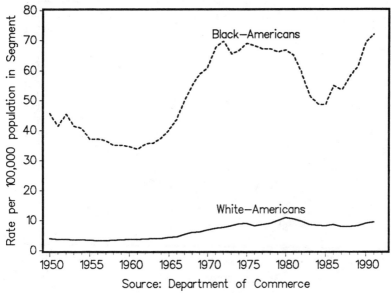

Source: Department of Commerce

FIGURE 17.5
Assaults and Robberies

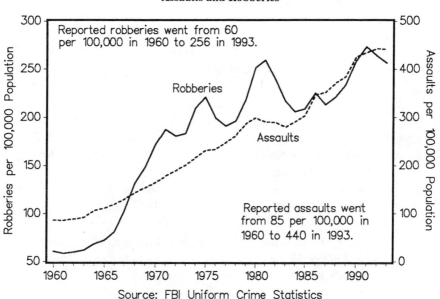

Reported robberies went from 60 per 100,000 in 1960 to 256 in 1993.

Robberies

Assaults

Reported assaults went from 85 per 100,000 in 1960 to 440 in 1993.

Source: FBI Uniform Crime Statistics

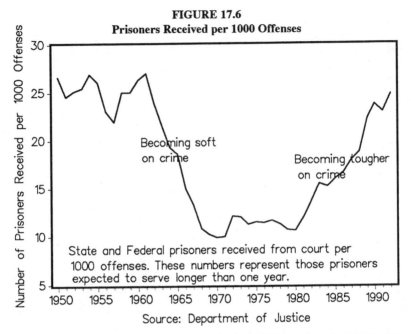

FIGURE 17.6
Prisoners Received per 1000 Offenses

Becoming soft
on crime

Becoming tougher
on crime

State and Federal prisoners received from court per
1000 offenses. These numbers represent those prisoners
expected to serve longer than one year.

Number of Prisoners Received per 1000 Offenses

Source: Department of Justice

rence won't be as effective as it was in the 1950s and early 1960s. Figure 17.6 shows the number of state and federal prisoners received from court per 1000 offenses committed who are expected to serve longer than one year. Offenses include both violent and property crime. Roughly twenty-five prisoners per each 1000 offenses were received during the 1950s. In other words, chances of spending time in a federal and state penitentiary after committing a crime was only 2.5 percent. Crime rates exploded in 1960s as the benefit/cost ratio favored the criminal. By 1970 less than ten prisoners per each 1000 offenses were received, which says the benefit/cost ratio tilted in favor of the criminal as the probability of jail time in a federal or state penitentiary fell to 1 percent. Starting in 1970, benefits of committing a criminal offense relative to costs stabilized, and in the 1980s costs—going to prison—started increasing as the United States became tougher on crime. This suggests that criminals, in the 1990s, face somewhat similar odds of going to prison after committing a crime as in the 1950s. If criminals in the 1990s respond as criminals did in the 1950s, a crime rate approaching that of the 1950s might have been expected, but since the violent crime rate continues to increase, it is obvious criminals don't. Changes in family and commu-

FIGURE 17.7
Illegitimate Births by Racial Group

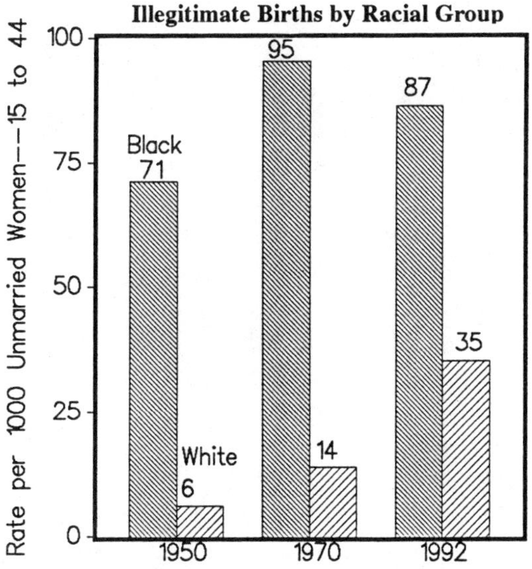

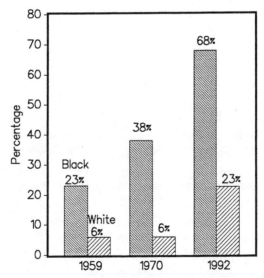

Source: Department of Commerce

FIGURE 17.8
Illegitimate Births as Percent of Total

Source: Department of Commerce

nity values appear to be the underlying reasons. As a result, the benefit/
cost ratio existing in the 1950s and early 1960s—that degree of tough-
ness—doesn't mean as much to criminals in the 1990s. A much tougher
approach to crime is required to convince criminals and potential criminals that crime doesn't pay. Evidence suggests that many criminals experience prison as simply a stopover in their life of crime, since many
crimes are committed by offenders who have already spent time in prison.

Changing family and community values can be illustrated by the high
rates of illegitimate births (figure 17.7). What wasn't acceptable at one
time in the United States is much more acceptable in the 1990s, in fact,
commonplace in some neighborhoods. These children, on average, are
at a relative disadvantage, and a higher proportion of them end up choosing the criminal life-style than children of a traditional family. Murray
suggests that part of this crisis is the relationship of illegitimate births to
overall births (figure 17.8).[10] Illegitimate births account for the majority
of black births, 68 percent, and 23 percent of white births. This rapid
increase in illegitimate births as a proportion of total births is no doubt
a major explanation for the higher incidence of crime among blacks and
also appears to be a major reason why benefit/cost ratios of the 1950s
and early 1960s aren't as effective in the 1990s.

Figure 17.9 illustrates the likelihood of people going to federal and
state prisons for more than a year after committing a violent crime in
1992. This reflects the incarceration rate relative to crimes reported to
police, not the incarceration rate relative to number of arrests. Fewer
than half of murder offenses end in prison time, while only 13.5 percent
of reported rapes end in prison time. Rapes are probably under-reported,
so the 13.5 percentage is likely on the high side, while homicide is almost always reported. Robberies and assaults seem to be relatively safe
for criminals—only 5.7 percent and 2.3 percent respectively end up going
to prison. Criminals commit multiple offenses, so percentages are not
quite as bad as they seem. However, the point that some criminals commit multiple offenses (so there may be a somewhat higher probability
of going to prison than the above numbers show) doesn't change the
point—crime pays; otherwise, it wouldn't be so prevalent.

The problem of parolees and repeat offenders has become a major
public issue as voters attempt to take control away from the legal system with referendums such as three strikes and you're out. "Most serious crime is committed by repeaters," according to Wilson.[11] Department

FIGURE 17.9
Violent Crime Pays

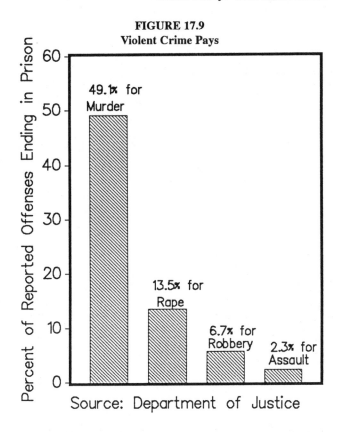

Source: Department of Justice

of Justice data shows that the number of parolees increased substantially during the 1980s.[12] In 1980 the rate of parolees was 136 per 100,000 adults, and by 1990 the number had increased to 287 per 100,000—a doubling of the rate. People previously sentenced to incarceration or probation keep showing up in prisons. A 1991 survey concluded that an astounding 80 percent of state-prison inmates had previously been sentenced to prison.[13] Criminals are *not* being deterred from committing crimes by costs of incarceration.

People talk about other factors influencing the rapid rise in crime. Some say a slow or stagnant standard of living in the United States influences the decision to become a criminal, but in the Great Depression the murder rate *fell* (figure 17.10). The overall crime rate as well as the subgroup of homicide rose rapidly in the 1960s, part of the U.S.

FIGURE 17.10
Murder Rate, 1900–1993

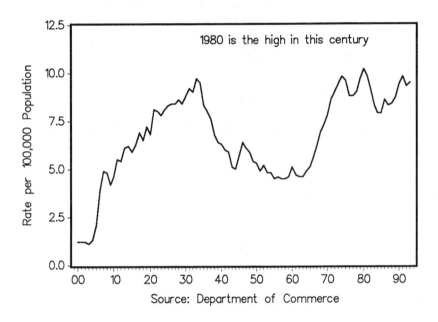

Source: Department of Commerce

golden age. Likewise, relatively poor countries around the world do not show that a pattern of poverty leads to high crime rates. Others say it is due to demographics. As mentioned, the increase in crime that began in the middle 1960s far exceeded what the age argument would have implied. Another factor that might explain an uptick for a few years is war. History, at times, suggests that sanctioned killing during war has a residual effect on the homicide level in peacetime society for a few years, before criminal activity returns to "normal." This factor may explain a pickup in homicide for a few years after Vietnam, as Archer and Gartner suggest.[14] However, there was no such effect after World War II.

Others point to an increase in guns as a major contributing factor to violent crimes. This is very unlikely as the cause and effect relationship is very weak—though the obvious does occur, which is that a high per-

FIGURE 17.11
Percent Murders Committed with Guns

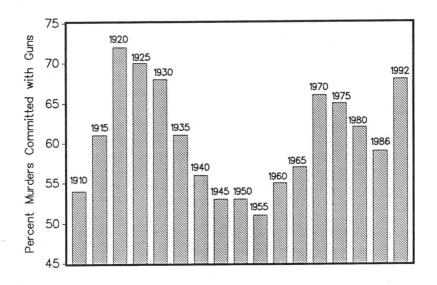

Source: Department of Commerce

centage of total homicides occurs by use of a gun as a weapon (figure 17.11)—but the rate of violent crime is high owing to the perceived benefit/cost ratio by criminals. While criminals may select guns as their weapon of choice to commit murder, guns do not *cause* the violent crime rate to be high. If they did, the violent crime rate would have been extremely high all through this century.[15]

Others point to increasing urbanization as a reason for an increasing crime rate. It is correct that relatively more violent crimes occur in large cities than in towns and rural areas, but among large cities it is not true that violent crime rates increase as city size increases. In other words, violent-crime rates are greater in metropolitan areas than in rural areas, but it does not follow that violent-crime rates increase as metropolitan areas increase in size, as Archer and Gartner point out.[16]

Increased drug use is an important contributor to crime, as criminals commit both property and violent crimes in connection with illegal aspects of drug distribution as well as with its use. But blaming crime on increased drug use misses the point. The basic question is, why has drug use increased? Lower rates of crime existed thirty years ago along with lower drug use. Drug use likely increased because of changed family and community values. A greater incidence of drug use in society is not something to be proud of. It begs the question to say increased drug use causes increased crime. A breakdown of both family and community values produces people who have difficulty distinguishing right from wrong, which leads to an increased crime rate as these people perceive a changed benefit/cost ratio. This leads more people to select the criminal life-style and results in increased drug use. Criminals and the subclass of potential drug users go through a process of calculating perceived benefit/cost ratios, and they see a different ratio because of the breakdown of family and community values. Legalizing drugs, which some call for, is therefore *not* a solution from society's viewpoint anymore than legalizing violent crimes would be. Legalizing homicide, rape, or robbery to reduce the crime rate doesn't resolve the basic right and wrong issue. Likewise, legalizing drug use doesn't resolve the basic problems of either right and wrong or family and community values.

18

Bounty Hunters and Fixed Penalties

Much of the United States is being altered by both crime and the fear of crime. This fear results in citizens attempting to privatize safety by altering their life-styles and forking over funds in an attempt to purchase security. It is probably safe to say that nearly everyone in the United States over the age of forty has significantly altered his or her life-style relative to fifteen to thirty years ago because of actual or threat of criminal activity. There are, perhaps, only relatively few Americans who have not been touched in some way by the increasing crime rate. This crime rate is influenced by changing family and community values that produces some people having an unacceptable understanding of benefits and costs. Such people perceive a benefit/cost ratio tilted in their favor, leading them to commit crimes. Benefit/cost ratios are moving back toward those of the 1950s and early 1960s, after shifting to favoring more crime in the later 1960s and in the 1970s. Changed family and community values suggest that the benefit/cost ratio needs to become even tougher on criminals than in the 1950s and early 1960s to have an effect. There are two direct methods for doing that: (1) make penalties for committing violent crime more severe and more definite, and (2) increase the likelihood of capture.

The major method of tilting the benefit/cost ratio against the criminal is to increase likelihood of capture. The 1990s, in certain ways, are reverting to the Old West (as explained in the previous chapter). In the Old West, citizens carried guns for protection. In modern times more and more people carry guns, Mace and/or some electronic device for protection. In addition, many provide protection for their auto or truck. Wanted posters with a reward were utilized in the Old West to help capture alleged criminals. That system encouraged the private sector to respond to a financial incentive in order to assist public law enforcement.

Such a system amounted to privatization of criminal capture with the private sector complementing public sector efforts. The United States, once again, needs to utilize private-sector criminal capture to complement public-sector efforts—similar to what was done in the Old West.

Public law enforcement can be expected to vigorously oppose attempts at privatizing capture of criminals. Public law enforcement has a monopoly franchise on this portion of the criminal justice system and will oppose private-sector efforts to pierce the monopoly franchise. As the NEA (see chapter 16), opposes efforts to privatize primary and secondary education because they fear competition, public law enforcement will also oppose entrance of private-sector firms because they do *not want* competition. Competition is likely to result in efficiencies and better service, which is precisely the reason the NEA is opposed to attempts to privatize education. The argument that public law enforcement will use against privatization is that the monopoly franchise is the most efficient market structure, and privatization would reduce benefits to society. If that were true, public law enforcement would have nothing to fear from privatization of capture of criminals as private firms couldn't profitably compete. Individual entrepreneurs and private firms are likely to enter the market effectively and add net benefits for society. There is no reason to think that public law enforcement is better for society when it has no competition than it would be in a situation that allows competition.

Privatization made major inroads in attempting to deter crime by increasing private security. *Forbes* reports that the private-security industry has 1.5 million employees and $52 billion in revenues originating from businesses, communities, and individuals, as entities attempt to protect themselves from crime.[1] Private-security employs more people than public law enforcement. Private security officers, in general, lack the sworn coercive authority from a public authority to enforce criminal law, which public police have. Private officers can ordinarily exercise only private powers to maintain order and protect private interests, but the private sector also contracts with public police officers who may exercise their sworn authority in off-duty employment. Other efforts at privatization of crime deterrence include activities such as the neighborhood crime-watch concept as well as purchasing products such as security systems for residences and businesses, personal electronic devices, Mace, weapons, and security systems for vehicles.

All of these efforts are attempts to privatize crime deterrence as the public crime-fighting effort isn't effective in halting violent-crime rate increases. Private-security forces can capture criminals, and private citizens can also participate in making a citizen's arrest. Substantial moves toward privatization have occurred for part of the public-safety function. But few inroads have been made into privatization of capture of criminals, which is the one aspect where major gains in crime deterrence can be accomplished for society. Once it becomes apparent to criminals and potential criminals that commission of a crime carries a higher likelihood of both capture and incarceration, one is likely to see a substantial decrease in the crime rate.

The theoretical rationale for the concept of privatization rests primarily on an expectation of greater efficiencies and net benefit gains for society. There are different types of privatization. One of these is contracting out; another is the use of vouchers. Contracting out is the most common form of privatization in this country. At the local government level, there are examples of nearly every activity having been contracted out to private contractors, including prisons, libraries, police service, and parole programs. La Miranda, California, a city of 41,000, has fifty-five government employees managing contracts for its services. Lakewood, California, has a total of eight city workers who manage its contracts. Scottsdale, Arizona, contracted out its fire service. In his book, *Sharing Power*, Kettl discusses these cities and also describes services most and least frequently contracted out by local government.[2] Examples of services most often contracted out include legal services, operation of homeless shelters, residential and commercial solid-waste disposal, street repair, drug and alcohol treatment facilities, and utility billing. Services less often contracted out include libraries, prisons and jails, fire, traffic control, payroll, and crime prevention and control. National defense, at the federal level, is an example of weapons production being contracted out. Some movement at the federal level to contract out apprehension of alleged criminals has occurred in a very select manner, for instance, the U.S. State Department providing rewards for terrorism information, according to *Time* magazine.[3] Another example is the FBI attempting to enlist citizen participation for help in finding fugitives on its most-wanted list.

In use of vouchers, another form of privatization, the government provides recipients with funding earmarked for use in shopping for services. The Food Stamp program is an example of voucher use. Use of wanted posters in the Old West was an effort to contract out capture of criminals by paying bounty hunters only if they captured the criminal. One can also think about the Old West reward system as a voucher system in which the bounty hunter attempted to collect the reward (voucher). Bounty hunters, in turn, used reward money to purchase whatever they wanted.

Bounty Hunter Alternative Models

There are alternative methods that can be followed to implement bounty hunting as a method to increase likelihood of capture of alleged criminals. Two different models are described below, either of which will work to complement public law enforcement, and there can be many variations of these two models.

One model would allow the private sector to complement public-sector efforts by opening the capture of criminals to competition through use of bounties. Commission of a violent crime typically results in a 911 call, and as a patrol car is usually then dispatched, the patrol officer is generally first on the scene. The patrol officer ascertains the situation, arrests the alleged criminal if he is present, and secures the crime scene. At that time, the proper people are notified within the violent-crimes division. The patrol officer may assist in providing security at the crime scene once detectives arrive but is generally out of the picture, unless a subpoena is later received by the patrol officer. After detectives gather data at the crime scene and identify the suspect, a bounty would be posted if the suspect has not been captured at the scene. The private sector would assist the public sector in capturing the alleged criminal. In this model the private sector could mean individual entrepreneurs as well as companies. The criminal-justice system would be subject to competition in capturing alleged criminals. Rewards would be paid only to licensed bounty hunters who capture alleged criminals alive. The requirement of capturing alleged criminals alive may eliminate some opposition to this approach, but substantial criticism will no doubt be leveled at this method, in particular from public law enforcement.

Three additional steps would be necessary for this model to work. First, a licensing process would be needed for bounty hunters, one that spells out such items as training, experience, and use of weapons. Private detectives go through a licensing process. Bounty hunters would also. National criteria would be established with local police departments implementing the criteria. The second step is that bounty hunters would need to use state-of-art stun guns to assist in capture of alleged criminals, and the third step is that information on crimes, data gathered, and descriptions would be part of a national database for bounty hunters with database access limited to licensed bounty hunters only. Bounty hunters would also need to be bonded and be subject to disciplinary action for false arrests. There would be no general media coverage or pictures or reward posting in newspaper or on television. If a family or company wanted to issue a reward in order to help find an alleged criminal, that would continue to operate. But the general public would be unaware of warrants issued, rewards, and/or captures other than that they are normally made aware of such activities by the media. Wanted posters in the Old West made the activity public. Modern communication systems no longer require that. It's essential that this model take full advantage of state-of-the-art communication systems to provide full information to bounty hunters. The only aspect that the public notices after implementation of this system is that the crime rate decreases over time.

No reward would be issued if for some reason the public sector entity wished to delay attempts to capture a criminal. U.S. guidelines would need to be established so that this alternative of no bounty was viewed as an exception to the general process of capture. For example, it could evolve at a crime scene that a potential suspect was a central figure in a wider investigation and public officials may not want bounty hunters tracking the suspect. In such a case, no bounty would be issued—no bounty, no reward. The same for capture of an alleged criminal by someone not a licensed bounty hunter. This latter guideline eliminates people not properly trained from attempting to obtain reward money by arresting someone who has had a warrant issued on them. An exception to this last rule would be an instance of someone who isn't a licensed bounty hunter making a citizens arrest if he or she happens to observe a crime-in-progress. Private citizens, not licensed, would be entitled to a reward for such an arrest.

Bounties paid for capture of criminals could start in the following ballpark ranges: murder—$800,000; rape, $100,000; robberies, $50,000; and assaults, $25,000. The bounty for murder is approximated from the

TABLE 18.1
Average Net Future Income

Age	
25	$900,000
35	$807,000
45	$654,000

Source: Northwestern Mutual Life Insurance Co of Milwaukee

human-life value approach that insurance companies utilize. A simplified approach involves the present value of future net incomes based on working-year expectancy of the individual. This approach, if logically carried out, would have different bounties depending on age, income level, and discount rate utilized. Table 18.1 presents a series of illustrative human-life values (rounded) at three ages under the assumption of constant net future income of $50,000 per year, a 5 percent discount rate, and retirement age of sixty-five.

People who are murdered each have a unique profile of characteristics, such as age and income earning potential, that could be utilized to calculate a unique reward. But rather than do that, it is suggested that the figure of $800,000 bounty be utilized across the board for all murders as a starting point. The size of reward may be sufficient to create an environment in which informants as well as criminals cooperate with bounty hunters to turn in other criminals, leading to higher arrest rates. Size of rewards could be increased at a later date if these amounts are not adequate. Bounties for rapes, robberies, and assaults do not have a direct approach to their calculation as murder does. However, each victim of a rape, robbery, or assault would have a unique set of cost factors and in the case of robbery, a monetary loss. The bounties for these crimes should certainly be less than for murder, but rewards need to be high enough to provide an inducement to the private sector to help capture the alleged criminal.

Rewards would be paid by the U.S. Treasury, so therefore the taxpayer pays the tab. Crime is a national problem and Congress can move to correct it by offering substantial awards for capture of alleged criminals committing violent crimes. This model is relatively easy for Congress to implement, is straightforward, and is likely to be very effective. Payment of rewards depends only on capture, not capture and conviction. It is not the bounty hunter's job to prove guilt.

The following numbers of violent crimes committed in 1993 are from the Uniform Crime Statistics: murder and non-negligent manslaughter—24,530; forcible rape—107,810; robbery—659,760; and aggravated assault—1,135,100.[4] The potential annual cost of bounties in this particular year (in the extreme and very unrealistic case that all criminals would be captured by bounty hunters) would be $92 billion, based on the following outlays: murder, $19.6 billion; rape, $10.5 billion; robbery, $33.6 billion; and aggravated assault, $28.4 billion. However, more realistic cost estimates can be obtained by first subtracting public law enforcement arrests. The following are the approximate percentage of arrests relative to number of offenses: murder, 65 percent; rape, 52 percent; robbery, 24 percent; and assault, 56 percent. Private-sector endeavors, in a very optimistic case and in addition to public-sector arrests, might identify and arrest 20 percent of murderers, 25 percent of rapists, 25 percent of robbers, and 30 percent of assaults. This private-sector arrest rate would then result in a total annual cost of nearly $23 billion, this more-realistic sum arrived at by the total of by-type-of-crime bounties for the following: murder, $3.9 billion; rape, $2.7 billion; robbery, $8.2 billion; and assault, $8.5 billion. The dollar amount is relatively small if the crime rate falls substantially because of private sector effectiveness. If bounty hunters were effective in bringing about a crime-rate reduction, citizens could begin to regain control of their communities.

Another model, not expected to be nearly as effective, would be for governments (federal, state, and local) to contract with private-security companies in order to attempt to improve capture of criminals. Private-security companies could go through a competitive bidding process for this activity. Companies would need to meet specified criteria to be eligible, the same as in bidding for other services. In this model there would not be a bounty placed on criminals. Instead, the service of capture would be contracted out just as with other governmental services. Companies might bid an annual fee but have incentives built-in if they capture a certain percentage of criminals. The activity could be segmented by type of violent crime to include only robberies and aggravated assault, only murders, or only rapes, or it could be across the board—or for first-time offenders for all violent crimes. There are many possible combinations. The process in this model would start at the same point as for the first model, and capture of criminals would be for profit. It would take time to evaluate the effectiveness of for-profit activities compared to those of the public sector. One variation of this system is for respective government entities to issue one license per geographic area to a company that would then chase alleged criminals only in that area. This is similar to issuing a franchise, but since criminals are highly mobile, this alternative doesn't appear to be workable.

Fixed Penalties

Penalties for committing violent crimes in the first half of this century were probably much clearer to everyone. Penalties are unclear in the 1990s for two reasons: (1) the value system of the family, community, and nation is changing, and potential criminals and actual criminals perceive that costs of crime are somewhat less and benefits somewhat more than in earlier years; and (2) there is a large variation in both sentencing that criminals may receive for what appears to be the same crime and in the amount of time they may serve before parole. These two reasons suggest that benefit/cost ratios present in the 1950s and early 1960s, which were effective then, are no longer effective. Criminals, for the same generic crime, need to be penalized the same. This enables everyone—criminals, victims and law-abiding Americans—to understand costs of committing violent crimes. In addition, it will likely allow taxpayers to feel that the legal system is there to serve and protect them, not the criminal.

Many taxpayers no doubt think the legal system is too easy on the criminal, which explains the interest in three-strikes-and-you're-out laws. The reason alternatives are being considered is that voters feel the present system doesn't work. Three-strikes-and-you're-out legislation would not be part of a national debate if voters felt the present system worked. It is an initial step by citizens to restructure the legal system so that people who are guilty remain in jail. Three strikes and you're out is a step in the right direction, but it doesn't go far enough. Severe automatic prison sentences are needed for people committing violent crimes. Everyone talks about the crime problem and the criminal-justice system is responding by moving benefit/cost ratios back toward levels of earlier years. But that won't be enough because of the changing value system and variation in sentences. A more decisive but evolutionary action would be mandatory prison sentences for violent crimes, which evolves out of three strikes and you're out. This step would make clear the cost of crime as sentencing concerns would be eliminated.

Three examples of violent-crime automatic penalties would be the following: (1) A person using a weapon in committing a robbery or aggravated assault would face an automatic minimum ten-year prison sentence for a first-time offense with no opportunity for parole during that ten years; (2) rapists would have an automatic minimum ten-year prison sentence with no parole for a first time offense; and (3) someone committing murder, if captured and convicted, would face either death or life in prison with no opportunity of parole.

There would be *no* alternatives. This would make clear to everyone—criminals, potential criminals, and law-abiding citizens—the costs of crime. Criminals committing crimes would understand what would happen if caught and proven guilty. The focus of the legal system could then be on the innocent-guilty issue. Such a process is necessary for criminals both to understand the costs and to remove the perception that they can somehow work the legal system to obtain a reduced sentence or early release from prison if they are captured and convicted.

Arguments people will use against this process will include that which claims a judge or jury may be hesitant to convict some people if they think there are extenuating circumstances, perhaps suggesting the criminal shouldn't receive the full mandatory sentence, but this is one reason why the crime rate will fall. Criminals will understand the certainty of punishment and judges and juries will no longer have the ability to lighten sentencing. The job of judges and juries is only the innocence-guilt issue in this new system.

Another argument will be that prisons would overflow because of the no-parole policy. However, fewer people will choose to become criminals and commit crimes once they understand that the cost side of crime is real. Criminals will be incarcerated for a longer time period, but the number of people committing crimes will decrease, resulting in the long run in relatively fewer criminals in jail. There are several alternatives if existing jail space does become a problem in the short run. One is for the taxpayer to build additional jails. Another is to speed up privatization of punishment facilities, namely, to turn more and more of correctional punishment over to the private sector in an attempt to gain efficiencies. In the juvenile segment the number of private programs has grown faster than public programs over the past thirty years.[5] Another alternative is to utilize POW-type facilities for whatever length of time necessary. There are many such alternatives available, including military facilities and oil tankers that aren't being utilized. Another alternative is establish POW camps in other countries, that is, the United States would simply privatize incarceration to other countries—the reverse of Guantanamo Bay, which in 1994 kept Cubans and Haitians in POW-style camps. States could send prisoners to some country that was in need of funds and hire them to keep prisoners in POW-type camps. Other countries would enter into a bidding process for the incarceration of U.S. prisoners. There is ample precedent for private prisons or prisons that are run by private contractors. Many prisons in England, in particular those located in smaller communities, were run by contractors for centuries. Profit was made by charging prisoners for room and board. Prisoners worked to produce products to earn money. During the American Revolution, the English needed temporary space for their prisoners and utilized naval vessels for what turned out to be approximately a fifty-year period to house prisoners until they could be transferred to other facilities. No prisoner should ever be given early parole because of space problems, as there are many low-cost alternatives to traditional prisons that could be utilized.

Two changes—automatic sentencing for persons committing violent crimes if found guilty and a higher arrest rate through privatizing capture—would make it clear to criminals and potential criminals that the United States is no longer accommodating crime. These changes would be a giant step in returning communities to citizens.

19

Symptoms of Broken Promises—Entitlements

An explosion in entitlements, overstatement of economic activity, excessive debt, demand for lawyers, and an appetite for gambling are symptoms of broken promises. Entitlements were utilized by politicians and voters to fill the gap between what the private economy could provide and what the expectations were of the golden years, such as a good education, decent job, and safe neighborhood. People feel that because they live in the United States, they are entitled to these, and they saw very ordinary Americans do well for many years. Suddenly, it was no longer true and transfer payments began to escalate. Transfer payments have a moral-hazard characteristic, as people on the receiving end want more and more and modify their behavior to that end.

Government transfer programs—such as Social Security, Medicare, Medicaid, food stamps, and welfare benefits—designed to alleviate economic difficulties, create perverse effects on family and community values. Social Security, in earlier decades, was viewed as a supplement to personal savings, but saving, for many, is now viewed as a supplement to the Social Security check. Personal saving, at one time, was viewed as a family and community value, but no longer. In 1940, Social Security expenditures totalled $1.1 billion. In 1994, total expenditures for Social Security, welfare, and income support were $940 billion at all levels of government. Social Security and welfare created a large mass of people dependent upon workers for support. Food stamps started in 1961 for 50,000 recipients at the cost of $825,000. By 1993, there were 27 million food-stamp recipients costing taxpayers $22 billion.[1] Welfare created many more dependents. Taxpayers, according to Fund, have forked over $5 trillion on means-tested welfare since 1965.[2] The result is the creation of a permanent welfare underclass. When government gives something away, people line up to receive it. And the bigger the piece of pie government gives away, the longer the lines. People modify their behavior to qualify for the program. People's response to government programs is similar to their response to medical insurance. The provision of medical insurance results in people modifying their behavior to use medical services more intensively than they would if there were no such provision. Consumers see a lower price because of co-insurance, and a third-party, either a private company or government unit, pays the full tab, which, of course, is ultimately paid by the worker or taxpayer. This is referred to as the moral hazard of insurance. Government programs also have a moral hazard. The very act of creating a government program generates a larger and larger demand for the program, and the tab is picked up by the taxpayer.

All or nearly all people accept and support a social-welfare function to a degree. A market economy has responsibility for helping those who are less fortunate and, in particular, those unable to help themselves. Social-welfare legislation was made a central theme in the New Deal by FDR and again by LBJ in the Great Society. All modern market economies accept a degree of responsibility for social welfare along with regulating business and redistributing income. But demand for entitlement programs by voters can never be met in an economy that is going through lean years and broken promises. In this environment people always want more. Retirees in the early 1990s were getting back three to five times what they paid into Social Security, according to Pete Peterson.[3] Medicare recipients may be getting back five to twenty times what they paid in, but even then, recipients can't get enough of these entitlement programs as a stagnant or declining standard of living does not provide that to which they expected they were entitled. Many transfer-payment recipients get back much more than they put in, which make entitlements equivalent to a free lunch for them. That means someone else has to pay, and that someone else is younger taxpayers.

Redistribution of income is, of course, one point underlying entitlement programs and as indicated, society has some degree of responsibility for those in need. In particular, society has a responsibility for helping those who cannot help themselves and for helping people until they are able to help themselves. Murray states, "Through 1964, the rationale for new social action programs was the one set by Kennedy: The government should take a more active role in helping people get on their feet."[4] Murray goes on to say, "Until July 1964 most whites (and most blacks) thought in terms of equal access to opportunity."[5]

By 1967 the rationale had changed from equality of opportunity to equality of outcome.[6] Opportunity is provided by a market economy. People sponsoring the Civil Rights Act of 1964 intended that act to help achieve equality of opportunity. Preferential treatment was not part of the legislation, but as Murray indicates, President Johnson, a year later, said civil rights would be a battle for "equality as a fact and equality as a result."[7] Executive Order 11246 was signed a few months later, requiring *affirmative action* to make the transition to equality. In the meantime, as the United States was in its golden years, floodgates were opened to new and expanded programs—Medicare (for low-income), food stamps, Medicaid, antipoverty programs, Supplemental Security Income, expansions in Social Security and public assistance, namely, Aid to Families with Dependent Children, with programs such as Medicare and food stamps dependent on income level while others such as Social Security dependent on an age test.

The years of plenty petered out in the 1970s as the standard of living for many began to stagnate and decline. This brought together two major forces—the standard of living problem and the equality-of-outcome issue. The latter, defined as society's responsibility, pushed aside individual responsibility and increased pressure on taxpayers to provide more at the time that the standard of living sputtered. The gap between expectations and what the economy could provide widened as the equality-of-outcome framework added more and more costs on the market economy. Equality of outcome is the antithesis of a market economy. *Opportunity* means that people have the opportunity to obtain a public education, the opportunity to find a job, the opportunity to earn money, the opportunity to save, the opportunity to invest—taking responsibility for their lives—but it doesn't follow that people have equal outcomes in areas such as education, jobs, and income.

All college football players have an opportunity to play professional football, but professional football can't meet a goal of equality of outcome and maintain top quality. Some players are just more talented than others. How many have the talent of Troy Aikman and Emmitt Smith? Many players have an opportunity to become professional football players, but only a short list make it. In reality, all college players don't even have an equal opportunity to become professional football players as their talent levels vary. In other words, probabilities for each college football player to become a professional football player are not equal because of different talent. Are people of each ethnic and minority segment entitled to be proportionally represented? Equality of outcome in professional football is silly—likewise, for the rest of the nation.

For example, take the cases of Fred Smith with Federal Express, Ray Kroc with McDonald's, Steve Jobs with Apple, Bill Gates with Microsoft, and Sam Walton with Walmart. Can equality of outcome be mandated in developing new businesses? Are people of each ethnic and minority segment entitled to be proportionally represented? A market economy can't do it. Courts can't do it without killing off the economy any more than they can do it in professional football without killing professional football. Do people even have an equal opportunity to do what Fred Smith, Ray Kroc, Steve Jobs, Sam Walton, Bill Gates, Emmitt Smith, or Troy Aikman did? Of course not. People are different. They have different skills. People with different skills have an opportunity to do something of value for themselves and society, but they do not even have equality of opportunity—much less equality of outcomes—to do the same function. Buzzwords such as equality of income, housing, and education are methods politicians utilize to garner votes, pitch population segment against segment, and polarize ethnic groups, but equality of outcome to earn the same education, income, and house is an *impossibility*. An economy can provide an opportunity to gain a quality education, a reasonable income, and an affordable house. An economy can do that by implementing policies aimed at having a strong educational system or making it easy to start a business, own a business, and hire workers, for example.

U.S. policies are *not* oriented in that direction (as explained in earlier chapters). Instead, policies are oriented toward entitlements that amount to equality of opportunity and outcome. Everyone, once they reach a certain age or fall below a certain income level, earns the same entitlement. Government entitlements meet both equality of opportunity and equality of outcome definitions. A market economy can't provide equality of outcome, but government can and does through entitlements. Voters want more and more entitlements, and politicians rush to provide more and more. Entitlements are becoming an increasing taxpayer burden because of the absolute size of entitlements relative to number of taxpayers.

Politicians sell entitlements under the guise of security, but those entitlements need to be paid for by someone. Entitlement spending results in government spending growing faster than income. This trend makes it unlikely that the United States can reverse its decline in the standard of living per job. Entitlements and mandates take away incentives for private-sector wealth generation. Entitlements and mandates make it harder and harder to generate wealth and therefore to meet the growing tax burden. It goes around and around. Larger entitlements and more mandates create demand for more entitlements and mandates. Larger Social Security payments mean people save less during their working lives. The less they save during their working lives, the greater the demand for larger Social Security payments. Income safety nets increased dramatically over the past few decades with Social Security, Medicare, Medicaid, unemployment compensation, food stamps, Supplemental Security Income, and welfare, for example. These were relatively small programs at the start, but politicians and recipients turned them into huge entitlement programs.

The Health Security Act proposed by President Clinton in 1993 was an example of a potentially huge entitlement program. Clinton's proposal was also an example of an attempt to mandate equality of opportunity as well as equality of outcome. Under the Clinton proposal, all people would be entitled to health care; thus, it provided equality of opportunity. A federal bureaucracy would have defined health-benefit packages for everyone, which would have met the equality of outcome goal. A market economy can't do this, but government could have with a mandate. The ability of people to earn a living is punished when government replaces the market.

Growth of entitlement programs continues to shift from an income safety net to an equality-of-outcome safety net. Inequality of income was important at one time, but traditional income-redistribution policies and entitlements eliminated many concerns about poverty. Perceived inequality—namely, among race, sex, and the handicapped—has instead become the major focus. Tremendous progress toward a color-blind society was made as some segments steadily improved their standard of living. Black Americans integrated into the dominant culture from the 1960s to the present. That middle-class entitlement was at least partially achieved. However, the emphasis shifted to equality of cultural outcomes—Mexican-American, black American, Asian-American, and others. Each wants its culture accepted, not integrated—that is, an entitlement of acceptance of cultures or equality-of-culture outcome—something a market economy cannot do. A market cannot make cultures equal or their acceptance equal, but government, through the educational system, can move toward it over time through cultural mandates such as courses in cultural awareness.

The dominant culture at one time had a set of values—the Protestant ethic—and had altruistic ideas of helping others not able to help themselves in addition to those of hard work, saving, and participating in a traditional family as well as community life. A market economy works well under such a set of values as ordinary people get pushed and pulled up the ladder. Entitlement programs such as Social Security, Medicare, Medicaid, unemployment, and welfare also work under such a value system, or they work as long as citizens receiving these benefits are part of this set of values. Through 1964, as pointed out above, government helped people get up on their feet as well as helping those unable to help themselves.

Social Security worked in earlier decades, when people saved a larger portion of their income for retirement. That was their set of values. Social Security was viewed as a supplement to their savings. For those not able to save much, Social Security ended up being a safety net—a relatively small one. Congress, over several decades, increased Social Security benefits in order to pull up the standard of living of those unable to save enough for retirement, that is, Congress increased the magnitude of the safety net. This process, even though well-intentioned, had the effect of allowing others—those who were saving—to decrease their personal-savings rate during their working years. Congress passed benefit increases of 7 percent in 1965, 13 percent in 1967, 15 percent in 1969, and indexed Social Security benefits to the Consumer Price Index (CPI) in 1972. Perhaps as early as the 1970s and for sure by the 1980s, many viewed personal savings as a supplement to the Social Security check (figure 19.1). It appears from figure 19.1 that a Social Security tax rate of perhaps 10 percent was the critical point at which people decided a government mandate altered the nation's personal-savings rate. President Nixon, in 1972, signed on to indexing of benefits to changes in the CPI just in time for major U.S. inflation increases during the remainder of the 1970s. The combined Social Security tax increased from 9.6 percent in 1970 to 12.26 percent in 1980, while the base jumped

FIGURE 19.1
Social Security Tax Rate vs. Personal Savings Rate

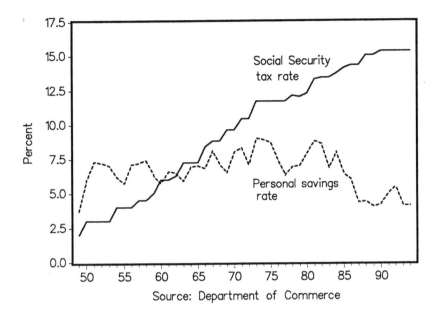

Source: Department of Commerce

from $7,800 to $25,900 over the same time period. These changes helped cement the process of turning Social Security from a saving supplement to a pension.

Social Security was run as a pay-as-you-go system for decades. People who would draw benefits at retirement paid for benefits to those who were drawing them at the time. This worked well as long as the ratio of employed to retired stayed about the same, and benefits of the retired didn't greatly change. It was obvious by the time President Carter arrived in Washington that major changes were occurring. The key ones were that a baby bust was underway which would impact, eventually, the ratio of employed to retired; relative to the 1960s, the employment level in percentage terms was reduced (unemployment was higher), which meant fewer relative workers paying in; and life spans were lengthening, which increased the amount of benefits paid. In addition to these factors, inflation increases ran wild during the 1970s, while real wages for the majority of jobs headed down. This was the first Social Security crisis. Congress and the administration agreed to gradual increases in the payroll tax, which was supposed to solve the Social Security crisis. That was a major shift toward the pension concept instead of a savings supplement that FDR had intended. By the time President Reagan appeared on the scene the crisis had worsened, and Reagan promised to keep Social Security as the major component of his income safety net.

In 1981 President Reagan appointed a bipartisan committee, chaired by Alan Greenspan, to study the problem and issue a report after the 1982 congressional elections. Based on the recommendations in this report, a law was signed in April 1983 demonstrating to Americans that higher tax rates and application of those taxes to higher base levels made Social Security a pension that retirees could count on.

Social Security may work for individuals, but it doesn't work for the U.S. economy as personal saving is reduced because of the expected certainty of Social Security; essentially, public mandates reduced private saving. Social Security is an example of a program established with the best of intentions that had an unintended outcome. It altered societal values—workers saved less. The Economic Recovery Tax Act of 1981 incorporated individual retirement accounts (IRA) that were supposedly going to increase the personal-savings rate. That didn't work. One obvious reason was that prosaving influences of IRAs were in direct competition with antisaving influences of Social Security reform. In addition, the tax system (see chapter 7) contributes to a low personal-savings rate.

Influence of other governmental transfer programs such as welfare programs on Protestant-ethic values has been well documented. Murray points to state policies such as welfare policy leading to broad shifts in cultural norms; for instance, single women are rewarded for having additional children. What once was considered unacceptable is now the norm. This has had expected effects on a core inner-city population of young people who have grown up with little or no parental supervision and very limited or poor education. Murray suggests that "illegitimacy is the single most important social problem of our time," and goes on to state it drives other problems in society such as crime and illiteracy.[8] It is also a major economic problem in that it is driven by economic incentives and requires taxpayer support as funds are thrown at problems originating from illegitimacy. Government programs create the conditions resulting in illegitimacy, which, in turn, creates the need for more programs to solve the problems resulting from illegitimacy—a vicious circle.

Black illegitimacy reached 68 percent of births to black women in 1992, while illegitimacy for whites was at 23 percent. Murray suggests that women with high-school educations or less account for 82 percent of illegitimate white births.[9] The future for many children born to single parents is grim. Consequences for the economy are well known and include the development of a segment of the population that has become a ward of the state and a long-term growing burden on society— an *underclass*.[10] Welfare is an excellent example of a program established with good intentions that created a monumental problem for society through altering values. Murray suggests that a solution involves having the state back away from interfering with natural forces of society.[11]

Mandates such as Environmental Protection Agency (EPA) and Labor Department regulations are well-intentioned and each has it merits, but the cumulative effect of mandates is that they create a business environment in which it is more difficult to start a business, expand a business, and hire workers. Unemployment benefits are needed to help tide unemployed workers over in the time period between jobs. Congress, in their effort to supposedly help employed workers, created a climate in which businesses find it necessary to unload the increased costs of doing business onto their workers in order to maintain profitability. Larger unemployment benefits and extended unemployment benefits are necessary to cope with the resulting anti-job-growth environment created. Congressional mandates are creating a situation in which it is harder and harder to follow through on the Protestant work ethic because entitlement programs, in altering the value system, move some segments away from the Protestant work ethic.

Progress toward the entitlement of a color-blind society can be found in a book entitled *Edge City: Life on the New Frontier* by Joel Garreau, in which the author chronicles the rapid expansion of the black middle class. In this book, middle class is defined in terms of income, the same standard as the dominant culture; that is, black Americans, in striving toward a color-blind society, moved to adopt values of the dominant culture. This new American black middle class may expand to become as large in percentage terms relative to total blacks as the white middle class is to the total white population in the 2010 decade.[12] Many blacks are doing like others in the United States—pulling themselves up by their bootstraps over a long period of time, as the Polish, Italian, and Irish immigrants did in earlier times.

Garreau estimates that approximately one-third of blacks are suburban middle class. Another third are what he calls the working class, people who do relatively well when unemployment rates are low, as they were in the 1980s.[13] Garreau also suggests that the remaining third of blacks live in poverty, and about one-third of that number—10 percent of the total black population—make up hopeless *underclass neighborhoods*.[14] These are neighborhoods dominated by unemployed high school dropouts and female-headed families having characteristics at the opposite end of the Protestant ethic. However, a large and growing number of blacks are in or moving into the middle class, and Garreau suggests that the poorer blacks can also pull themselves up the income scale over time as well.[15]

Garreau fails to mention a major obstacle in the road to major gains by poverty-level people. Immigrants in the earlier part of this century lived in an economy where many very ordinary people experienced a rapidly rising standard of living in subsequent decades—except for the 1930s. Immigrants in the 1920s and their succeeding generations moved through a strong education system. Education is more of a key to future success for a country and its citizens than ever before. An average high-school graduate in the 1990s is ill-prepared to obtain a decent-paying job or to go to college. In comparison, an average high-school graduate in the 1920s or even the 1950s was much better equipped for a decent-paying job or for entering college. It is difficult to expect people in the 1990s to make the rapid progress that immigrants and their descendants did in the early part of this century as the economy is much more rigid in the 1990s. Another major difference is that in the 1990s the income safety net is large, and some proportion of people of all ethnic segments may not have the economic incentive to pull themselves up by their bootstraps. In earlier decades there was a major incentive to pull oneself up—that was to keep food on the table. That incentive is not nearly as strong in the 1990s. In addition, for those attempting to pull themselves up, it is much more difficult to obtain a quality public education, live in safety, and find a decent-paying job.

The Protestant ethic led to a materialistic culture which a healthy market economy delivered for many. The focus has shifted from a color-blind society to equality of outcomes for separate cultures. Different cultures have different rules, and a market economy founded on the Protestant ethic can't function nearly as well as it once did in that new environment. Government mandates on developing curriculum in the U.S. educational system, such as in the Excellence in Education Act, can move this country toward equality of different cultures over time. Movement away from the dominant culture toward an array of subcultures means the economy doesn't work as well as before, and the broken promises of this past decade are likely to be continued for many more. It is one thing to talk about citizens of a country moving toward one dominant culture when there are commonly understood rules; it is quite another to learn a new set of rules and attempt to force the economy to fit those rules, which seems likely to result in disappointment for many.

Other examples also illustrate how silly the objective of equality of outcome has become. Taller people tend to earn higher incomes than shorter people. Is Congress going to pass legislation requiring that people can't be discriminated against because of height? Good-looking people have an advantage over ugly people. Is Congress going to require that attractive women marry ugly men in order to breed-out ugliness? Or are ugly people going to demand plastic surgery under the Americans for Disability Act? Are fat people discriminated against relative to people who are not overweight? One can argue that each of these situations is not an equal outcome. Lawsuits are filed on issues such as height and weight as there are people that are actually serious about this stuff. A market economy provides an opportunity to progress educationally and professionally in life, but some of the above groups do relatively better than others, such as tall people versus short people.

Progress of ethnic groups during the past thirty years suggests major success in moving toward the dominant culture. Tremendous progress toward entitlement of a color-blind society was achieved. Congress passed the Civil Rights Act of 1964, prohibiting discrimination in employment and public accommodations. President Eisenhower earlier signed the Voting Rights Act of 1960, which authorized federal courts to appoint voting referees to register black voters. Progress in the past thirty years for ethnic groups was perhaps equal to that of the integration of Polish-Americans, Italian-Americans, and Irish-Americans into the dominant culture in the period from 1910 to 1940. It is an entirely different situation, however, as a society moves toward equality of different minority groups and cultures. This movement has picked up momentum, and society is being driven along a road filled with dissatisfaction, as the war over cultures with its polarization of ethnic groups builds and perhaps becomes the cold war replacement. The educational system, already a problem, is apt to deteriorate more as it mandates its way toward cultural awareness—with federal mandates such as *Goals 2000* and the Excellence in Education Act—and away from basic knowledge. Educational problems in the past have been localized in the primary and secondary public-school systems. Movement toward a culturally and ethnic-group-blind society impacts colleges as they include more courses in cultural and minority-group awareness and perhaps move away from basic knowledge and skill courses.

Why the push toward a culturally and minority-group-blind society? The dominant culture was primarily that comprised of the Protestant-ethic values—obtaining a good education, working hard, and enjoying a rising standard of living. Fighting the cold war and its impact on the standard of living hit about the time the entitlement system was in place, and entitlements grew rapidly. Entitlement programs, as described above by Murray, as well as the push toward equality of outcomes in general, have been slowly tearing apart basic family and community values. In its place is a movement toward a culturally or minority-group-blind society that has as its premise no dominant culture but rather the equality of many cultures. Teaching cultural and minority-group awareness and acceptance in grade schools, high schools, and the university system suggests that it may take a generation or more before those lessons become imbedded. Reasons for this movement apparently have to do with ethnic and minority groups not wanting to adopt values of the dominant culture and instead to have their cultures be viewed as equal to the dominant culture.

One can speculate on reasons for this movement, and some of these considerations include (1) the desire to keep their own culture or minority group identity; (2) a dislike of dominant culture values; (3) a dislike of the Protestant ethic; (4) an inability for some to pull themselves up by their bootstraps to be in the dominant culture or "sour grapes"; and (5) the motives of leaders of ethnic and minority groups not wanting their followers to integrate because ethnic and minority-group leaders would then be out of jobs.

Examples of cultures and minority groups include Mexican-American, black American, native American, Indian-American, Asian-American, feminists, the elderly, the poor, the rich, the physically and mentally disabled, the uninsured, people with diseases, preschoolers, teenagers, single parents, divorced singles, gays, inner-city youth, smokers, religious groups, small business, minority business, new businesses, big business, farmers, blue-collar workers, and on and on. Groups, cultures, and their representatives want entitlements ranging from a monthly check to a parking space, from a subsidy to grow tobacco to a place to smoke, and from a decrease in capital-gains tax to a mortgage-interest deduction. The United States is moving toward this entitlement of equality of cultures and minority segments. It is not working well and it won't since it depends on mandates and entitlements—a what's-in-it-for-me mentality.

Entitlements work if everyone is playing by the same rules—namely, those governing working, saving, and family and community life, and such—and the list of entitlements that people ask for is short. Under equality of cultures and minority segments, there is an endless list of demands. Entitlements won't work because different cultures and groups have alternative rules. In particular, all groups want entitlements, but not all groups contribute to the tax base, family base, community base, and saving base of a country whose economy evolved along the lines of the Protestant ethic. Premises of the Protestant ethic allowed ordinary people to do very well and progress rapidly. Mandated social and economic progress make it very difficult for ordinary people to do well. That is what broken promises are about. Ordinary people resort more and more to governmental mandates to dole out largess and to ensure that each culture and minority group gets their fair share. In establishing mandates, voters and elected officials, to date, have allowed costs to be pushed to either the ultimate consumer or onto the backs of workers, the productive segment of society that allows U.S. business to earn an adequate rate of return and be competitive.

20

More Symptoms

Entitlement growth resulted in politicians at the federal level setting outlays independently of tax revenue from the 1970s onward. In comparison, entities at the state and local level need to balance their budgets. Government outlays growing faster than the economy eventually leads to slowing economic growth, which, in turn, constrains tax revenue. In the 1950s and 1960s, politicians at the federal level set spending levels so that they had some relation to tax revenue, and they were able to do so because the U.S. economy was strong. The economic vulnerability of the United States was brought home after 1973, and broken promises were apparent. Elected officials moved away from fiscal responsibility because voters wanted entitlements more than fiscal responsibility. It is more difficult for politicians to control federal expenditures when the private sector of the economy is unable to deliver on people's expectations.

Tocqueville's observation in *Democracy in America*, first published in 1840, still stands.

> There are always a multitude of men engaged in difficult or novel undertakings, which they follow by themselves without shackling themselves to their fellows. Such persons will admit, as a general principle, that the public authority ought not to interfere in private concerns; but, by an exception [to] that rule, each of them craves its assistance in the particular concern on which he is engaged and seeks to draw upon the influence of the government for his own benefit, although he would restrict it on all other occasions. If a large number of men applies this particular exception to a great variety of different purposes, the sphere of the central power extends itself imperceptibly in all directions, although everyone wishes it to be circumscribed."[1]

An economy that fails to deliver a rising standard of living finds that public-sector growth overwhelms the private sector because more and more voters want assistance from government for their particular concerns. Both the decline in the standard of living for many and the broken promises set in motion a process which led to overstatement of U.S. economic activity, a large demand for lawyers, and explosive growth of lotteries.

Overstatement of Economic Activity

The chapters on education and safety illustrated a major difficulty with government outlays—they are not productive. Real spending per capita increases rapidly, but quality of service declines or doesn't improve. This results in economic activity being overstated because of the method from which the government portion of economic activity is derived. Economic activity is calculated by three different methods—the spending, income, and production methods—which result in the same level of economic activity—over $6.7 trillion in 1994. The following briefly summarizes these three different methods.

The spending method is the most widely discussed method. In it economic activity ($6.7 trillion) is viewed as measure of demand for U.S. output in terms of four major components—consumption, investment, government purchases, and net exports. The income method is the flip side of the spending method in that whatever is spent on U.S. output becomes income, dividends, rent, taxes, or depreciation to someone, all of which, in this method, can be utilized to obtain economic activity or gross domestic product. The production method adds what is produced by three sectors—business, nonprofit institutions and households, and general government (federal, state, and local)—to obtain economic activity.

These three different methods provide the same level of economic activity as well as providing a check on business-sector activity but not that of government. For instance, employees at Compaq computer are compensated for their work. The outlay of compensation for employees in the economy along with that for rent, taxes, and other outlays can be compared to spending. Compaq-produced computers are sold in the marketplace at a price that customers pay. This allows matching of production with spending. Customers don't purchase products that are not useful to them, and that being the case, production of the product or service would decrease. That would mean fewer employees needed by Compaq for production. Spending, in this case, falls, but so do compensation and production. The different methods of calculating economic activity act as a check on each other for that portion of the economy producing goods and services sold to customers.

Government production is an entirely different situation. Functions of government, such as education, safety, and Congress, provide services that can't be measured as the services are not directly sold in the marketplace. Government employees, in general, are involved in activities that are not measured. Employees of Compaq computer produce a product or service sold in the marketplace. Government activities, in comparison, are not directly valued. Instead, the value assigned to government functions is based on an input basis—what people are paid. In other words, the more Congress pays themselves, the higher the U.S. economic activity. Similarly for other government functions such as safety and education, an increase in salaries means that U.S. economic activity increases. The relative increase in salaries in safety, education, and all government services and functions over past decades means that U.S. economic activity originating from those sectors has increased, even though the quality of what was produced has decreased. This means U.S. economic activity is overstated in that higher salaries for government employees and more government employees mean increases in economic activity, while the quality of what is produced declines or stagnates. The author estimates that U.S. economic activity may be overstated by 10 percent or more.

A method to pump up the reported level of economic activity is to hire more government employees at federal, state, and local levels, but it is very misleading as services produced are of questionable value. Overstatements of economic activity occur because of the entitlement mentality resulting from broken promises. Whenever a question arises about a slowdown in national economic activity, programs are passed by legislators to pump up economic activity. Hiring more government workers results in increased economic activity. Such programs have been hailed as a success for pumping up economic activity, but economic activity didn't go up by producing a product or service that a customer bought but by hiring more government workers. The Crime Bill of 1994 had that effect as government payrolls increased. Hiring more government workers is an artificial method to inflate national economic activity and lower the unemployment rate, as nothing of value is produced. Programs such as those contained in the Crime Bill appear to be prima-

FIGURE 20.1
Annual Federal Deficit

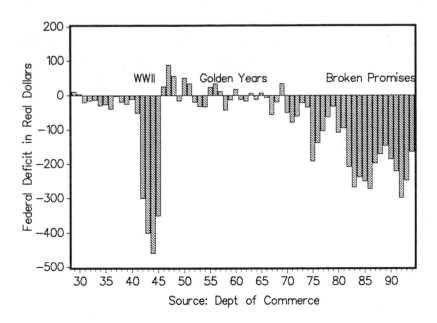

Source: Dept of Commerce

rily make-work programs aimed at pumping up reported economic activity, while nothing is produced.

Debt

Broken promises result in more and more citizens wanting benefits from government, even though these same people may profess to want limited government. Government expenditures bring with them intrusion via mandates that affect all segments of the economy, which further burdens the economy, making it more difficult to grow and expand. Elected officials respond with deficits that are a back-door method of hiking future taxes. (See figure 20.1, which illustrates voter demand for federal expenditures.) Politicians began setting expenditures independent of revenues in the 1970s resulting in large annual deficits. Deficits disappeared after World War II when the United States entered its golden age. Voters didn't feel the need to turn to government for help during the golden age because citizens enjoyed a rapidly rising standard of living, and politicians didn't feel the need to overpromise. That changed with a declining purchasing power for many private-sector jobs. People turned to the public sector for assistance, but more governmental intrusion creates a situation in which the economy grows slower, thereby creating more pressure to increase government outlays.

Pressure to increase government outlays is always present, and figure 20.2 illustrates the long-term upward drift in expenditures relative to national income. (Government outlays in figure 20.2 are federal plus state plus local government outlays.) Pressures to increase governmental outlays are greater when the economy is relatively weak. Most people and sectors of the economy have their hands in the trough, and government expenditures per dollar of income have spiraled upward from twenty-six cents in 1950 to forty-two cents in 1994. It is very difficult to reverse the trend in figure 20.2, because even though people know that benefits ought to be limited, they believe that they should be limited only for others. That makes slowing or reducing benefits potentially politically explosive. Politicians run for cover if slowing or reducing Social Security benefits is mentioned, because voters vote with their feet. Another alternative is to increase taxes, but the American taxpayers are already overtaxed, taxpayers know it, and they vote with their feet on this issue too. Another alternative is the one being followed, which is borrow more, but the U.S. fiscal house is already in disarray. The last option is print money.

Meanwhile the revenue side presents a picture (figure 20.3) in which the revenue-generating ability of the economy is running out of steam because of the heavy tax burden on taxpayers. Revenue per dollar of income tended to flatten from 1970 onward under a tax system of both high and low marginal tax rates. Marginal income-tax rates remained at 70 percent during the 1970s, while the Social Security combined tax rate increased from 9.6 percent in 1970 to 12.26 percent in 1979. During the 1980s the top federal statutory marginal personal income-tax rate decreased from 70 percent in 1970 to 28 percent in 1988, while the Social Security combined tax rate was at 15.02 percent in 1989 and 15.3 percent in 1990 (also the 1994 level). The Social Security maximum

FIGURE 20.2
Government Expenditures per Dollar of Income

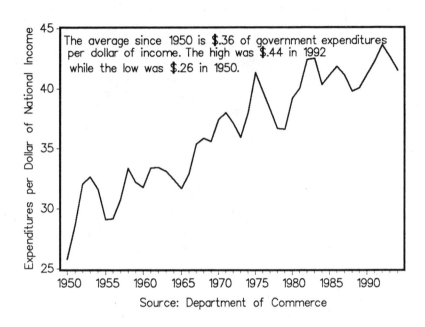

The average since 1950 is $.36 of government expenditures per dollar of income. The high was $.44 in 1992 while the low was $.26 in 1950.

Source: Department of Commerce

base income went from $25,900 in 1980 to $51,300 in 1990 and to $60,600 in 1994. These and other changes to the tax code for the median four-person family resulted in federal average tax rates moving from near 16 percent in 1970 to almost 25 percent in 1994. The average federal tax burden increased during that time period in addition to the combined state and local burden. Voters wanted benefits to be doled out from government. Politicians, in order to pay for that, continued hiking taxes at not only the federal level but also the state and local levels. Tax revenue didn't keep pace with expenditures, as economic activity suffered because of the high-tax burden.

Annual deficits are a method to provide current benefits to voters but are an obligation for taxpayers down the road. Annual deficits result in a very large outstanding federal real per capita debt (as illustrated in

FIGURE 20.3
Government Revenues per Dollar of Income

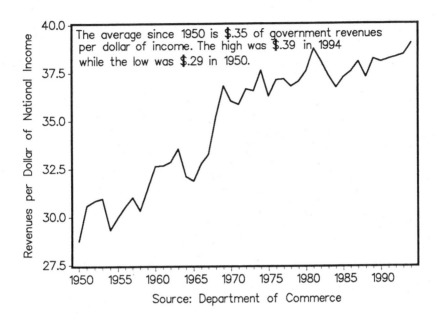

The average since 1950 is $.35 of government revenues per dollar of income. The high was $.39 in 1994 while the low was $.29 in 1950.

Source: Department of Commerce

figure 20.4). At the end of World War II, the United States had over $15,000 of outstanding federal debt for each man, woman, and child. Per capita outstanding federal debt in 1994 was $17,700 per person. Domestic entitlements expanded rapidly since outstanding federal debt hit its low of $6,800 per capita in 1974. Broken promises came home to roost in the form of increasing government outlays per dollar of economic activity. Annual deficits and cumulative federal debt are delayed taxes that someone pays, either through actual tax increases or through loss of purchasing power of the dollar. Excessive expansion of the money supply leads to loss of purchasing power, and it is a method some central governments choose to pay off the outstanding-debt burden.

Inflation is an expensive method to pay off debt, but it may become the only politically acceptable outcome for some countries. The nomi-

FIGURE 20.4
Outstanding Federal Per Capita Debt

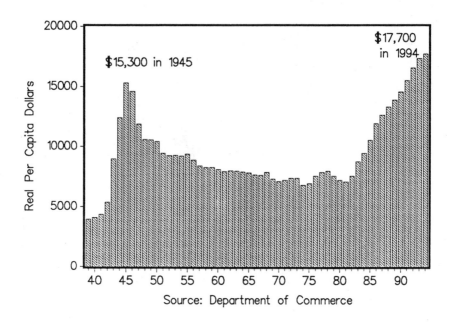

Source: Department of Commerce

nal economic pie becomes much larger with higher rates of inflation. In turn, that makes the face value of Treasury debt issued in previous years worth much less in today's dollars. A relatively large per capita federal outstanding debt is but one problem for society. Less obvious problems created for society at the federal level are the proliferation in size and number of federal programs and entities that create taxpayer exposure—$14 trillion (figure 20.5). Federal debt outstanding is shown as one problem area. Goodies having unfunded liabilities are postponed tax burdens. It's a method politicians follow to provide benefits but delay the tax collector. Programs with unfunded liabilities (promises to pay) include Social Security, federal employee retirement and disability benefits, nuclear waste disposal, and crop insurance. Unfunded liabilities are a method to win votes while delay-

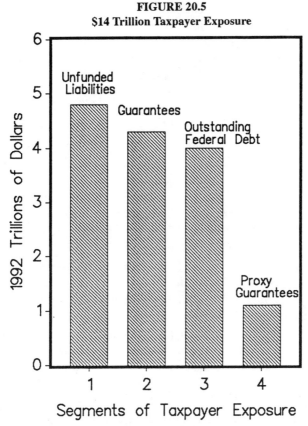

FIGURE 20.5
$14 Trillion Taxpayer Exposure

Segments of Taxpayer Exposure

ing the time the tax collector comes through the front door. Roy Webb of the Federal Reserve Bank of Richmond estimated unfunded liabilities of the federal government at $4.2 trillion and suggested that estimate was probably on the low side, though the $4 trillion is an amount equal to the total outstanding federal debt.[2] Lawrence Lindsey, a member of the Board of Governors of the Federal Reserve, places unfunded liabilities of Social Security in 1994 at $6.7 trillion, an amount in excess of the Federal debt outstanding.[3]

Another method Congress utilizes to dole out benefits without setting off the ire of taxpayers is through guarantees, which are off-budget items backed 100 percent by taxpayers. But guarantees don't appear in the federal budget until the taxpayer is brought in. This is one more method of extending federal programs and involvement without increasing federal outlays. Deposit insurance is the largest federal guarantee. In Roy Webb's study cited above, deposits insured amounted to $2.8 trillion, this amount being only the official amount insured in federally insured institutions. Behavior of regulators suggests depositors have come to expect to be paid off regardless of the amount, in particular when it's a large institution, but taxpayers are only legally committed to the $2.8 trillion. Problems, when talking about guarantees, seem to stay under wraps as long as possible. In 1989 people such as William Seidman, former head of the Resolution Trust Corporation, implied that trends in the Savings and Loan (S and L) industry were pretty good. People were talking positively until shortly before costs to U.S. taxpayers of the S and L bailout became publicly known. When a guarantee such as deposit insurance goes bad, it slides over to the unfunded liability category. Then the Treasury sells bonds, and taxpayer money pays off depositors.

Other guarantees include the Government National Mortgage Association, Federal Housing Administration, and Veterans Administration. The sum of these other guarantees may have potential exposure of $1 trillion. These agencies are large bureaucracies that can lead to increasing exposure and duplicate private-sector functions. Voters and their elected representatives apparently want to help segments of society purchase houses via these programs. It would entail much less cost as well as risk to provide those segments a tax credit or outright gift and allow the private sector to make the loans. A government-sponsored enterprise (GSE) is another method that Congress utilizes to provide benefits to their constituencies without increasing taxes. GSEs are federally chartered institutions and not subject to state and local taxation. They have a cost advantage and can be considered near monopolies. Examples of GSEs include Federal National Mortgage Association, Federal Home Loan Mortgage Corporation, and Farm Credit Banks.

Lawyers

The world-leadership position held by the United States over the past fifty years weakened the U.S. economy relative to other economies that U.S. policies helped strengthen. Politicians responded to voter concerns by increasing government outlays and by intervening in the economy.

When the standard of living is increasing rapidly, the majority of people feel they have an opportunity to improve their lot in life. John F. Kennedy said it best: "A rising tide lifts all boats." The United States enjoyed such a period from World War II until 1973. When the majority of people feel their opportunity is more limited, as it has been since 1973, they turn to government as well as to the legal system for goodies.

People tend to reach out for assistance if they think the future is not what it once was. People want some degree of security, and if the job market doesn't provide it, people turn elsewhere. Lawyers, as a profession, were well suited to attempt to fill the gap between the private economy and people's expectations. A sputtering economy led to increasing legislation for entitlements that Congress, comprised mostly of lawyers, passed. Entitlements and laws need to be enforced, which increased demand for lawyers. The more people felt the economy didn't provide opportunity, the more they utilized the legal system. Figure 20.6 illustrates the fact that prior to the 1970s, demand for lawyers, while increasing, was increasing rather slowly. Post-1970 the demand for lawyers increased rapidly as the standard of living stagnated. Figure 20.6 can be looked at two ways: (1) productivity of lawyers decreased in the sense that one lawyer could provide services to twice as many people prior to 1970 than he or she did in 1991, or (2) demand for lawyers increased sharply as improvement in the standard of living slowed. People become lawyers for the same reason that people choose other professions—they find it attractive. Post-1970 many more people chose to become lawyers because the profession was more attractive relative to other professions.

It didn't happen overnight but the point is that a relative increase in the number of lawyers in the post-1970 period indicates an economy in difficulty. More relative lawyers is a sign of an economy that does not provide security of opportunity. An economy that attempts to provide that security to people through the legal system is an indication of problems. More laws, entitlements, and governmental intrusion in the economy increase demand for lawyers. People turn to lawyers to obtain their entitlement, whether that is a mandated entitlement or an entitlement of equality of culture or entitlement of income from a lawsuit. Tort reform addresses the result, not the cause. In addition, the fact that there are more criminals means more lawyers needed to defend them as well as more need trying to convict them.

FIGURE 20.6
Lawyer Productivity

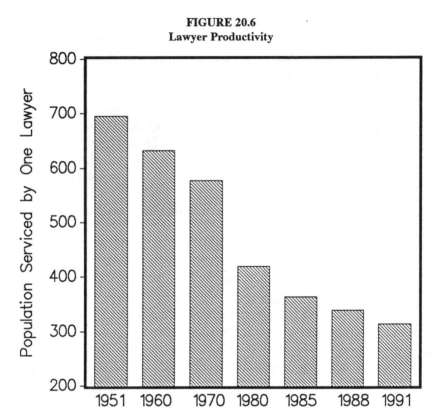

Source: Statistical Abstract

Lotteries

Lotteries are not new in the United States as lotteries. They were used to help finance ventures in colonial days such as schools, roads, and bridges. Opposition to lotteries increased in the nineteenth century because lotteries, it was felt, had harmful effects on low-income groups and gambling was deemed to be morally wrong. There were no government-sponsored lotteries from 1894 to 1964. New Hampshire, in 1964, was the first state in this century to enact a lottery. State lotteries rely on the pure dependence of randomly drawn numbers and do not require active player participation. The New Hampshire lottery was adopted with the purpose of slowing the increase in the local property-tax rates with revenues earmarked for education. New York, in 1968, became the second lottery state. In the 1970s and 1980s, government-sponsored lotteries spread across the United States. In 1990 only eighteen states were without lotteries, and thirteen of those were located in the south and southwest. Lotteries are usually perceived as regressive, but if tax revenues are earmarked for education, then low-income groups benefit, which tends to make lotteries more proportional in their incidence.

The rapid spread of lotteries reflected the need of states to increase tax revenue without actually calling the lottery a tax. The ability of the states' economies to handle additional tax burdens was already being questioned twenty years ago. States started going after additional tax revenue by sneaking in the back door. But the major driving force of lotteries is demand, as lottery participants feel lotteries give them a chance to get ahead—not a realistic chance but a chance. The rapid increase in lotteries since the 1970s reflects the sputtering standard of living. In turn, this has resulted in voters asking state governments to give them a lottery for a chance at "easy-street." States do not have the power to print money, so lotteries are a source of tax revenue in addition to allowing lottery participants to do what they want, which is to try and get ahead.

Part III

The Future—Change?

21

The Future?

Policies the United States implements are a highly useful predictor of the future's broad outline. This has been the case for the major thrust of foreign and domestic policy over the past fifty years. The classic foreign-policy example, described in this book, is the world-leadership role taken by the United States after World War II in order to encourage development of strong market economies around the globe to contain the Soviet Union. Large government transfer programs having a moral-hazard characteristic also shared wealth internally. This set of external and internal wealth-sharing policies led to both lean years and broken promises for workers and taxpayers and helped to erode basic institutions such as family, community, work, saving, education, and safety. Once basic institutions began their meltdown, the decline of the United States relative to other countries was not far behind.

That meltdown process was underway in the 1960s for African-American families and slowly spread across society. Adverse macroeconomic numbers in the 1970s such as high inflation and oil prices—in addition to the ongoing cold war—covered over bubbling problems in U.S. economic and social institutions. The ending of the cold war laid bare the breaking apart of the underlying economic-social consumer-sector fabric for everyone to see in the 1990s.

These changes appear to suggest a dichotomy as U.S. business continues to do about as well as always (chapters 14 and 15). Still, many people encounter lean years and broken promises as fundamental institutions in this economy break apart. Business as well as financial markets did well in the 1980s, yet many people did not participate in the upswing. That theme was one of the cornerstones of Clinton's 1992 campaign. It is a popular theme, but, of course, it is aimed at the wealth-generating part of the United States—business. The culprit is not business but centralized social and economic programs that were rolled out over the past fifty years to help U.S. citizens as well foreign countries—wealth-sharing programs.

There are two reasons for this apparent dichotomy. One is that politicians, to date, have been clever enough to pass mandates and laws that affect the business sector that business, for the most part, has been able to off-load on customers and employees. That means individuals bore the full burden of external and internal wealth-sharing policies that led to broken promises. Punish business through such mechanisms as price controls to pinch both profit margins and cash flow so that business shares broken promises, and the downhill slide of the economy becomes rapid. But the consumer sector can experience broken promises for decades without necessarily generating changes that might lead to a major upheaval.

Another reason for the dichotomy is that as Peter Drucker states, companies are in the business of creating and satisfying customers. Business adapts to changing environments by making necessary changes, as shown in individual businesses operating in many different countries having different cultures. A business is a flexible dynamic institution. Companies that don't or can't adapt go out of business. As long as a company satisfies its customers and maintains its internal discipline, a business can operate in various domestic environments as well as foreign countries. Companies adjust or else—unless the state steps in to prop them up. Changes in business always result in short-term dislocations of human and physical capital, but for the economy as a whole, such changes are part of the normal process of evolution.

Evolve or go out of business, however, is not the case for basic institutions such as the family, community, and society mores. A corporation can make many changes in its products or services, where it does business, and its organization, yet it can continue to function effectively. But the family unit, the community, and social mores, while slowly changing over time, seem to have limitations on the degree of change. A simple example is personal saving. Government attempted through Social Security to remove that responsibility for people. That grand experiment placed severe strains on the economy as the government learned it runs into problems when it attempts to replace individual responsibility for saving. Personal saving also suffered because the tax system punishes savers (as explained in chapter 7). Saving is a responsibility that seems to work best when individuals do it and is a necessary one for an economy to function. Aid to families with dependent children is another example in which government attempted to socialize individual responsibility by paying the head of the family to have and take care of her children, and that experiment has had an adverse effect on individual responsibility. Once change goes too far, the economic and social building blocks become stretched, torn, and dysfunctional. That seems to be the position the United States is in during the 1990s.

Popularity of business ethics is an example illustrating concerns many have with family and community values. Business is doing what it has always done—provide products and services to customers. The array of products and services is no doubt of better quality, on average, than twenty years ago. The quantity of products and services produced has also increased as business responded to customer demands. Business is doing its job, yet the cry for more business ethics grows louder, and businesses and educational institutions have moved to incorporate business ethics into classrooms and daily operations.

Universities across the United States have installed business-ethics courses as part of their curricula. Corporations have adopted more policy guidelines on ethical behavior as well as employing people whose full-time job is to cope with ethical problems. The idea of all this is apparently to try and teach people seventeen to eighteen- years old, as well as those in their twenties and thirties and older, something about ethics, ethical behavior, and ethical problems that arise once they have a job. It is assumed that many people reach the age of going off to college or accepting a job without a code of ethics of individual behavior. Businesses issue manuals on ethical guidelines and establish ethical departments to cope with employees who never learned individual ethics. This illustrates the very point that both the family and community life of the United States are being torn apart. Individual ethics is something learned early in life by being a member of a family and community. A void of learning and experiencing accepted ethical behavior in early years of life means a breakdown at some level later in life. The effect of government programs and evolution of mores during the 1960s started the breakdown. People from that generation are now running business and government. These leaders talk about ethics and importance of teaching ethics, but ethics is something learned in family and community life. Most people, by the time they are teenagers and probably much earlier, have their base set of mores and values that they carry around with them through life.

In 1982 Peter Drucker made the following observation that is as pertinent in the 1990s as it was then:

> There is only one code of ethics, that of individual behavior, for prince and pauper, for rich and poor, for the mighty and the meek alike. Ethics, in the Judao-Christian tradition, is the affirmation that all men and women are alike creatures—whether the Creator be called God, Nature, or Society. And this fundamental axiom business ethics denies. Viewed from the mainstream of traditional ethics, business ethics is not ethics at all, whatever else it may be. For it asserts that acts that are not immoral or illegal if done by ordinary folk become immoral or illegal if done by business.[1]

> Clearly, one major element of the peculiar stew that goes by the name of business ethics is plain old-fashioned hostility to business and to economic activity altogether—one of the oldest of American traditions.... And business ethics may be good politics or good electioneering. But that is all. For ethics deals with the right actions of individuals. And then it surely makes no difference whether the setting is a community hospital [or] National Universal General Corporation [or] a quality control manager.[2]

This latter argument of antimarket orientation by Drucker is an explanation utilized by some to explain the British relative decline (as pointed out in chapter 1).

The reason society wants business ethics taught is because many people no longer have the traditional family experience in which to learn a value system. The family, the fundamental building block in a society, is undergoing erosion, and as a result, an attempt is being made to transfer the responsibility of teaching ethics to business and the educational system. We are witnessing an attempt to socialize ethics, which, at one time, took place in families and communities. Discussions of the importance of teaching ethics are a way for leaders to put their heads in the sand and ignore the fundamental problem, which is that the social and economic fabric in the United States is unravelling. The state is attempting to place the burden of behavior on both business and the educational system when individual ethics should be learned in family and community life, and those institutions are being pulled apart. This may be inevitable as countries mature—the breakdown of both basic institutions and the discipline necessary to transact family and community relationships. This breakdown may, in time, result in a situation in which enough degrees of freedom are taken away that some other form of government evolves.

The antismoking campaign underway in the United States is another attempt to target a social behavior—smoking—as unethical. Society concluded that an individual can't be trusted to make his or her own decision not to smoke. Should smoking be banned in private residences? Other products are likely to come under fire, as there are many food products that should not be consumed for optimal health, such as candy and food with a high-fat content. But is it society's concern if people want to consume commercial products such as a Big Mac, fries, and Coke that, perhaps, they shouldn't for optimal health? People who consume large quantities of cheeseburgers, french fries, milk shakes, steak, pork chops, and bacon and eggs are more likely to die from colon cancer or heart attack than those who don't, but does that mean that consumers shouldn't be allowed to purchase these items or companies to produce them? Nearly 45,000 people per year die in auto accidents. Does that mean the auto industry should be closed down?

Released and distributed movies are an example of what the entertainment business deems customers want. Elected representatives and many others bash the movie and television industry not only for the amount of violence and sex in their productions but also for showing an odd collection of family and community relationships. Many in society talk about lack of ethics and bemoan what is occurring in the entertainment industry, but that industry is responding to perceived needs. One may think those needs reflect a dysfunctional social and economic structure, but until and unless those dysfunctional needs are addressed, that is part of what will be provided since public wants are being met. An alternative is the step of socializing people's television-viewing habits by a board of federal regulators.

President Clinton's 1993 Health Security Act was an example of this ongoing move to shift decision making to the state and away from individuals, families, and communities—an attempt to move from reliance on the marketplace for health care to reliance on government entities. The proposal would have taken the ability to choose away from the individual and family. Under the Clinton proposal, one would not have had the option of freely purchasing health care, as is the case for other products and services.

Health care would have been treated like Social Security in one respect. Private-sector workers (except railroad workers) do not have the option of rejecting participation in Social Security. Everyone working is taxed. Clinton's health-care proposal would have been like Social Security in that regard. However, with Social Security one can continue to save additional funds for retirement—that is not illegal. But the Clinton health-care proposal would have declared illegal any purchase of additional health insurance, and in this regard the health-care proposal was much more restrictive than Social Security as it proposed taking away consumer choice. One of the stated reasons for the Clinton proposal—providing health care to the 15 percent uninsured—could also be applied to such industries in the United States as housing, for example, when people are in substandard housing or are homeless. The Clinton proposal was a new model for the United States, one in which government would have established a command and control system requiring everyone to participate and making it illegal to use alternative systems.

Choice was tossed out. Past world powers such as the Soviet Union, England, France, and Germany have moved further than the United States in this direction, but the Western European countries, like the United States, have maintained a positive business environment. The ability of economies to function would cease without maintaining this positive business environment, and the United States is likely to do the same, that is, attempt to maintain an environment in which businesses can continue to do relatively well. Without this wealth creation, society would rapidly wind down. Politicians and their constituencies continue to whine and moan about business, but without a vibrant and strong business sector, society as we know it would whither away.

Soviet leaders learned what happens when you don't maintain a strong business sector. The Chinese are moving toward a positive business environment. Societies can continue for centuries—*if* the business environment is favorable. That appears to be the direction the United States is headed with a two-pronged domestic strategy: (1) maintaining a healthy business environment, while dishing out verbal attacks on business; and (2) allowing and encouraging erosion of underlying nonbusiness institutions through government policies—slowly moving away from choice toward the socialization of individual decision making as basic economic and social values erode. This direction is *not yet* etched in stone, and instead of socialization of individual decision making, the United States could move toward decentralization through a direct-democracy concept utilizing the information highway.

Erosion of nonbusiness institutions seems inevitable with the additional involvement of government into more and more aspects of society, unless it is halted by a direct-democracy push. Further erosion of basic parameters means more and more pressure to socialize or take away individual freedom of choice. It is a vicious circle. Government expansion through laws, regulations, standards, taxes, and interpretations by the court system results in the process of slowly but surely displacing individual, family, and community responsibility and replacing that with state responsibility. The state keeps the private sector alive so that it (the state) won't go hungry, but a larger and larger state results in more people dependent upon the state, society becomes more rigid, and more and more of a burden is placed on the individual.

The direction for the United States over the next ten to twenty years is nearly etched in stone for those wanting to read it. A change in policies is necessary to go in a different direction, and that requires a change in the decision-making structure of government. It is of little benefit to change people in the chairs without changing the organization—the bureaucracy. Company after company found this out in attempts to reorganize, downsize, rightsize, restructure, move closer to the customer or whatever buzzword is used. Going through motions of restructuring or moving closer to the customer is of little use without fundamentally altering the organization and bureaucracy to implement the revised strategy. A company's board of directors can appoint a new chairman to reverse fortunes, but without fundamentally changing the organization's structure to implement revised strategies, it is of little value. Bureaucracies resist change.

The same for the federal government or other government entity. It is of limited effectiveness to vote in a president and new members of Congress without fundamentally altering the structure of the federal government to implement alternative policies. Reducing Congressional staffs is equivalent to slimming down the corporate pyramid. Unless the pyramid is completely altered, such attempts usually amount to window dressing. To change the structure, one needs to be able to answer the following six representative questions in the affirmative. (1) Will Congress make major changes in the method they utilize to carry out their duties to their constituents (see chapter 22)? If the answer is yes, then perhaps the United States can reverse its relative decline. (2) Will Congress implement bounties as a method to encourage the private sector to help capture criminals ? (3) Are regulations, mandates, and laws—and the thinking the court system uses to interpret those laws going to change? (4) Congress and other governmental entities measure their success by the number of laws, mandates, and regulations they pass. Is Congress going to start measuring success by the number of regulations, laws, and mandates thrown out? (5) Is Congress going to suggest or make it easy for local school districts to implement school choice and pay for performance? (6) Is the total tax burden (federal, state and local) going to be reduced?

Members of Congress will change and presidents will come and go, but there will be no major shifts in policy implementation unless the organizational structure of the federal bureaucracy changes. Major policy shifts will be proposed, but unless and until Congress alters the way in which it does business, no major changes will occur. Congress represents itself, not the public. Voter turnout would be much higher if Congress represented the public. People are disenfranchised from the political system. The structure of the two-party system, as we know it today in Washington, D.C., does not function for people.

The analysis set forth in chapters 1 to 20 concerning the U.S. golden age, the move to lean years, and broken promises is perhaps difficult to accept. Many Americans remain in denial that the United States is in a relative decline. The United States was the dominant economic power as recently as the 1950s and 1960s. Yet during the Gulf War Secretary of State James Baker ran around hat-in-hand taking up a collection to fund the U.S. military effort. Is that the signal of a dominant economic power? During the 1993 NAFTA debate, many people in the United States were shaking in their boots that their country would be economically beaten by competing with Mexico on a level playing field. Is that a signal of a dominant economic power or one in relative decline? Mexico's economy amounts to roughly 10 percent of the U.S. economy. Competing with Mexico or Japan or West Germany would not have raised an eyebrow in the 1950s because the U.S. economy was dominant.

It is different in the 1990s. Americans are afraid of the future because many countries have grown more rapidly than the U.S. economy over the past fifty years, reflecting, in part, U.S. policies. The United States, for instance, was larger than the Japanese economy by a factor of nearly 12 in 1950. By 1994 the U.S. economy was larger than Japan's by a factor of only 1.5. People are afraid the same competitive situation may occur with other countries. A major difference is that the United States had explicit building blocs to promote growth in Japan's economy as well as other countries over the past fifty years. If Mexico can maintain political stability and pro-growth economic policies, it could perhaps demonstrate large relative growth over the next fifty years, but Mexico and Japan are not countries for the United States to be concerned about for its future. The future of the United States is determined by U.S. policies, not those of Japan and Mexico. In addition, China is the country to be concerned about in terms of a country being in a position to challenge the United States in the next century militarily and economically. If the United States wants to reverse its relative economic decline, then it means making major policy shifts.

22

Change

There is an enormous political and economic vacuum to be filled in the last years of the twentieth century and early years of the twenty-first century. The cold war ended with Soviet economic and political defeat and the United States in relative economic decline. A country's military is only as strong as its taxpayers. The Soviets discovered that. The U.S. military is the only superpower left but U.S. taxpayers are tapped out and can no longer fund that status. The military, along with the economy, can be expected to continue in relative decline in coming years. More and more countries are likely to attempt to alter their boundaries by force and will feel that without a superpower looking over their shoulder, they can do so. Countries that can afford to do so will, in effect, rent the U.S. military to protect their boundaries, similar to what occurred in the Middle East in 1990–1991. But U.S. taxpayers will drag their feet on military support as their focus will be on internal difficulties.

Broken promises are *the cost of winning* as the United States shared her wealth with other market economies around the globe and also its own people helping them get on their feet. From the 1960s internal wealth sharing has been geared toward attempts to achieve equality of outcomes. The U.S. economy provided a rapid increase in the standard of living for its citizens and at the same time built the world economy during the golden years. Eventually foreign and domestic wealth sharing led to declining real wages for the majority of U.S. private-sector jobs. Many families, in an attempt to stay whole, needed two or more workers per family. This process contributed to family and community erosion—with more and more time spent outside the family and community. In a 1994 editorial in the *Wall Street Journal*, Peter Drucker addresses these issues:

> What, then, will family mean tomorrow, if these trends persist? And what will this mean for community and for society?

283

But this development, well outside of anything that traditional economics, sociology and political science ever considered to be within their purviews, may well be seen a century hence as the distinctive social innovation of the 20th century. It is a reversal of all history and tradition.[1]

The family, church, parent-teacher relationship, and school-related social events like basketball and football dominated much of U.S. life in the 1950s. This strong sense of family and community took place within an economic environment of a rapidly increasing standard of living. Social norms in the 1950s centered around family and community values, and an intolerance existed for people outside that perceived basic set of values wrapped around family, community, and belief in God. One effect of this intolerance was that those on the outside were driven toward sharing that common set of values in order to be accepted.

People enjoying an increasing standard of living wanted to share their good fortune with others through new and larger entitlement programs— with unexpected results. Daniel Patrick Moynihan, one of the pioneers on the social effects of domestic wealth-sharing programs, noted the adverse effect of entitlement programs on African-American family values in the early 1960s.[2] Charles Murray's book, *Losing Ground: American Social Policy, 1950–1980*, broadened Moynihan's premise to society in general. The public sector is good at redistribution of wealth. The private sector is good at creating wealth. Growth of the public sector outstripped private-sector growth in order to achieve wealth-sharing objectives.

Domestic public-sector wealth sharing didn't work well in the past, and modern technology and communication make state planning and social-investment spending obsolete concepts. Development of new industries cannot be planned in the twenty-first century any more than they could have been in the twentieth century. Variation in life cycles, rapid changes in technology, and a global community broken into region states connected by communication networks make state planning and wealth sharing much less effective. The United States, to revitalize itself, needs to create wealth. Can the United States create wealth and revitalize itself? Yes. One building block could act as the foundation necessary for bringing about changes necessary for the domestic U.S. economy to evolve into one characterized by opportunities for advancement in both quality of life and standard of living.

Suggestions which follow are evolutionary in nature, do not require constitutional amendments, and are designed to move away from centralized government bureaucracy and power, allowing the private sector to regain importance in U.S. life. The fundamental building block for change to occur is a restructuring of the federal bureaucracy. This restructuring requires Congressional leadership. Business continually restructures to deliver better products and services to its customers. The federal bureaucracy needs to do the same. This evolutionary change is unlikely to occur as bureaucracies in general—and, in particular, the Washington, D.C., bureaucracy—do not want to give up power. Many companies encounter bureaucratic roadblocks in attempting to rightsize, restructure, and move closer to the customer. The bureaucracy inside the Beltway in Washington, D.C., is much larger and much more difficult to restructure than any company has encountered and may be as difficult to restructure as the USSR bureaucracy.

The *Beltway-bureaucracy* customers are other participants in the bureaucracy, not individual voters. Companies have shareholders, customers, and competitors that encourage change. Customers of the Beltway-bureaucracy are other members of that elite organization. There are no shareholders, only stakeholders. Stakeholders are large dependent constituencies feeding off taxpayers. There is no incentive to change other than to grow larger. We have only to look at the government funded and nurtured educational bureaucracy to see the resistance to change, even in the face of dismal school performance. Changing players in the chairs doesn't do much as long as the bureaucracy remains in place. A restructuring of the federal bureaucracy would mean the United States would have an opportunity to become the first major power in the history of the world to revitalize itself, thereby avoiding decades of continuing relative decline. Congress can do mankind a great service by exhibiting leadership and implementing the following building block.

Building Block—Restructuring Congress

Restructuring of the federal bureaucracy in the manner suggested is fundamental to rvitalizing the U.S. economy relative to global competitors. The following five restructuring steps are evolutionary as they take advantage of modern technology to move government closer to voters and break the federal stranglehold on the U.S. economy.

1. Congress needs to restructure itself out of Washington, D.C., and meet for a maximum of three to four months per year at a different site

each year in order for a U.S. revitalization to take place. Congress could adopt a ten-year schedule of meeting sites at different cities around the country. A three or four-month period allows members adequate time to discuss and act on major policies prepared over the preceding nine months as well as discuss the agenda for the upcoming year.

2. During the remainder of the year, members can remain in contact with their main constituents—voters—as well as other participants in the bureaucracy. Required actions and votes during the remaining eight or nine months of the year can be handled by electronic means. A cable channel and information highway can assist this process and incorporate more town-hall meetings, which would lead to more voter participation and much more of a direct participatory democracy.

3. A key element of this restructured foundation for change is that all Congressional staff members must work in the respective districts of each member. Their salaries are paid by taxpayers, and they need to be in the respective home districts of the voters for whom they work.

4. Term limits or balanced-budget amendments are not necessary if the above steps are undertaken. One would not think of placing term limits on people in business or restricting households or businesses from going into debt. Business and households respond to the marketplace. The reason term limits and a balanced-budget amendment are on the agenda is because Congress doesn't work in its present form. Term limits and a balanced-budget amendment address the result, not the cause— which is that the Congressional bureaucracy is unresponsive to individual voters and responsive only to large highly dependent constituencies like the elderly. The only way to correct this is to restructure the bureaucracy. That is a given. Anyone who has done any serious work with large organizations knows that.

5. Much of the remaining federal establishment also needs to be shut down and/or privatized and dispersed. Dispersion of Congress, their staffs, and the federal establishment would necessitate taking advantage of state-of-the-art communication systems to bring them closer to customers, yet remain in contact with other parts of the bureaucracy. Agencies such as HUD, Treasury, Transportation, Commerce, Labor, Energy, Health and Human Services, Education, Interior, Veterans Affairs, and Agriculture need to be shut down and/or privatized and dispersed across the United States. Companies relocate headquarters. There is no reason government agencies, privatized or not, can't relocate given today's advanced com-

munications systems. Taxpayers foot the tab for the federal bureaucracy that is strangling the U.S. economy. Simply by moving out of Washington, D.C., Congress is likely to become more responsive to the taxpayer and be willing to make decisions on the remainder of the federal bureaucracy. The following should perhaps remain in the District of Columbia area in proximity to the White House—State Department, Defense Department, CIA, and the Attorney General.

Suggested policies to be implemented by the restructured Congress follow. These policies are instrumental to revitalization of the United States. The point is, however, that only after restructuring occurs, would Congress and the president be willing to implement policies for revitalization, not before.

Tax Policy to Revitalize America

There are two major tax-policy areas—personal income-tax policy and the Social Security system—that require immediate action if the United States is to reverse its decline. Regarding the first, personal income-tax policy, the action required is to eliminate the current complex personal income-tax code. The personal income tax has had the desired effect—it helped win the cold war, but the cold war is over and it is way past time to institute a tax code that will revitalize the U.S. economy. The current personal income tax and capital-gains tax ensure the relative decline of the U.S. economy. (This process was described in detail in chapter 7.) They tax what we need more of—income—and capital. One does not tax that which one needs in greater amount.

There are many other disadvantages of the personal income tax system—it is complex, costly to comply with, perceived as unfair, penalizes capital formation, promotes economic growth in other countries at expense of the United States, inhibits work, promotes debt use, and hits low-income segments especially hard in that the tax system acts as a major roadblock to the advancement of these segments, the ones most in need of capital. On top of all that, the tax code is customer unfriendly. It is inexcusable that many Americans need help to comply with the tax code. It is a make-work program for many people in this country. FDR had make work programs to employ people during the Great Depression. The U.S. personal tax code is the largest make-work program that the United States has and is a national disgrace.

A transaction tax should replace the personal income tax. A transactions tax is a national sales tax on final goods and services. It would be easy to comply with, difficult to avoid, highly visible, and could generate the same amount of revenue as the current personal-tax system. Requirements of a tax code to replace the personal income tax are that it needs to be highly visible, simple, and easy both to implement and collect. Since the transactions tax would be highly visible, people would associate taxes paid with government outlays, which would help them to judge if they are getting their money's worth. When people purchase a product or service, they associate the price with benefits of that product or service, which is the reason taxes need to be highly visible. The transactions tax is easy to implement and requires no filing or withholding on the part of individuals. The incidence of the transactions tax would be, of course, on the transaction, which means that it is a consumption tax on final goods and services and is a fair tax in that people pay only when they purchase. If an individual does not wish to pay the tax, he or she need make no purchase.

A transactions consumption tax would apply to all nonfood transactions, including services purchased by the final consumer, for example motor vehicles and parts, motor vehicle maintenance and repairs, tires, travel services (such as airline/boat tickets), taxis, mass transit, furniture, household equipment, clothing, shoes, jewelry, personal care items, gasoline, oil, medical services, health insurance, household utilities, telephone, personal business services (such as legal services), books, magazines, newspapers, videos, computers, televisions, television repair, lottery tickets, and admissions to spectator amusements, in addition to many others. Exclusion of food means the exclusion would apply only to food purchased for off-premise consumption. *Food*, as used here, does not include many items that can be purchased at the local supermarket such as tobacco products, beverages, household furnishings, and other nonedible or non-nutritional products. Purchased meals and beverages would be taxed. Businesses would collect tax revenues and reimburse those receipts to the U.S. Treasury. A transactions tax, of course, means no tax deductions for items such as the mortgage-interest deduction for homeowners or payments for state and local taxes. A national sales tax would allow citizens to take home more of what they make, but purchased goods and services would be more expensive by 15 percent or more in order to be revenue neutral.

It perhaps is a moot point to discuss elimination of the corporate income tax. Like all business expenses, it is shifted to customers and employees, but, nonetheless, opposition to elimination would be major. President Reagan floated the idea once and met heavy criticism. Likewise, it is a nonstarter to discuss elimination of the capital-gains tax unless it were to be replaced by a capital-transactions tax. A transactions tax or sales tax on capital transactions would harm efficiency of capital markets. An alternative would be to index the capital-gains tax at a lower rate such as 10 percent and have it apply to both short and long-term gains. This tax would then amount to a *gains* tax.

The second major tax-policy area that requires action is that of the Social Security tax. As indicated earlier (see chapter 19), the Social Security system resulted in socialization of saving. A method of providing incentives for people to regain their sense of saving is to privatize Social Security and to eliminate, completely, the cost-of-living adjustment as well as delaying the traditional retirement age until the age of seventy. The cost-of-living change should be made immediately, while the adjustment in the normal retirement age to seventy could take effect in the year 2000. This would represent a broken promise, but a country in relative decline has to break promises if it ever hopes to stop the decline. IBM had to break its lifetime-employment promise by terminating a substantial percentage of its workers, but because of that broken promise in conjunction with the reengineering of its businesses, it looks as if IBM has been revitalized. If so, IBM can create new jobs and products and make a contribution. The United States is in the same boat—it is breaking promises, has to break many more, and, most importantly, reengineer the federal bureaucracy before the United States can be revitalized. To privatize, young workers would be precluded from entering the system, and those in the system would have their monies returned in the form of an IRA with interest. This latter action, however, would need to be phased in as funds are not available. To date, one country, Chile, has privatized, and another, Argentina, has started, so it is a feasible solution.

Social Security benefits, as long as the system is in effect, would increase only because of net gains in retirees. Doing away with the cost-of-living adjustment and delaying the traditional retirement age to seventy would help reduce the unfunded liability problem of Social Security. Two advantages of these steps: first, it reintroduces the importance of personal saving, and secondly, it would create a large and powerful constituency to support the Federal Reserve effort to maintain the stable purchasing power of the dollar. A stable price level would eliminate need for cost-of-living increases in Social Security payments. However, a major risk is that Congress, if it doesn't reengineer itself, may eventually restructure the Federal Reserve in a way that the central bank would attempt in time to inflate its way out of the U.S. outstanding debt burden. The Federal Reserve was created by Congress in 1913, and Congress can therefore alter the Federal Reserve if it so wishes. Germany's central bank, in comparison, has an independent status as part of their constitution.

Reclaim Cities and Towns

Segments of many cities and towns have literally been taken over by crime, and nearly all cities and towns are adversely impacted by fear of crime. This fear results in citizens' attempting to privatize their safety through private security in addition to altering their life-styles. Chapter 18 explains the steps necessary for law-abiding citizens to reclaim cities and towns—bounty hunters and fixed penalties.

Welfare

A policy for revitalization of low-income areas of cities along with a reduction in the welfare rolls involves the following steps. Elimination of the corporate income tax in low-income and poverty areas is a straightforward method of encouraging companies to locate and expand there, thus promoting job growth. Elimination of the employer-paid portion of the Social Security tax for each person hired would further encourage companies to hire people off welfare rolls and others from the low-income area. This step would effectively reduce the cost to the company of each person hired and/or increase the take-home pay of workers. The final step would be to eliminate the capital-gains tax on gains from investment dollars in these designated areas. These steps could easily be implemented by Congress for low-income areas on a nationwide basis. It makes no sense to talk about throwing people off welfare without implementing a job-creation program such as this.

As indicated above, there are potentially ten federal agencies needing to be dispersed. These agencies would provide a major anchor in the ten cities having the largest concentration of people on welfare. Federal agencies could be relocated to the very worst areas within cities and serve as a catalyst for employment growth. Entry-level people from welfare or below the poverty line could be hired from the immediate area and trained. It is important in doing this that the programs outlined to reduce the crime rate be implemented.

Revitalization of cities having large concentrations of low-income and welfare populations involves a similar approach to that for early-stage developing countries. Low-income segments of cities, as with developing countries, require (1) a strong educational system; (2) reduced tax rates and changed regulations, which make it easy to start and expand businesses that can produce goods, services, and information for export; and (3) relative freedom from violence so that people can live in the area. As explained in earlier chapters, the U.S. economy is much more rigid in the 1990s than in earlier decades, which makes it very difficult for people to achieve upward mobility, and the three steps listed above would make the economy more fluid for both low-income people and people on welfare, the same as in a developing country.

Education Policy

There are two major problems in education (see chapter 16). One is the National Educational Association (NEA) and according to Toch, a misrepresentation on their part of issues facing local school systems.[3] The NEA is also opposed to most steps that might improve educational quality such as school choice. Another major problem is the lack of parental involvement both at-home and at-school. A point that appears to be a certainty is that inadequate funding is not a problem in creating the mediocre educational system at the primary and secondary level. The NEA is part of the bureaucracy in Washington, D.C., and, again according to Toch, is one of the strongest political forces in the United States.[4] Milton Friedman, Nobel prize-winning economist, suggested adoption of school vouchers and school choice during the 1960s.[5] Forty years later schools are in worse shape. School choice may be somewhat closer to being a reality but the power of the NEA suggests school choice may not become a reality except on a small scale. Even so, school choice is not a panacea. Parents need to be involved both at-home and at-school.

One potential solution to lack of parental involvement is that each child be entitled to an advocate (chapter 16, suggested by Joe Gorman).[6] The advocate would be a concerned adult who would ensure that the child is learning, completing homework, and attending school. The breakdown of the traditional family and community values may suggest that parental involvement may never be present, and an advocate may be a method to cope with that. Governmental policies contributed to the breakdown of values, and if not changed, the twenty-first century may see a much larger movement to socialization of child rearing and education by the state. If policies similar to those outlined in this chapter are not implemented, the future offers state socialization of the child-care center and boarding-school concept from birth through high school with children visiting their parent(s) on an occasional basis. The concept could be altered somewhat to follow the European model, in which brighter students are selected to go to college while those in the lower part of the bell curve receive other training such as vocational education.

Trade Policy

Three most important elements of a successful long-term trade policy are (1) a high-quality educational system relative to our competitors; (2) elimination of the personal income tax and replacement with a transactions tax; and (3) negotiation of free-trade agreements with Far East countries.

Foreign Policy

Major ingredients of a strong long-term foreign policy are the points discussed to revitalize the domestic U.S. economy. Has there ever been a country with a strong long-term foreign policy without a strong domestic economy? The post-cold war U.S. foreign policy will evolve over time into a positive one if the U.S. can revitalize its domestic economy. Mainland China is looming on the horizon as a potential world leader perhaps to replace the Soviet Union in another cold war. The United States may have botched what should have been no cold war with China by not implementing up-to-date domestic economic policies and by entering into a NAFTA-type agreement with China.

No Change

If action is not taken to implement changes such as those discussed in this chapter, the United States will continue its relative decline. Foreign policy will become a mirror image of domestic trends. Denial of this trend is probably much like that of a drug addict. This is especially difficult to accept in the United States because it was the dominant economic power not so many years ago. Denial may well last into the next century until another power, probably China, militarily and economically challenges the United States.

Priorities for Change

The United States won the cold war through implementation of economic policies to shape global development. And the cost of winning is broken domestic promises. The cold war is over. The United States needs to change policies in order to arrive at a future that once again presents opportunities for ordinary Americans.

The following six points are the author's suggested minimum policy guidelines to arrive at a future of opportunity for ordinary Americans. (1) A restructuring of Congress, its staffs, and the accompanying bureaucracy out of Washington, D.C., must take place for the United States to implement post-cold war policies to revitalize itself. At that point the role of government in helping the United States to arrive at the future can be decided. Government will again represent voters. (2) Privatize capture of alleged criminals through bounty hunters, and implement mandatory sentences for all persons convicted of committing a violent crime. (3) Eliminate the personal federal income tax and replace it with a transaction tax. (4) Implement school choice and pay tied to performance. Competition will reduce the monopoly power of the National Education Association and improve the quality of primary and secondary education. (5) Create areas of economic opportunity in low-income portions of cities through elimination of the corporate income tax and the employer portion of Social Security. (6) Privatize Social Security. In the meantime, immediately eliminate the cost-of-living adjustment and change the traditional retirement age to seventy effective in the year 2000.

It is the author's belief that action on these six priorities is essential, and that only then will the United States begin to be able to redeem its broken promises.

Notes

Introduction

1. Paul Kennedy, *The Rise and Fall of the Great Powers* (Random House, 1987), 362.
2. Dean Acheson, *Present at the Creation* (W. W. Norton & Company, 1969), 1.
3. Joseph M. Jones, *The Fifteen Weeks (February 21-June 5, 1947)*, (The Viking Press, 1955), 107.
4. John D. Rockefeller, III, "Japan Tackles Her Problems," *Foreign Affairs* (July, 1954): 579, 586.

Chapter 1: It Has Happened Before

1. Kennedy, *Rise and Fall*, 362.
2. A.H.M. Jones, *The Roman Economy* (Basil Blackwell, 1974).
3. Sidney Homer and Richard Sylla, *A History of Interest Rates* (Rutgers University Press, 1991), 46.
4. Ibid., 49.
5. Edmund Henry Oliver, *Roman Economic Conditions to the Close of the Empire* (University of Toronto Library, 1907), 165.
6. W. D. Rubinstein, *Capitalism, Culture, and Decline in Britain 1750–1990* (Routledge, 1993), 5.
7. Ibid., 2.
8. Ibid., 4.
9. Ibid., 24.
10. Francis Williams, *Twilight of Empire, Memoirs of Prime Minister Clement Attlee* (Greenwood Press, 1960), 1.

Chapter 2: The Foundation Years

1. Milton Friedman and Anna Jacobson Schwartz, "Money and Business Cycles," Supplement, *Reviews of Economics and Statistics*, vol. 45, no. 1, part 2 (February 1963): 34.
2. Kennedy, *Rise and Fall*, 202.

Chapter 3: Prelude to the Creation

1. Acheson, *Present at the Creation*, 55.
2. Ibid., 83.

3. John Taft, *American Power, the Rise and Decline of U.S. Globalism, 1918–1988* (Harper & Row, 1989), 76.
4. George F. Kennan, *Memoirs* (Little, Brown and Company, 1967), 213.
5. Ibid., 213.
6. Taft, *American Power*, 77.
7. Kennan, *Memoirs*, 17.
8. Ibid., 61.
9. Ibid., 84.
10. Ibid., 219.
11. Ibid.
12. Ibid., 299.
13. Ibid., 310–11.
14. Acheson, *Present at the Creation*, 192.
15. Kennan, *Memoirs*, 320.
16. Ibid., 321.
17. Ibid., 357–59.
18. Eduard Mark, "The Question of Containment: A Reply to John Lewis Gaddis," *Foreign Affairs* (January 1978): 432.
19. Kennan, *Memoirs*, 364.

Chapter 4: The Creation—Building Bloc I, the Marshall Plan

1. Kennedy, *The Rise and Fall*, 362.
2. Jones, *The Fifteen Weeks*, 107.
3. Ibid., 107.
4. Ibid., 109.
5. Ibid., 112.
6. Ibid., 223.
7. Kennan, *Memoirs*, 343.
8. John Gimbel, *The Origins of the Marshall Plan* (Stanford University Press, 1976), 6.
9. Jones, *The Fifteen Weeks*, 281–84.
10. Robert A. Pollard, *Economic Security and the Origins of the Cold War, 1945–1950* (Columbia University Press, 1985), 151.

Chapter 5: The Creation—Building Bloc II, Trade Policy

1. Pollard, *Economic Security*, 166.
2. Council of Economic Advisers, *Economic Report of the President 1989*, 153.
3. Pollard, *Economic Security*, 60.
4. Council, *Economic Report*, 155.
5. Jacob Viner, "Conflicts of Principle in Drafting A Trade Charter," *Foreign Affairs* (July 1947): 613.
6. Pollard, *Economic Security*, 163.
7. Raymond Vernon, "Foreign Trade and National Defense," *Foreign Affairs* (October 1955): 79.
8. Ibid., 77.
9. Ibid., 78.

10. Ibid., 79.
11. Averell W. Harriman, "Leadership in World Affairs," *Foreign Affairs* (July 1954): 529.
12. Kennan, *Memoirs*, 372.
13. Ibid., 373.
14. Ibid., 374.
15. Ibid., 376.
16. Pollard, *Economic Security*, 175.
17. Kennan, *Memoirs*, 381.
18. Ibid., 388.
19. Pollard, *Economic Security*, 186.
20. Kennan, *Memoirs*, 391.
21. Ibid., 393.
22. Rockefeller, "Japan Tackles Her Problems," 579.
23. Ibid., 586.
24. Saburo Okita, "Japan's Economic Prospects," *Foreign Affairs* (October 1960): 125.
25. Peter F. Drucker, "Trade Lessons from the World Economy," *Foreign Affairs* (January-February 1994): 105.
26. Council, *Economic Report*, 148.

Chapter 6: The Creation—Building Bloc III, Military

1. John Lewis Gaddis, "Was the Truman Doctrine A Real Turning Point?" *Foreign Affairs* (January 1974): 394.
2. Zbigniew Brzezinski, "How the Cold War Was Played," *Foreign Affairs* (October 1972): 181.
3. W .W. Rostow, "Containment: 40 Years Later," *Foreign Affairs* (Spring 1987): 837.
4. Pollard, *Economic Security*, 166.
5. Acheson, *Present at the Creation*, 151.
6. Brzezinski, "How the Cold War Was Played," 184.
7. Acheson, *Present at the Creation*, 380.
8. Ibid., 380.
9. Harriman, "Leadership in World Affairs," 531.
10. Brzezinski, "How the Cold War Was Played," 189.
11. Ibid., 192.
12. Kennedy, *The Rise and Fall*, 389.
13. Robert A. Pollard and Samuel F. Wells, Jr., "1945-1960: The Era of American Economic Hegemony," in *Economics and World Power*," eds. William H. Becker and Samuel F. Wells, Jr., (Columbia University Press, 1984), 358.

Chapter 7: The Creation—Building Bloc IV, Tax Policy

1. Carolyn Webber and Aaron Wildavsky, *A History of Taxation and Expenditures in the Western World* (Simon and Schuster, 1986), 378.
2. Charles P. Kindleberger, *Historical Economics* (University of California Press, 1990), 207.
3. Webber and Wildavsky, *A History of Taxation*, 418.

4. Ibid., 416.
5. Ibid., 423.
6. Kindleberger, *Historical Economics*, 211.
7. Ibid., 211.
8. Lewis H. Kimmel, *Taxes and Economic Incentives* (The Brookings Institution, 1950), 79.
9. Ibid., 70.
10. Ibid., 71.
11. Ibid., 78.
12. Ibid., 93.
13. Ibid., 99.
14. Ibid., 38.
15. National Bureau of Economic Research and the Brookings Institution, "Foreign Tax Policies and Economic Growth" (A Conference Report distributed by Columbia University Press, 1966): 39–159.
16. Ibid., 211.
17. The Committee for Economic Development, *Reducing Tax Rates for Production and Growth* (New York, 1962).

Chapter 8: The Creation—Building Bloc V, Oil

1. Pollard, *Economic Security*, 213.
2. Ibid., 214.
3. Ibid.
4. Ibid., 215.
5. Daniel Yergin, *The Prize* (Simon & Schuster, 1991), 476.
6. Ibid., 521.
7. Ibid., 544.
8. Ibid.
9. Ibid., 545.
10. Ibid.
11. Ibid., 546.
12. Ibid.
13. Pollard and Wells, *Era of American Economic Hegemony*, 365.

Chapter 9: British and American Golden Ages

1. Kennedy, *The Rise and Fall*, 228.
2. Ibid., 228.
3. Ibid., 229.
4. Andrew Gamble, *Britain in Decline: Economic Policy, Political Strategy, and the British State* (Beacon Press, 1982), 46.
5. Ibid., 47.
6. John Maynard Keynes, *A Tract of Monetary Reform* (Macmillan & Company, Ltd., 1923), 11.
7. Webber and Wildavsky, *A History of Taxation*, 342.
8. Ibid., 347.
9. Ibid., 354.

Chapter 10: Crumbling Foundation, 1971–1985

1. Brzezinski, "How the Cold War Was Played," 197.
2. Ibid., 197.
3. Yergin, *The Prize*, 591.
4. James Akins, "The Oil Crisis: This Time the Wolf is Here," *Foreign Affairs*, (April 1973):
5. Yergin, *The Prize*, 595.
6. Ibid., 607.
7. Ibid., 614.
8. Ibid., 614.

Chapter 11: The Lean Years, 1985 to ...

1. Joint Economic Committee, *Capital Crimes: How Higher Capital Gains Tax Rates Have Cost the U.S. Economy and the Federal Government Billions of Dollars* (December 1993), 4.
2. Jeffrey Frankel and Wei Shang-Jin, "A Pacific Economic Bloc: Is There Such an Animal?" *Federal Reserve Bank of San Francisco Weekly*, 12 November 1993.
3. Stephen E. Ambrose, *Eisenhower* (Simon and Schuster, 1983), 251.

Chapter 14: Loss of High Paying Jobs—A Broken Promise

1. Alison Butler, "Is the United States Losing Its Dominance in High-Technology Industries?" *St. Louis Federal Reserve Review* (November-December 1992): 23.
2. Central Intelligence Agency, *Handbook of International Economic Statistics*, (Washington, D.C., 1994), and ibid., 19-34.
3. Michael E. Porter, *The Competitive Advantage of Nations*, (Free Press, 1990), 368.

Chapter 15: Creation of Jobs—A Broken Promise

1. Michael W. Cox and Richard Alm, "The Churn," *Federal Reserve Bank of Dallas* (1992 Annual Report): 11.
2. Clark S. Judge, "Thresholds of Pain," an editorial in the *Wall Street Journal*, 10 August 1994.
3. Kristin M. Roberts and Mark E. Schweitzer, "Looking Back at Slow Employment Growth," *Federal Reserve Bank of Cleveland*, (15 August 1994): 3.
4. Neal Templin, "Auto Plants, Hiring Again, Are Demanding Higher-Skilled Labor," *Wall Street Journal* (March 11, 1994):
5. Graef S. Crystal, *In Search of Excess: the Overcompensation of American Executives* (Norton, 1991), 205.

Chapter 16: Public Education—A Broken Promise

1. David Jackson, "Postwar Revolution," article in the *Dallas Morning News*, in which he quotes Peter Drucker, (22 June 1994).
2. Thomas Toch, *In the Name of Excellence* (Oxford University Press, 1991), 8.

3. U.S. Department of Education, National Center for Education Statistics, *Digest of Educational Statistics 1994*, Table 27.
4. Ibid., table 23.
5. Ibid., table 28.
6. Toch, *In the Name of Excellence*, 152.
7. Peter Brimelow and Leslie Spencer, "The End of Arrogance," *Forbes*, 13 February 1995): 121.
8. Toch, *In the Name of Excellence*, 153.
9. Ibid., 153.
10. Ibid., 178.
11. Ibid., 157.
12. Ibid., 179.
13. Ibid., 181.
14. Ibid., 186.
15. Peter Brimelow and Leslie Spencer, "The National Extortion Association?" *Forbes* (7 June 1993): 72-84.
16. Myron Lieberman, *Public Education: An Autopsy* (Harvard University Press, 1993), 2.
17. Milton Friedman, *Capitalism and Freedom* (University of Chicago Press, 1962), 85-107.
18. Sarah Lubman, "Schools Tie Salaries to Pupil Performance," an article in the *Wall Street Journal* (10 March 1995).
19. Bruno V. Manno, "Deliver US From Clinton's Schools Bill," editorial, *Wall Street Journal* (22 June 1993).
20. Marshall Loeb discusses Joe Gorman thoughts on the public school system, "Let's Get on with the Revolution," *Fortune* (12 December 1994).

Chapter 17: Public Safety—A Broken Promise

1. Gary Becker, "Crime and Punishment: An Economic Approach," *Journal of Political Economy* (March 1968): 168-217.
2. Charles Murray, *Losing Ground* (Basic Books, Inc. 1984), 114.
3. President's Commission on Law Enforcement and Administration of Justice, *Task Force Report: Crime and Its Impact—An Assessment* (1967): Appendix D.
4. James Q. Wilson, ed., *Crime and Public Policy* (Institute for Contemporary Studies, San Francisco, California, 1983), 14.
5. Michael J. Mandel and Paul Magnusson, "The Economics of Crime," *Business Week* (13 December 1993), 72.
6. Wilson, *Crime and Public Policy*, 15.
7. James Q. Wilson, *Thinking about Crime* (Basic Books, 1975), 17.
8. Murray, *Losing Ground*, 117.
9. Wilson, *Thinking about Crime*, 6.
10. Murray, *Losing Ground*, 126.
11. Wilson, *Thinking about Crime*, 199.
12. U.S. Department of Justice, Office of Justice Programs, *Sourcebook of Criminal Justice Statistics, 1992*, table 6.113.
13. U.S. Department of Commerce, Bureau of the Census *Statistical Abstract of the United States—1993*, No. 345, p. 211.

14. Dane Archer and Rosemary Gartner, *Violence and Crime in Cross National Perspective* (Yale University Press, 1984), 96.
15. James A. Inciardi and Charles, E. Faupel, *History and Crime: Implications for Criminal Justice Policy* (Sage Publications, 1980), 126.
16. Archer and Gartner, *Violence and Crime* , 116.

Chapter 18: Bounty Hunters and Fixed Penalties

1. Nina Munk, "Rent-a-cops," *Forbes* (10 October 1994), 106.
2. Donald F. Kettl, *Sharing Power* (The Brookings Institution, 1993), 158.
3. Comments by Janice Castro in "The Terrorists Bounty Hunters," *Time* (10 August 1992): 11.
4. U.S. Department of Justice, Federal Bureau of Investigation, "Uniform Crime Reports: 1993," table 1.
5. William T. Gormley, Jr., ed., *Privatization and Its Alternatives* (The University of Wisconsin Press, 1991), 200.

Chapter 19: Symptoms of Broken Promises—Entitlements

1. Walter E. Williams, "How to Really Help People Escape Poverty," editorial in the *Dallas Morning News* (2 July 1994).
2. John H. Fund, "Welfare: Putting People First," editorial in the *Wall Street Journal* (Tuesday, 14 June 1994).
3. Peter G. Peterson, *Facing Up: How to Restore the Economy from Crunching Debt and Restore the American Dream* (Simon and Schuster, 1993), 458.
4. Murray, *Losing Ground*, 24.
5. Ibid., 33.
6. Ibid., 43.
7. Ibid., 43.
8. Charles Murray, "The Coming White Underclass," an editorial in the *Wall Street Journal* (29 October 1993).
9. Ibid.
10. Ibid.
11. Ibid.
12. Joel Garreau, *Edge City: Life on the New Frontier* (Doubleday, 1991), 150.
13. Ibid.
14. Ibid.
15. Ibid.

Chapter 20: More Symptoms

1. Alexis de Tocqueville, *Democracy in America* (Knopf, 1945), 294.
2. Roy H. Webb, "The Stealth Budget: Unfunded Liabilities of the Federal Government," *Economic Review* (Federal Reserve Bank of Richmond, May/June 1991), 23–32.
3. Lawrence Lindsey, "The Big Black Hole," *Forbes* (21 November 1994).

Chapter 21: The Future?

1. Peter F. Drucker, *The Changing World of the Executive* (Times Books, 1982), 237.
2. Ibid., 254.

Chapter 22: Change

1. Peter F. Drucker, "The Continuing Feminist Experiment," an editorial in the *Wall Street Journal* (Monday, 17 October 1994).
2. Daniel P. Moynihan, *The Negro Family: The Case for National Action* (Office of Policy Planning and Research, United States Department of Labor, March 1965).
3. Toch, *In the Name of Excellence* (see chap. 16, n. 2), 181.
4. Ibid., 152.
5. Friedman, *Capitalism and Freedom* (see chap. 16, n. 16), 85–107.
6. Loeb, "Let's Get on with the Revolution," (see chap. 16, n. 18).

Sources and Notes for Figures and Tables

Chapter 1: It Has Happened Before

Figure 1.1   U.S. Department of Commerce, Economics and Statistics Administration, *National Income and Product Accounts of the United States*, vols. 1 and 2, tables 1.15 and 3.1; *Survey of Current Business*, tables 1.9 and 3.1.

Chapter 2: The Foundation Years

Figure 2.1   Department of Commerce, Economics and Statistics Administration, *National Income and Product Accounts*, vol. 1, table 1.2; percent unemployment is from U.S. Bureau of Labor Statistics, Division of Labor Force Statistics, fax dated 15 July 1993 from Abraham T. Mosisa.

Chapter 4: The Creation—Building Bloc I, the Marshall Plan

Figure 4.1   Kennedy, *Rise and Fall* (see introd., n. 1), 369.
Figure 4.2   Ibid.

Chapter 5: The Creation—Building Bloc II, Trade Policy

Figure 5.1   Council of Economic Advisers, *Economic Report of the President 1989*, 151.
Figure 5.2   U.S. Department of Commerce, Bureau of the Census, Foreign Trade Division, fax dated 2 August 1993 from Blake Sanders; U.S. Department of Commerce, Economics and Statistics Administration, *Survey of Current Business*, table 10.a.
Table 5.1   Central Intelligence Agency, *Handbook of International Economic Statistics*, tables 90 and 91, 138–40.
Table 5.2   Michael H. Cosgrove, "Success of Developing Countries' Export Strategies and World Trade Structure," *Seoul Journal of Economics*, vol. 4 (March 1991): 87.

Chapter 6: The Creation—Building Bloc III, Military

Figure 6.1   Kennedy, *Rise and Fall*, 384.

Figure 6.2   U.S. Department of Commerce, Economics and Statistics Administra-
              tion, *National Income and Product Accounts*, vols. 1 and 2, table 3.2;
              Survey of Current Business, table 3.2.
Table 6.1   Webber and Wildavsky, *A History of Taxation*, 474.
Table 6.2   See figure 6.1 note above.

Chapter 7: The Creation—Building Bloc IV, Tax Policy

Figure 7.1   Committee on Ways and Means, U.S. House of Representatives, *Over-
              view of the Federal Tax System* (1993 Edition), tables 1 and updates.
Figure 7.2   Allen H. Lerman, *Average and Marginal Federal Income Tax, Social
              Security, and Medicare Tax Rates for Four-Person Families at the Same
              Relative Positions in the Income Distribution, 1955–1994* (Department
              of the Treasury, 18 April 1995), table 1.
Table 7.1   Kimmel, *Taxes and Economic Incentives* (see chap. 8, n. 8), 80.
Table 7.2   Ibid., 81.
Table 7.3   Calculated.

Chapter 8: The Creation—Building Bloc V, Oil

Figure 8.1   DeGolyer and MacNaughton, *Twentieth Century Petroleum Statistics,
              1994* (Dallas, TX), 105; data for after 1973 from Energy Information
              Administration, *Monthly Energy Review*, table 9.2.
Figure 8.2   DeGolyer and MacNaughton, *Twentieth Century Petroleum Statistics,
              1994*, 4.
Figure 8.3   Ibid., 15; data for 1973 from Energy Information Administration, *Inter-
              national Petroleum Statistics Report* (November 1994), table 4.6.
Figure 8.4   DeGolyer and MacNaughton, *Twentieth Century Petroleum Statistics,
              1994*, 63; data for 1973 and later from Energy Information Administra-
              tion, *International Petroleum Statistics Report*, table 3.1a.

Chapter 9: British and American Golden Ages

Figure 9.1   David Hale, Kemper Financial Services, *The Twilight of Anglo-Ameri-
              can Power* (June 1987), chart 3; data for 1991 from J.P. Morgan, *World
              Financial Markets* (September/October 1992), 28; data for 1993 from
              Organization for Economic Co-operation and Development, *Statistics
              on the Member Countries 1994*, 24–25.
Table 9.1   Kennedy, *Rise and Fall*, 202.
Table 9.2   Council of Economic Advisers, *Economic Report of the President 1989*,
              150.

Chapter 10: Crumbling Foundation, 1971–1985

Figure 10.1   DeGolyer and MacNaughton, *Twentieth Century Petroleum Statistics,
              1994*, 52; data after 1973 from Energy Information Administration,
              Monthly Energy Review, table 3.1b.

Figure 10.2   Council of Economic Advisers, *Economic Report of the President 1995*, table B-47.
Figure 10.3   Ibid., table B-45.

Chapter 11: The Lean Years, 1985 to...

Figure 11.1   Energy Information Administration, *Historical Monthly Energy Review, 1973-1992; Monthly Energy Review*, table 9.2.
Figure 11.2   Norman S. Fieleke, "One Trading World, or Many: The Issue of Regional Trading Blocs," *New England Economic Review* (Federal Reserve Bank of Boston, May/June 1992): 14.
Figure 11.3   Ibid., 15.
Figure 11.4   Ibid., 14-15.
Table 11.1   International Monetary Fund, *International Financial Statistics Yearbook* (1989 and 1994).

Chapter 12: Government Taxes and Outlays

Figure 12.1   U.S. Department of Commerce, Economics and Statistics Administration, *National Income and Product Accounts*, tables 1.15 and 3.1.
Figure 12.2   U.S. Department of Commerce, Economics and Statistics Administration, *National Income and Product Accounts*, table 3.1; population data from Council of Economic Advisers, *Economic Report of the President 1995*, table B-32.
Figure 12.3   U.S. Department of Commerce, Economics and Statistics Administration, *National Income and Product Accounts*, table 3.1.
Figure 12.4   U.S. Department of Commerce, Economics and Statistics Administration, *National Income and Product Accounts*, table 3.2.
Figure 12.5   Ibid., table 3.1.
Figure 12.6   Ibid., table 3.15.
Figure 12.7, Ibid.
Figure 12.8   Ibid.
Figure 12.9   Ibid.
Figure 12.10 Ibid.

Chapter 13: Purchasing Power Broken Promise

Figure 13.1   Council of Economic Advisers, *Economic Report of the President 1995*, table B-45; the top line for all workers is from Jeff Kunkel, Social Security Administration, Office of the Actuary, fax dated 19 December 1994.
          The lower line referring to nonsupervisory workers is a series produced by the Bureau of Labor Statistics, Department of Labor, calculated on a sample of approximately 360,000 private, nonagricultural business establishments, reflecting the composition of businesses throughout the country. Wages are reported by establishments, not individuals, and are reported on a *per job* basis. All current pay is reflected including overtime, holidays, vacations, and sick leave. Bonuses, tips, and payments in kind are excluded. This measure also excludes supervisory work-

ers and, in addition, white-collar workers in goods-producing businesses not directly involved in production and design.

The top line referring to all workers is tabulated by the Social Security Administration and is based on all wages reported by employers in W-2's; therefore, it reflects all wage and salary workers in the country. This measure is computed on a *per person* basis, and all earnings during the year for workers with more than one job are included, but the worker is only counted once. All wages, tips, and bonuses are reflected in this measure.

Figure 13.2   Council of Economic Advisers, *Economic Report of the President 1995*, table B-37.

Figure 13.3   U.S. Department of Commerce, Bureau of the Census, *Income, Poverty and Valuation of Noncash Benefits, 1994* (P60-188 Series), Appendix.

Figure 13.4   Calculated from table 13.3.

Figure 13.5   Government Transfer Payments from U.S. Department of Commerce, Economics and Statistics Administration, *National Income and Product Accounts*, table 3.1; wages and salaries from Council of Economic Advisers, *Economic Report of the President 1995*, table B-26.

Chapter 14: Loss of High Paying Jobs—A Broken Promise

Figure 14.1   U.S. Department of Commerce, Economics and Statistics Administration, *National Income and Product Accounts*; *Survey of Current Business*, table 1.14.

Figure 14.2   Calculated from previous table (see fig. 14.1 above).

Figure 14.3   Council of Economic Advisers, *Economic Report of the President 1995*, table B-44.

Figure 14.4   Ibid., table B-45.

Figure 14.5   Central Intelligence Agency, *Handbook of International Economic Statistics*, 158.

Figure 14.6   Ibid., 159.

Figure 14.7   Lehman Brothers, *Exchange Rate Trends* (New York, June 1993); Federal Reserve Statistical release, G.5.

Table 14.1   Butler, "Is the United States Losing Its Dominance?" (see chap. 14, n. 2), 29; market share for machine tools and robotics is from Central Intelligence Agency, *Handbook of International Economic Statistics*, table 124.

Table 14.2   Central Intelligence Agency, *Handbook of International Economic Statistics*, table 86.

Table 14.3   Ibid., table 87.

Table 14.4   Ibid.

Chapter 15: Creation of Jobs—A Broken Promise

Figure 15.1   Board of Governors of the Federal Reserve System, *Flow of Funds Accounts*, Z.1 (7 December 1994).

Figure 15.2   Income Statistics Branch, Bureau of the Census, *Current Population Survey* (P60 Series), historical data from table 33A.

Table 15.1   Cox and Alm, "The Churn" (see chap. 15, n. 1), 11.

Chapter 16: Public Education—A Broken Promise

Figure 16.1   *Council of Economic Advisers, Economic Report of the President 1995,* Table B-45; data for high-school graduates from National Center for Education Statistics, U.S. Department of Education, *Digest of Educational Statistics, 1994,* table 99.

Figure 16.2   National Center for Education Statistics, U.S. Department of Education, *Digest of Educational Statistics, 1994,* table 165.

Figure 16.3   Ibid., tables 127 and 165.

Figure 16.4   Ibid., table 128.

Figure 16.5   Ibid.

Figure 16.6   National Center for Education Statistics, U.S. Department of Education, *Digest of Educational Statistics, 1994,* table 82.

Figure 16.7   Ibid.

Figure 16.8   Income Statistics Branch, Bureau of the Census, *Current Population Survey* (P60 Series), historical data from Table 33A.

Figure 16.9   National Center for Education Statistics, U.S. Department of Education, *Digest of Educational Statistics, 1994,* table 3.

Table 16.1   Manno, "Deliver US From Clinton's Schools" (see chap. 16, n. 19).

Table 16.2   National Center for Education Statistics, U.S. Department of Education, *Digest of Educational Statistics, 1993,* table 395.

Chapter 17: Public Safety—A Broken Promise

Figure 17.1   U.S. Department of Justice, Federal Bureau of Investigation, *Uniform Crime Reports for the United States: 1993,* table 1.

Figure 17.2   Ibid.

Figure 17.3   Ibid.

Figure 17.4   U.S. Department of Commerce, Economics and Statistics Division, *Statistical Abstract of the United States, 1994,* table 307.

Figure 17.5   U.S. Department of Justice, Federal Bureau of Investigation, *Uniform Crime Reports: 1993,* table 1.

Figure 17.6   U.S. Department of Commerce, Economics and Statistics Division, *Statistical Abstract, 1994,* table 340.

Figure 17.7   Ibid., table 100.

Figure 17.8   Ibid.

Figure 17.9   U.S. Department of Justice, Bureau of Justice Statistics, *Felony Sentences in State Courts, 1992* (January 1995), 5.

Figure 17.10 U.S. Department of Commerce, Bureau of the Census, *Historical Statistics of the United States* (Series H), 971–986.

Figure 17.11 Ibid.

Chapter 18: Bounty Hunters and Fixed Penalties

Table 18.1   Northwestern Mutual Life Insurance Company, fax dated 2 November 1994 from Beth Henderson.

Chapter 19: Symptoms of Broken Promises—Entitlements

Figure 19.1   U.S. Department of Commerce, Economics and Statistics Administration, *National Income and Product Accounts*, table 2.9; Social Security maximum tax rate includes the tax rate for the Federal Old-Age and Survivors Insurance and Disability Insurance Trust Fund plus Part A of Medicare. Tax rates are from the board of trustees of the Federal Old-Age and Survivors Insurance and Disability Insurance Trust Fund, *Federal Old-Age and Survivors Insurance and Disability Insurance Trust Funds*, House Document 102-279 (Washington, 3 April 1992), table II.B.1 and updates.

Chapter 20: More Symptoms

Figure 20.1   U.S. Department of Commerce, Economics and Statistics Administration, *National Income and Product Accounts*; *Survey of Current Business*, table 3.2.
Figure 20.2   Ibid., 3.2.
Figure 20.3   Ibid.
Figure 20.4   Ibid.
Figure 20.5   Webb, "The Stealth Budget" (see chap. 20, n.2).
Figure 20.6   U.S. Department of Commerce, Economics and Statistics Division, *Statistical Abstract, 1994*, table 327.

Index

Acheson, Dean, 27-28, 37, 42-50, 69, 71
AFDC, 275
affirmative action, 245
Agricultural Adjustment Administration, 24
Airline Deregulation Act, 128
airplane, 189
Akins, James, 122
Alabama, 220
Algeria, 102
Allies, 95
Anglo-American Petroleum Agreement, 98
antismoking campaign, 277
Aramco, 98-99
Archer, Dane, 230-231
Argentina, 66, 173
arms race, 71
atomic bomb, 68, 70
Attlee, Clement, 11
Australia, 66
automobile, 189
  production, global market share, *183 table*
Axis powers, 95
Ayatollah Khomeini, 133-135

baby boomers, 151, 186-189, 195, 219
Baker, James, 142, 280
balanced-budget amendment, 286
Bank Holiday, 23
Battle of Lexington, 108
Battle of Waterloo, 108
Becker, Gary, 217
Beer-Wine Revenue Act, 23-24
Berlin Blockade, 70
Berlin Wall, 70, 75
Big Four, 39, 72
blacks

homicide rates for, 223, *225 table*
illegitimate births, 227, 228, 251
middle class, 251-252
SAT scores, 203-205
Black Thursday, 19
blue-collar workers, 185-186, 195
Bohlen, Charles "Chip," 45-46
bounty hunters, 236-240
Brandeis, Louis, 15, 17
Brazil, 66, 173
Bretton Woods, 28-31, 43, 121
British Empire, 107-114
Brzezinski, Zbigniew, 67, 69-72, 120
Bullitt, William C., 32-33
bureaucratic growth, 157-159, *159 table*
Bush, George, 12, 74, 130, 147-148, 167
business, 273-276
  positive environment for, 278
  restructuring of, 279
business debt, *188 table*
business ethics, 275-276
Business Week, 223
Buy-Sell Program, 125
Byrnes, James F., 36

California, 220
Canada, 76, 85, 137-139, 143
capital formation, 90-92, 136, *136 table*
capital gains tax, 89-90, 135, 287
Carter, Jimmy, 128, 142, 167, 208, 249
Chandler, Alfred, 103
chief executives, 195
China, 59, 71, 74, 141-143, 173, 278, 281, 292-293
Churchill, Winston, 11, 29, 32-33
Civilian Conservation Corps, 24
Civil Rights Act (1964), 193-194, 245, 253
Civil War, 78, 110
Clayton, Will, 45-46, 52, 54, 56

309

National System of Interstate and Defense Highways, 145
NATO, 70, 72
Navy, U.S., 68
Netherlands, 91, 123
New Deal (Roosevelt), 22–27, 147, 244
New Economic Policy (Nixon), 120–121
New Freedom (Wilson), 15, 17
New Hampshire lottery, 268
New York lottery, 268–269
Nigeria, 102
Nixon, Richard, 24, 74, 120–123, 125, 183, 248
North Korea, 70
North Vietnam, 74

OECD market shares, *180 table*
oil
    annual consumption, U.S., *105 table*
    economic history of, 95–106
    embargo, 161, 200
    imports as percent of consumption, U.S., *124 table*
    low-priced, 152, 174
    price rise in 1970s, 121–128, 133–135, *134 table*, 161–164, 176
    real and nominal prices, *100 table*
    total consumption, U.S., *104 table*
    world crude production, *100 table*
Okita, Saburo, 62
Old West, 220–222, 233, 236–237
Omnibus Budget Reconciliation Act of 1993, 167
OPEC, 143, 186
    economic leadership grab in 1970s, 121–128
    formation of, 101–102
    oil embargo of, 133–135, 161–162
opportunity, 185
output and export growth, *117 table*

Paley, William, 109–110
parolees, 228–229
Pasvolsky, Leo, 27–28
Payne-Aldrich Tariff, 16
PCs, 189
Pentagon, 76
personal savings, 248, *249 table*, 274–275

Peterson, Pete, 244
Petroleum Price and Allocation Decontrol Act, 128
Petroleum Reserves Corporation, 97
Philippines, 60, 71
plunder, 4
Poland, 26, 33
Pollard, Robert, 51, 61, 75
POW camps, 241–242
Pravda, 32
President's Crime Commission, 219
prisoners
    incarceration rate, *229 table*
    received per 1000 offenses, *226 table*
private education, 213–214, *214 table*
private security, 222–223, 234–235
productivity, *127 table*
progressive income tax, 10
Prohibition, 25
Project Independence, 125
protectionism, 64
Protestant ethic, 253–255
public education, 199–216
    expenditure per pupil by country, *216 table*
    expenditure per pupil by state, *215 table*
    expenditures per pupil, *202 table*
    high school graduates, real income of males, *213 table*
    high school graduates vs. standard of living, *201 table*
    private school enrollment, *214 table*
    SAT scores, verbal by ethnic group, *205 table*
    SAT scores for college-bound seniors, *203 table*
    SAT scores in math by ethnic group, *204 table*
    students per school employee, *210 table*
    teachers as percent of school employees, *209 table*
public safety, 217–232
    expenditures vs. violent crime, *221 table*
    frequency of violent and property crimes, *218 table*
    violent and property crimes, frequency of, *218 table*

Heterick Memorial Library
Ohio Northern University

DUE	RETURNED	DUE	RETURNED
1.		13.	
2.		14.	
3.		15.	
4.		16.	
5.		17.	
6.		18.	
7.		19.	
8.		20.	
9.		21.	
10.		22.	
11.		23.	
12.		24.